Disarming Your Inner Critic

Disarming Your Inner Critic

James Elliott, Ph.D.
with Kathryn Elliott, Ph.D.

ANTHETICS INSTITUTE PRESS
P.O. Box 81097, Lafayette LA 70598
(318) 261-3322 or (337) 261-3322
Anthetics@AOL.com

Copyright © 2000, Anthetics Institute Press

All rights reserved. No part of this book may be used or reproduced in any manner whatsoever without payment of licensing fees and receipt of written permission from Anthetics Institute Press except in the case of brief quotations in reviews for inclusion in a magazine, newspaper, or broadcast.

Publisher's Cataloging-in-Publication
(Provided by Quality Books, Inc.)

Elliott, James (James Emerson), 1928-
 Disarming your inner critic / James Elliott ; with Kathryn Elliott -- 1st ed.
 p. cm.
 Includes bibliographical references and index.

 1. Criticism, Personal. 2. Self-talk.
 I. Elliott, Kathryn   II. Title

BF637.C74E45.1999   158.1
                                     QBI99-1488

Library of Congress Catalog Card Number
99-75563

Printed in the United States of America

To order, please contact
Anthetics Institute Press
P.O. Box 81097, Lafayette, LA 70598
(318) 261-3322
After 1/1/00: (337) 261-3322
E-mail: Anthetics@AOL.com

Disclaimer

This book is designed to provide general information about Anthetic Therapy methods for disarming one's Inner Critic. In view of the complex and specific nature of psychological problems, it is not meant as a substitute for professional therapy, nor can it be used as such a substitute.

The purpose of the book is threefold. Its first purpose is to provide an introduction to Anthetic Therapy so the reader can make an informed decision as to whether to seek out a therapist who has been certified to provide this kind of therapy. Its second purpose is to serve as an adjunct to the process of Anthetic Therapy by offering detailed information about the many issues that may be encountered in learning Anthetic Inner Critic challenging. Its third purpose is to serve as an introduction for mental health professionals so they can make an informed decision as to whether to apply for professional training in Anthetic Therapy.

Warning: Clinical experience has shown that the methods described herein are powerful and effective. However the reader should be aware that the book cannot be used as a guide for doing therapy or counseling by mental health professionals who have not completed the Professional Training Program offered by Anthetics Institute. The procedures described appear deceptively simple, but they will not be effective unless they are offered by a practitioner trained and certified by Anthetics Institute and, in fact, may even make things worse because of the unconscious influence of the untrained practitioner's Inner Critic.

Since the purpose of the book is only that of educating the reader, the authors and publisher expressly disclaim any liability or responsibility to any person or entity with respect to any loss or damage caused or alleged to be caused directly or indirectly by the information contained in this book.

If you agree to the above, please retain this book; if you do not wish to be bound by the above, please write for information as to how to return this book.

■ An Important Note to The Reader

Despite our care in presenting our ideas as clearly (and even redundantly) as possible, there is one way our message has been misunderstood in the past and might be misunderstood by some readers of this book.

We might be misunderstood as proposing a kind of moral anarchy.

Therefore, we want to say as forcefully as possible that this is not at all what we propose.

Instead, we propose an ethic of responsible living based on the rock-solid values of love, caring behavior, and empathic relating.

The solidity of this foundation comes from the fact that Anthetic values are based on what comes from a person's heart, not what comes from her or his Inner Critic. Values based on the Inner Critic inevitably lead not only to dysfunctional relationships but also to most of the evils of society.

Anthetic values are mentioned throughout the book and are described in a focused way in Chapter 17.

Contents

1 A Revolutionary New Paradigm..................... 1
- How Inner Critic work can help you
- Why most therapy bypasses the Inner Critic
- Results of Anthetic Inner Critic work

2 What Is The Inner Critic?............................. 16
- Your Inner Critic imposes shoulds and inflicts punishment if the shoulds are disobeyed
- You may think you don't have an Inner Critic
- Everything is grist for the Inner Critic's mill

3 Origins of The Inner Critic.......................... 27
- It's not trauma; it's dysfunctional learning
- Prototypes: It wasn't just your family of origin
- The Black Hole and where it came from

4 How The Inner Critic Functions.................... 41
- Imperative shoulds vs. wants
- Imperative shoulds vs. recipe shoulds
- The electric fence that supposedly protects you

5 The Five Emotional Punishments Inflicted By Your Inner Critic.................................... 50
- Feelings of defectiveness, shame, guilt, inferiority, and magnified fear
- Challenging the experts about guilt and shame

6 How Your Inner Critic Creates Reactivity....... 75
- From the natural self to the devalued self
- The compensatory self and its buffers
- Addictions to buffers
- The buffer training you get in childhood
- Reactive vs. Anthetic self-esteem
- The protective self as a suit of armor

- Machinery, stuff, the trance, and the player piano

7 Consequences of Living by Inner Critic Shoulds..96
Some General Disadvantages
- Emotional pain and suffering
- Not enough pleasure
- Overreactions and mood swings
- Depression
- Living by other people's rules
- Not knowing what you really want
- Difficulty listening to feedback and criticism
- Problems with drugs or alcohol
- Insomnia
- Stress
- Idealization of other people
- Living by shoulds doesn't work
- Having to hide your natural self

Relationship Problems
- Addiction to love
- Self-pretzelization to gain approval
- Difficulty with assertiveness
- Vulnerability to pressure from others
- Self-centeredness
- Feeling suffocated in a relationship
- Inability to really connect with others
- Judgmentalism, anger, and a drive for revenge
- Nervousness and tension in relationships
- Feeling unequal to others in personal power
- Feeling as though you don't belong
- Making the wrong choice of a life partner
- Sexual problems
- Difficulty handling other people's feelings
- Problems with jealousy
- Inability to express love to others

Problems that Block Your Effectiveness
- Low energy
- Difficulties in reaching your goals
- Fear of taking risks
- Fear of success

- Stage fright, test anxiety
- Procrastination
- Feeling like an impostor even when you do succeed
- Difficulty in making decisions
- Perfectionism
- Difficulties with learning
- Difficulty in following orders or directions
- Blocked creativity
- Vocational problems

Problems that Block Your Growth
- Being out of touch with your feelings
- Reluctance to begin counseling or therapy
- A tendency to blame others for your problems
- Belief that your problems are due to terminal traits
- Attempting to polish and improve your reactive self

8 Clues to Inner Critic Functioning...............121
Ego-Dystonic Clues
- Self-condemnatory statements
- Emotional twinges
- Feelings of discomfort
- Obvious Inner Critic language
- "Should" language
- More complex Inner Critic language
- "Why" attacks
- "Who" attacks
- Issues about being wrong
- Anger at yourself
- Self-discounts
- Self-critical body language
- Victim feelings and beliefs
- Responsibility language
- Confusion and indecisiveness
- "Buts"
- Feeling worried or anxious
- Inability to forgive yourself

Ego-Syntonic Clues
- "Lowering yourself" issues
- Pride issues
- Judgmentalism

- Feeling put off
- Feeling hurt or betrayed
- Anger
- Reluctance
- Dislikes, aversions, and "I hate" statements
- Dislike of being labelled
- Compulsion to explain, justify, or defend yourself
- Feeling taken advantage of

9 Challenging Methods: Making Releasing Statements..................131
- General principles of making releasing statements
- The "What You Call" tehnique
- The "YASNY" technique
- The "Good Person" technique
- Making releasing extensions
- More releasing statements
- Overcoming fear and anxiety
- Don't use your buffers to challenge
- Anthetic master affirmations
- How to tell if challenging is working

10 Eleven More Challenging Methods................149
- The de-fusing method
- De-fusing conceptual fusions
- Adding the JB challenge to your releasing statements
- De-fusing the T-self from a buffer
- Disengaging the present from the past
- Challenging negative comparisons
- Challenging perfectionistic demands
- Declaring your importance
- Resisting pressure from others
- Reducing your concern about what people might think
- Challenging responsibility commands
- Challenging guilt feelings about the present
- Challenging guilt feelings about the past
- Challenging negative predictions
- Overcoming worry

11 Putting It All Together: Some Examples........160

- Overcoming depression
- Overcoming writers' problems
- Overcoming fear of success
- Overcoming aphilia (the inability to be loving)

12 Suggestions for Making Your Challenging More Effective..........173
- How to think about your Inner Critic
- How to think about the disarming process
- Dehypnotizing the devalued self
- The process of challenging
- Why challenging must come first
- Prerequisites for successful challenging
- Values necessary for successful challenging
- Values you will have to give up
- You must be willing to create new values
- Anthetic practice in everyday life

13 Strategies That Don't Always Work.............186
- Forgiving yourself
- Converting the should into a preference
- Giving yourself permission
- Experiential disconfirmation
- Thought stopping
- Replacing negative thoughts with positive affirmations

14 How to challenge your Inner Critic's Propaganda Messages...................... 201
- 16 propaganda messages your Inner Critic uses to keep you enslaved; how to challenge them

15 Overcoming the Problems and Pitfalls of Challenging........................ 214
- New shoulds your Inner Critic will think up
- Inner Critic backlash
- How to do troubleshooting
- The need for feedback
- Problems of Catch-22
- Pseudochallenging

- Problems doing critical thinking
- Theoretical positions that interfere with learning to challenge
- More statements that indicate problems in challenging

16 Overcoming Fears that May Block You From Effective Challenging 242
- Fear of becoming an uncaring person
- Fear of freedom
- Fear of being overwhelmed by emerging feelings
- Fear of self-image disconfirmation
- Fear of confronting your Inner Critic
- Fear of loss of a self-part
- Fear of sadness
- Fear of happiness
- Fear of loss of identity
- Fear of making mistakes if you become yourself
- Fear of what other people will think
- Fear of God's retaliation
- Fear of becoming a lazy bum
- Fear of giving up all standards
- Fear of growing up
- Fear of hurting other people's feelings
- Fear of losing relationships
- It may feel uncomfortable at first
- Your growing edges

17 Toward A New Foundation for Morality 256
- Discovery #1: Judgmentalism, Anger, Vengeance
- Discovery #2: Anthetic Love
- Discovery #3: Anthetic Caring
- Living a responsible life
- Discovery #4: Genuine Connectedness
- Discovery #5: Critical Thinking as A Prerequisite
- Discovery #6: How to Reverse The Decline in Morality
- Anthetics as moral training
- "Ultimates" and "penultimates"
- The need for moral renewal

18 Some Final Words 270

19 Epilogue: The Rat Story............................ 278

Appendix A: Training Programs..................... 281

Appendix B: The High-Voltage Relationship.......283

Appendix C: "PsychotherapyToday"................ 286

References..289

Index...297

1

A Revolutionary New Paradigm

IN THIS BOOK WE INVITE YOU to embark on an extraordinary journey leading to a whole new way of life. What we're going to describe is a philosophy so powerful, it can bring you freedom from all the negative programming that has been sabotaging your effectiveness, your happiness, and your feelings of well-being.

If you choose to adopt this philosophy as your own, you will find more success, more peace of mind, and more vitality than you've ever experienced before.

We are well aware that this seems like an extravagant claim, yet we persist in making it. We have seen it fulfilled with so many of our psychotherapy clients that we hesitate to moderate our language.

Right from the start we want to tell you that we're not going to offer the usual recycled formulas. Instead, we're going to describe an approach so new and revolutionary that you may feel distinctly uncomfortable as you read about it. It may really shake you up.

It's an approach we have developed in our work with groups and individuals over the past 35 years (Jim) and 10 years (Kathy). It's an approach that may require a 180-degree shift in your belief system, so be prepared for some surprising proposals.

As you read these pages, we're going to ask you to challenge the core ideas you have about yourself. We're going to show you that perhaps some of the beliefs that you cherish the most are the very ones that have been sabotaging your life and making you feel unhappy.

Your Inner Critic

The basic idea of this book is simple: inside each of us is a negative influence that is responsible for 99% of our psychological problems.[1] That negative influence is the Inner Critic

If your Inner Critic wasn't interfering in your life, you would enjoy serene self-confidence, you would be able to achieve whatever goals you chose, and you would experience an ongoing feeling of deep satisfaction and contentment.

But because your Inner Critic has taken over much of your life (probably without your awareness), you have personal problems that seem puzzling and difficult to overcome: fears and anxieties, unsatisfying relationships, depression, blocked effectiveness, and other forms of reactive living.[2]

The first step toward freeing yourself from the sabotage caused by your Inner Critic is recognizing its voice. Once you have learned to do this, you can begin the work of Anthetic challenging, which consists of a series of steps designed to neutralize and disarm your Inner Critic.

The more you are able to do this work, the more the inner process of your life will be free to unfold naturally, the way it was meant to.

As this inner process unfolds, and as you learn to focus and deploy the energies that are released, good things will start happening in your life:

■ Your self-esteem will rise;

■ Your relationships will become more harmonious and deeply satisfying; and

■ You will find yourself becoming more effective in working toward your goals.

The result is that you will begin to experience, perhaps for the first time, what it means to live a truly free, creative, zestful, and happy life.

These are the things we tell the people in our Anthetic training workshops. And then we add an important comment:

"If this sounds easy," we say, "it isn't. For some people, it's difficult. It requires a shift in values that may at first glance seem to contradict the rules of civilized society. It requires a firm commitment to value inner freedom above all other values. And it's not without a certain amount of discomfort at first. But the methods we'll be describing will begin to pay off immediately, the instant you put them to work.[3]

"And each time you challenge your Inner Critic, it will become easier and more comfortable. You'll see immediate results in increased options available to you, greater aliveness, and genuine happiness.

"The more you do Anthetic challenging, the more your life will be transformed from a dull routine into an exciting adventure.

"These are the results reported by people who have learned these challenging skills, and these are the results you can have for yourself."

In this book we're going to draw on years of clinical experience and explain exactly how your Inner Critic has been sabotaging your life and what you can do about it, just as we tell our psychotherapy clients and workshop participants.

Therapy Usually Bypasses The Inner Critic

If you've ever been in therapy, chances are your therapist hasn't focused much on your Inner Critic. Most therapists don't know about this inner voice, and some who do might even encourage you to befriend it and obey it. But even among therapists who recognize its negative effects, few can teach you the skills to challenge it effectively.[4]

Therefore, there's a good chance your Inner Critic will be bypassed in your therapy. The result is that its negative messages will be woven into the work you do. That is, the Inner Critic will become a contaminating factor in your journey toward wholeness and self-fulfillment, and you will not have enough of the very thing you need as the foundation of all your efforts at personal growth: inner freedom.

How This Book Was Written

This book evolved out of a number of handouts I (Jim) gave to my clients and workshop participants. It ultimately became my doctoral dissertation. Now, in a thoroughly revised form, it has been written as a basic manual designed to be used in conjunction with counseling and psychotherapy. Its goal is to provide you with information that will guide you in achieving freedom from the influence of your Inner Critic.

You'll Need To Experience Anthetic Dialogue

Although this book presents step-by-step sequences for disarming the Inner Critic, it may be difficult for many people to feel the full impact of these new methods simply by reading about them.

In other words, this book cannot serve as a substitute for professional help, nor can it teach you the challenging skills the way you'd learn them in individual sessions of Anthetic Therapy or in an Anthetic training group. However, the book can provide you with enough information to begin to do your own challenging so you can get an idea of the power of this work.

Because Anthetic Therapy is such a radical approach, learning to challenge your Inner Critic can be a bit tricky, since your old way of life may interfere, creating resistance. If done correctly, however, challenging is a skill that anyone can learn—provided the problems in learning are carefully addressed and overcome. Once you learn the skill, it will be available to you the rest of your life.

In these pages we've tried to help you overcome every possible problem you may have in getting free from your Inner Critic. In any case, we suggest you read this book in conjunction with your work with a Certified Anthetic Therapist.

A Note To Psychotherapists

This book was also written for the psychotherapist. It's designed as a concise, comprehensive training manual—a text for use in our Professional Training Program.

But now a warning: Clinical experience has shown that the methods described here are powerful and effective when used properly. However, there are many pitfalls in their use—that is, many ways that mistakes can be made so that, for example, the client may wind up with even more blocks and dysfunctional beliefs than before.[5]

Although the Anthetic challenging methods appear to be simple, our experience has been that counselors or therapists cannot teach the skills correctly without extensive training in Anthetic Therapy.

To therapists, then, we have the following message: If you try to apply these methods in your practice without going through our training program, you may discover that often they will seem not to work. You may then come to believe that this approach is ineffective. And all because you have not learned the complexities involved in applying the methods. Remember: this book is a manual designed to accompany the professional training program. You cannot learn to do Anthetic Therapy by reading this book (or any book). One reason is that learning to do Anthetic Therapy requires a personal transformation that can only be achieved in a training workshop. (If you'd like more information on what is involved in this transformation, please write us.)

What This Book Offers You

In this book we're going to tell you where your Inner Critic came from, how it functions, and how it punishes you whenever you disobey it. Next, we're going to describe at great length the dysfunctionality (we call it reactivity) that occurs in your life as a result of Inner Critic oppression. People are usually astonished when they learn how the Inner Critic has affected practically all aspects of their lives.

We want you to see all the negative consequences that result from believing what your Inner Critic says. It's important for you to understand these consequences fully; otherwise, you may simply agree intellectually with our statements and close the book still believing that if you just keep trying harder to follow your old rules, you'll be able to solve your personal problems and live a happy life.

After describing the consequences of living a life constricted by your Inner Critic, we're going to give you some step-by-step instructions that you can use right away to get a taste of what disarming your Inner Critic means. Finally, we're going to tell you how to overcome many of the problems people have in using this disarming process.

How to Get
The Most
From This Book

This book offers a new paradigm, a new model of what has heretofore been called mental health. To understand this new paradigm, you must temporarily suspend any attachments you may have to what you have read or been taught somewhere else.

Because the Anthetic paradigm is so revolutionary, it will be difficult for you to understand it if you view it from *within* whatever model you are presently using. You must step outside that model and read with what Zen Buddhists call a beginner's mind. The beginner's mind is one that is as free as possible from preconceptions.

Suzuki contrasted the beginner's mind with the expert's mind and declared that the problem with the expert's mind is that it contains fewer possibilities. In the beginner's mind there are many. "The mind of the beginner is empty," he writes, "free of the habits of the expert, ready to accept, to doubt, and open to all the possibilities" (1970, pp. 13f). Unless you can read with such an unattached mind, this book may not make much sense to you.[6]

Therefore, we suggest that you bracket all your attachments to other theories—that is, temporarily put them out of play—and read this book as if you knew nothing about psychotherapy, recovery theory, and personal growth.

Let go of whatever structures you have already created, so you can move forward into the new vision that Anthetic Therapy will reveal. Don't assume that, as an expert, you know The Truth. Give yourself permission to start with a beginner's mind.

How to Read
This Book

Some of our colleagues who have read this book in manuscript form found it overwhelming. "It's like an encyclopedia," one therapist friend told us. "People may need to read it several times."

Said another colleague: "You have to read the whole thing all the way through to understand how the parts fit together. As you read it, you'll have a lot of questions, but the questions will ultimately be answered. So tell your readers to be patient until the complete system unfolds itself."

"It's not full of fluff, like most self-help books," said a third colleague. "And it doesn't just describe problems, it tells you what to do about them. I'd certainly recommend it to my patients, but I'd warn them that they need to read it with an open mind, because the ideas are so new."

So our recommendation is to read the whole book through, keeping track of anything you disagree with. We've included answers to all the questions people typically ask, as well as responses to a great many common objections.

Once you have a sense of the complete system of thought presented here, you might want to go back and try some of the challenging skills.

If You Feel Uncomfortable

You may be one of the people for whom this book comes as a welcome and pleasant revelation—a doorway to a new and happier world. On the other hand, you may find yourself feeling some jangly resistance or other uncomfortable feelings as you read about the ideas presented here.

From time to time we're going to ask you to think critically about what the experts have been telling you. When we challenge other people in the field, we do it not to judge their intentions or their characters. We believe that every writer of psychotherapy books sets forth ideas that she or he sincerely believes will be helpful. Issues, not personalities, are what we will be examining. We believe everyone (including ourselves) should be held accountable for what they write, and we think you have the right to know how our work relates to that of others, whether that relationship is one of agreement or disagreement.

In any case, because we will be challenging conventional wisdom, you may have a sense that some of your most comfortable beliefs are being attacked. You may even feel indignant.

If so, we suggest that you consider the possibility that this feeling is a clue that your Inner Critic is fighting back, trying to maintain its sabotaging grip on your life.

We want to make it very clear what we don't mean. We don't mean that if you disagree with what is written here, you are just resisting. What we're saying is best captured by the words of one of our group members: "When I first heard your ideas, I got annoyed, because you were contradicting some of the leading authorities in the field. You were also contradicting what I had learned in years of therapy, and I had a lot invested in thinking my therapist was right, even though I never did make the amount of progress I wanted. But I thought, if my therapist was wrong, I had been wasting a lot of time, and I didn't want to face that. Now I see that I was just putting those so-called experts up on pedestals and not thinking critically about what they were teaching. Once I was able to disengage from their ideas, I became open to what you were saying, and I discovered that the methods you taught really worked. From then on, I was able to make progress real fast. Everything was accelerated."

As you read this book, we want you to take a second look at a lot of things you thought were all settled. Our clients in Anthetic Therapy report that this "second look" becomes pleasurable and exciting once they loosen their attachment to old ways of thought. We'll do our best in this book to help you make this shift.

What Is Anthetic Therapy?

The term comes from the Greek *anthesis*, referring to the growth and blossoming of a flower. Once the Inner Critic is neutralized, the person will be free to grow and blossom in her or his own way. Of course, there's more to Anthetic Therapy (AT) than Inner Critic work. As a matter of fact, Inner Critic work represents a small part of what AT is all about.

Briefly stated, AT is a school of therapy that views the therapeutic process in terms of inner figures. Inner figures are the various parts of a person that seem to have personal characteristics and a certain degree of autonomy. You can have an idea of what these parts are like by thinking about the decisions you've found it hard to make. You probably thought, "Part of me wants this; another part of me wants that." Those parts are your inner figures. [7]

What Is Anthetic Dialogue?

An important method used in Anthetic Therapy is Anthetic Dialogue (AD).[8] An adaptation of the Gestalt empty chair method,

AD differs from conventional empty chair work in that it does not rely on back-and-forth dialogue between two chairs but uses several chairs (as many as eight or ten) to reveal a number of inner figures.

In our clinical practice, AD has proven to be far superior to both journaling and the two-chair method in eliciting and working with inner figures. Moreover, AD is not only a therapeutic procedure, it is also a research method.[9] That is, it can be used to understand the various configurations that inner figures form, together with the dynamic forces among the inner figures. This kind of research has given us new insights into the structures of such emotions as anger, vengefulness, and judgmentalism.

Anthetics

Anthetic Therapy is one application of a more general field of study called Anthetics. Anthetics is a broad philosophical framework that is competitive with such philosophies as behaviorism, existentialism, and materialism. Anthetics includes ontological, epistemological, and ethical positions.

It's important to realize that Anthetics is more than a therapy. It's difficult at first to see how broad and deep it is. Here are the comments of Kathy, my wife and colleague: "When I first heard your lecture on Anthetic Therapy, I thought, 'Sure, the Inner Critic is the internal voice that criticizes a person. So what? No big deal.' As I learned more about this work, I saw that the Inner Critic not only was the source of criticism, it was also the source of blocks. At that point I got more interested: here was something that could be useful in doing what I call block work.

"Then I saw that the Inner Critic was the source of emotional punishments—as you say, feelings of defectiveness, shame, guilt, inferiority, and magnified fear. Now I had a way of understanding these negative feelings, and I saw that Anthetic Therapy was much more than I thought at first.

"As I continued to learn, I began to see the connections between almost every personal problem and the Inner Critic. Finally, I realized that the Inner Critic was behind most social problems, too: war, prejudice, crime, and oppression of women.

"But it took a personal experience with Anthetic Dialogue for me to truly understand the Inner Critic and see all these connections. I now do Anthetic Therapy in my private practice with individuals and couples, and I also teach it in my graduate courses. And I see now that Anthetics has the potential to change the whole world for the better. You might want to tell your readers it's much more than a school of therapy."

Case Studies

The personal stories that appear in this book have been gathered from thousands of therapy clients and participants in our groups, including seminars for the general public and training workshops for mental health professionals. To protect the identities of the individuals involved, all names have been changed, and biographical details have been disguised. In some cases, stories have been combined to form composites.

Where These Ideas Came From

My creation of Anthetic Therapy has a long history. I (Jim) began the study of psychotherapy in 1947 when I read Karen Horney's books and learned of the importance of "shoulds," basic anxiety, and the three personality styles: compliant, detached, and expansive.

I became aware of the superego from reading Freud (the original discoverer of what I call the Inner Critic), but it took me a while to realize how important this entity was.

In the 1960s I discovered Transactional Analysis and attended Eric Berne's social psychiatry seminars, where I learned about the Parent, Adult, and Child. Reading Edmund Bergler's books gave me an idea of the pervasiveness and destructiveness of the superego.

I watched Fritz Perls do empty chair work at a convention of the American Psychological Association and was impressed by the speed with which clients enacted and explored their problems.

From Stewart B. Shapiro (1962, 1976) I learned about "the critic" and about empty chair work that used multiple chairs.

From an article by Louis Paul (1970) I got the idea that empty chair work could be used to disarm the Inner Critic. As I continued to use this approach, I modified it considerably and named it Anthetic Dialogue.

From Albert Ellis, Aaron T. Beck, and other Cognitive-Behavioral Therapists I learned how one's beliefs played an important role in dysfunctional behavior, and I integrated many of the insights of

A REVOLUTIONARY NEW PARADIGM 11

CBT into Anthetic Therapy.

From reading the works of Alfred Adler I learned about compensation, a concept that appers in my theory of buffers, although the Anthetic theory of compensation contradicts Adler in important respects.

I would like to acknowledge my intellectual debt to all these pioneers, although in every case I have radically revised their ideas, left out what I thought was not useful, and added many new concepts and methods.

Although AT owes a debt to these writers, it is primarily derived from my work with groups and individuals since 1964, and it is to these people that this book is lovingly dedicated.

About Kathryn (Kathy)

In January 1989, in my doctoral program, I met Kathy, and seven months later we were married. I taught Kathy to do Anthetic Therapy, and we began to build a practice in Lafayette, Louisiana, where we now specialize in work with couples and conduct a trainining program in AT for mental health professionals. As a professor of psychology at the University of Southwestern Louisiana, Kathy offers Anthetic principles and methods in her graduate classes, where she trains counselors.

From time to time in this book I use the pronouns "I" and "my" to refer to my own clinical work. I use "we" and "our" when referring to what we have both learned as therapists.

I might add parenthetically that we use Anthetic skills in our marriage, and they work beautifully. In fact, we are now still experiencing the excitement of our honeymoon stage. We would like to write more about this topic, but that will have to wait for another time and another book.

QUESTION: Is AT a combination of several schools of therapy?

ANSWER: Not in the sense that it simply combines the ideas and methods of several therapies. While AT appears to be similar to Cognitive-Behavioral Therapy, Gestalt Therapy, Voice Dialogue, Voice Therapy, Adlerian Therapy, Horney Psychoanalysis, Transactional Analysis, Jungian Analysis, and Primal Therapy, it is not at all a synthesis of those therapies.

Although it has theoretical connections with each of these schools of thought and can encompass some of their concepts and methods, AT differs considerably from them and, in some cases, holds views that are diametrically opposed to the views found in those therapies.

Results of Anthetic Inner Critic Work

It's common to hear our clients say, as one man did, "When I challenged my Inner Critic, it was like a burden was lifted off my shoulders. I felt lighter. In fact, I could almost levitate."

As people get released from the oppressiveness of the Inner Critic, they feel bursts of joy, often expressed in great peals of laughter. "It's an Anthetic satori," reported one man who had done a lot of Zen meditation, "only it takes much less time to achieve."

As our clients learned to recognize and disarm their Inner Critics, they reported results such as the following:

■ **"I feel more energetic and creative."** "It feels like some creative energy got released inside me," one woman said. "Something that had been blocked for years is now flowing freely. It feels like I'm no longer driving with the brakes on."

■ **"I can now work my way out of feeling depressed."** Before learning the skills of Anthetic Therapy, people saw their feelings of depression as puzzling and mysterious. Afterwards, our clients could easily trace them to the Inner Critic, whereupon they knew exactly what skills were needed to overcome the depression. "I knew something was wrong," one woman said, "but I didn't know what it was. Now I know what's happening when I get depressed. And I know what to do about it. My 'down' feelings used to last several days. Now they last only a few minutes, or an hour at most."

■ **"I find myself becoming more assertive and effective."** No longer blocked by guilt, fear, or shame, our clients and group members could learn the skills of self-empowerment as a foundation for assertiveness. They learned to spot when they were giving away their personal power to other people, and now they had the skills necessary to reclaim it.

Take Katie, for example, one of whose problems was anger. She and her husband John had come to me (Jim) for couple counseling, and we were talking about making requests. "I can't make any requests of John," she said, "because I've been taught in a workshop on Recovery from Codependency that I shouldn't try to change other people. I should only work on changing myself."

I taught Katie Anthetic challenging, pointed out the should (in this case, a "shouldn't"), and asked her to challenge it. She did so successfully and took back her right to make requests of her husband, a process that began a rapid positive change in their relationship.

"The recovery 'should' made me unassertive," she said. "No wonder I've been so angry."

"Right!" I said. "When you buy into any should, no matter where it comes from, you'll disempower yourself. And anger is the inevitable result of self-disempowerment."

■ **"I'm able to resist pressure from other people."** Because they became more centered in themselves, more in touch with what they wanted, people were able to spot manipulative attempts by others, and they had the skills to resist those attempts.

■ **"I'm much less addicted to other people's approval."** Once they were trained in the Anthetic skills, people could *enjoy* others' approval but no longer *craved* it so much, no longer saw it as a "fix" they had to have in order to feel OK.

Although they were considerate of others, they no longer felt so concerned about what people might think of what they said or did.

■ **"I can now confront others' strong feelings."** The people who learned the skills were much less affected by others' anger, judgmentalism, and hurt feelings. "My buttons don't get pushed as often," one man said, "and when they do, I know what kind of work to do on myself so I can get free."

■ **"My marriage is improving enormously."** One of the most powerful applications of Anthetic Therapy is in couple relationships. It's common for a couple to come to us for counseling and say, "We've tried many kinds of couple therapy, but nothing seems to work. The therapist just listens and says 'umm-hmm.' Or gives advice."

After only four or five sessions of Anthetic Therapy, couples often show dramatic improvement in their ability to reduce their judgmentalism, anger, and nagging. It comes as a great surprise to couples when they realize that their Inner Critics have all along been responsible for the problems they have been having.

■ **"I can now do things that used to seem impossible."** As people liberated the energies of their natural selves, more choices now seemed open to them. Some people switched jobs (or even careers). Others broke through emotional barriers and finally left home, applied for college, asked for a raise, learned to give public lectures, started their own businesses, or got married. Women left abusive relationships. In each case, what had held them back was the Inner Critic, although they weren't aware of it.

Once they used Anthetic challenging to disarm this internal saboteur, they felt free to actualize their deepest wishes and longings.

■ **"Anthetic Therapy is like a good road map; I know exactly what to do with my clients, and it's exciting to see how rapidly the methods bring about therapeutic progress."** This is a common report of psychotherapists who have had professional training in Anthetic Therapy. "I used to fumble around, not knowing what to do," one therapist told us. "Now I'm never at a loss. Anthetic Dialogue is so powerful. I'm amazed at the quick results my clients get from it. What used to take months of work can now be done in three or four sessions."

What You'll Need to Do

Here's what you'll need to do in order to build a solid foundation for learning the Anthetic challenging skills:

☐ You must temporarily set aside any preconceptions you may have about psychotherapy, recovery theory, and personal growth, so you can approach this work on its own terms, rather than refracted through the lens of another theory.

In the next chapter, let's take a closer look at that sabotaging force we have been calling the Inner Critic.

NOTES

1. The Inner Critic is not the sole cause of all personal problems. It does, however, appear to be the primary cause of many problems and is implicated to some extent in practically every problem. *[From p. 2]*

2. "Reactive" is a term we propose as a substitute for such terms as "neurotic" and "mentally ill." Reactivity includes all the self-structure created in response to the Inner Critic's messages. *[From p. 2]*

3. For some people, Anthetic challenging (the method described in this

book) seems quite magical. Prior to one of our Inner Critic workshops, a woman said, "I know there's no magic key to solving my problems." After the workshop, she said, "I discovered that there really *is* a magic key!"

In individual sessions the Anthetic Therapist teaches the challenging skills using an intensive approach. Occasionally, only one or two sessions are needed. More often, it takes longer—especially for people who find it difficult to make the shift to valuing inner freedom (i.e., freedom from the Inner Critic) as a primary value. *[From p. 3]*

4. If you've been in therapy a long time, and you haven't been making much progress, it's probably because you haven't been learning the skills necessary to free yourself from your Inner Critic's oppression. Once you begin learning these skills, the process of therapy becomes greatly accelerated. *[From p. 3]*

5. For example, these methods cannot be used successfully if the therapist is in any way judgmental; the judgmentalism will simply add new shoulds to the burden the client is already carrying. Unfortunately, therapists, along with people in general, are often judgmental and almost always not aware of their judgmentalism. *[From p. 5]*

6. A forthcoming book, *Anthetics*, will describe methods for adopting the beginner's mind. *[From p. 6]*

7. Inner figures will be the subject of a future book. Its tentative title is *Disarming Your Inner Saboteurs with Anthetic Therapy. [From p. 8]*

8. For more information on Anthetic Dialogue, see Elliott (1992b). *[From p. 8]*

9. Our research using Anthetic Dialogue reveals the Inner Critic as one of a number of inner figures. Another inner figure is the Inner Guide. Unlike the Inner Critic, the Inner Guide is a positive figure that offers unconditional love and gentle guidance. Among the other inner figures we've discovered are The Blob, The Warrior, The Avenger, and The Witch. In addition, there are about twelve Inner Child figures. Of all these, the Inner Critic is a key figure, since it has a negative impact on all the other inner figures. Rowan (1990) has written a useful history of inner figure theory. *[From p. 9]*

2

What Is The Inner Critic?

To BEGIN WITH, YOUR INNER CRITIC is the source of all your negative self-talk.[1] It's a voice inside you that criticizes you, calls you stupid when you don't know something, and provides a running negative commentary on all your thoughts, feelings, behavior, hopes, and plans.

Your Inner Critic Does More Than Criticize

The Inner Critic might well be called the Inner Saboteur, since it does much more than criticize. Its chief self-appointed task is to impose the "shoulds" (and "shouldn'ts") that constrict your life. Each time you disobey one of these shoulds, your Inner Critic will give you a twinge (or jolt) of emotional punishment in the form of feelings of:

- Defectiveness ("There's something wrong with me")
- Shame ("Someone has discovered [or will discover] my defectiveness")
- Guilt ("I've committed a crime or transgressed in some way.")
- Inferiority ("Because of my defectiveness, I'm less than other people: less important, less powerful, less valuable") and
- Magnified fear.[2]

To put this another way, whenever you feel one of these five negative feelings, you can be sure of two things:

WHAT IS THE INNER CRITIC? 17

1. The feeling is a punishment that has come from your Inner Critic, and
2. It has resulted from your disobedience to a should.

Like a hidden enemy inside you, your Inner Critic constricts your life and blocks you from trying to satisfy wants and needs that are perfectly normal and healthy, calling them weird and abnormal. In this way it undermines your full humanity and contributes to your disempowerment, lack of fulfillment, and general unhappiness.

Through its relentless threats of punishment, your Inner Critic launches powerful attacks on your self-confidence, your ability to think clearly, and your effectiveness in reaching your goals. Moreover, it may wreck your relationships, since it is indirectly responsible for your anger, judgmentalism, defensiveness, vengefulness, and inability to sustain a successful relationship.

Your Inner Critic thinks it has a noble purpose: that of protecting you from the dangers it envisions were you to stray from the constricted life it proposes for you. However, in the service of this goal, it does its best to squelch the vibrant aliveness, boundless energy, and sparkling creativity that you were born with and that still lie hidden away inside you.

Everyday Coping With The Inner Critic

Fearful of the threat of emotional punishment, people cope with the Inner Critic in a variety of ways. Some use alcohol and drugs to put the Inner Critic to sleep. Others may use absorbing work to distract themselves from hearing its voice. Still others may achieve financial success, which gives the illusion of mental health and buys off the Inner Critic for a while. None of these methods works very well.

Unless you face the Inner Critic head on and disarm it, it will continue to have a negative impact on your life—perhaps conspicuously, perhaps in ways you don't even know about.

QUESTION: Is the Inner Critic the same as the conscience?

ANSWER: It's what might be called a *negative* conscience. It controls you through its threats to punish you if you disobey it. In later chapters you'll learn about your Inner Guide, a *positive* conscience that is the source of gentle and loving guidance.

QUESTION: Is the Inner Critic the same as the Freudian superego?

ANSWER: Not exactly. In his early writings, Freud (1914/1949, p. 52) saw the superego as composed of two parts: the ego ideal, which sets standards, and the conscience, which punishes the person for not meeting those standards.[3] Anthetic Therapy's concept of the Inner Critic is similar: the "shoulds" are the standards (ego ideal), which are imposed by the Inner Critic (the punitive conscience).

However, Freud offered so many different versions of the superego and ego ideal that there is no uniformity among present-day Freudians as to the meanings of these terms.[4] Many Freudians now see the ego ideal as a positive force. Some also believe that the superego can be beneficial, as well as punitive, and should be integrated into the personality.

Anthetic Therapy, on the other hand, *defines* the Inner Critic as the source of all emotional punishments. AT holds that if you integrate a punitive superego into your personality, you'll be integrating mental suffering into your life. Who needs that?

Your Inner Critic As Propagandist

To top the whole thing off, your Inner Critic will try to brainwash you into thinking that it's working in your best interests—when all along it is simply oppressing you and constricting your life, preventing you from making the best use of your talents and abilities. And because you believe the Inner Critic's propaganda, its tyranny may not sound like tyranny at all; it may sound perfectly reasonable to you.

The Inner Critic Is an Internal Reality

Your Inner Critic is a real element in your mind, a living reality inside you that seems to have a life of its own, along with its own purposes. If you're like most people, you're already aware of its voice; if not, you'll probably be able to recognize it with only a little training.[5]

You May Think You Don't Have An Inner Critic

When Kathy and I give lectures, we usually ask for a show of hands of those people who can hear the Inner Critic's voice. Whether we're speaking to professional or lay audiences, from 80% to 90% of those present raise their hands. It has become clear to us that the overwhelming majority of people are aware of the Inner Critic's sabotaging voice.

If you are not aware of that voice, it may be because your Inner Critic is buried so deeply in the unconscious part of your mind that it's difficult to identify. You may not even know it's there.[6] You may think you don't have an Inner Critic at all. All you may know are some of the consequences to be mentioned in Chapter 7.

Those consequences are clues to Inner Critic functioning. If your problems are puzzling to you, it's probably because you are not aware that their source is your Inner Critic. You may think all that's needed to overcome a problem is a little more willpower. It may be even more puzzling when the extra willpower doesn't always work.[7]

Your Inner Critic May Masquerade As You Yourself

When your Inner Critic produces its negative thinking, it may sound as though you yourself are the source of that thinking. You may say, for example:

- "What a dumb thing I did!"
- "It's too scary to try that new thing. I'll probably fail."
- "I shouldn't be the way I am."

In each case, it sounds like the negative thought is yours, and that it has been yours all along. We want to assure you, however, that the original source of every negative thought you have is *not you at all*. Every negative thought you have came from a *part* of you—your Inner Critic. It became *your* negative thought when you bought into it. It can stop being yours when you decide to buy out of it, using the skills we'll describe in later chapters.

Under the guidance of an Anthetic Therapist, the first skill you need to learn is that of disengaging from your Inner Critic and hearing it as a separate voice. Once you learn this skill, you can begin to see how your Inner Critic has been sabotaging your life—often without any awareness on your part at all.

This point bears repeating: **Like most people, you may be totally unaware of the extent to which you have fallen under the life-constricting influence of your Inner Critic.**

You May Externalize Your Inner Critic

Your Inner Critic is sneaky. From its secret position deep in the hidden part of your mind, it may tell you that other people or external events are the causes of your negative feelings.

For example, if someone criticizes you, and you feel hurt, you may think the cause of your hurt feelings is what the other person said.

If you lose your job and you feel depressed, you may think your depression was caused by the loss of your job. If somebody asks you a question and you feel embarrassed because you don't know the answer, you may believe that your embarrassment was caused by the questioner.

In each of the above cases you externalize your Inner Critic by assuming that the primary cause of your negative feelings is the external event.

In each case, however, the primary cause of your negative feelings is your Inner Critic: a hidden mechanism, deep inside your mind, that got *triggered* by the external event. It's as though you are sown with land mines, and when someone says something to you, or a negative event happens to you, one or more of those land mines explodes.

Later on, we'll tell you exactly how an Anthetic Therapist can help you dismantle those land mines so you can feel good about yourself no matter what someone says and no matter what external event happens. You will then have reclaimed your personal power—the power to feel good—power you have been giving away to other people or events.

You May Project Your Inner Critic

As mentioned above, externalizing your Inner Critic means seeing the source of your negative feelings as outside yourself. Externalizing occurs when there is a real external event that impacts one of your land mines.

But you may also project your Inner Critic onto other people when there is no negative triggering event at all. That is, you may hear the most neutral and innocent comments as attacks and accusations. This happens when your hypersensitive Inner Critic misinterprets the situation by projecting itself into the other person. If this happens, other people may seem to be your enemies, when in fact they are not.

Everything Is Grist For Your Inner Critic's Mill

Having read this far, you may be feeling a few twinges of self-criticalness about *having* an Inner Critic. Many people do. We want to assure you that those twinges are caused by your Inner Critic itself, which has the ability to take any neutral or helpful statement and convert it into a self-blaming statement.

Take, for example, a question that a woman asked at one of our lectures: "Do you mean I'm as bad as all that? That I'm to blame for all my negative feelings?"

"Not at all," I (Jim) replied. "We're giving you factual information about a process inside people that sabotages their efforts to be happy. That sabotaging process has its source in your Inner Critic. Unfortunately, your Inner Critic has the ability to take that information we gave you and convert it into self-blame.

"I can say to you, for example, that you are wearing glasses—just a statement of fact. And your Inner Critic will probably convert that into a criticism: 'He's telling me there's something wrong with wearing glasses!,' when such is not the case.

"Your Inner Critic is wily, devious, and sneaky. The best rule of thumb is that every negative feeling you might have is caused by your Inner Critic—even the negative feelings that get triggered as I talk to you about the Inner Critic."

We hope this point is very clear, because as you get deeper into this book, you'll read many things that your Inner Critic may convert into self-blaming statements. As you continue reading, you may feel some twinges of guilt. You may feel indignant. You may even feel insulted. You may feel offended by what you think of as the negative quality of this book. We want to assure you that in each case, these feelings are caused by your Inner Critic, struggling to get you not to look at anything that might weaken its power.

As you continue reading this book, we are going to ask you to do something that may be difficult: we want you to consider the possibility that these feelings are simply material to work with, not sources of truth about reality. You will then be in an excellent position to get free from the sneaky forms of self-sabotage that your Inner Critic is so expert at inflicting.

Does Everyone Have An Inner Critic?

The answer is Yes. Having an Inner Critic seems to be a necessary part of growing up. The Inner Critic serves the temporary function of protecting the young child from danger and helping it quickly adapt to life.

We've never met anyone who didn't show signs of Inner Critic functioning, although we've met a number of people who claimed they didn't have an Inner Critic. Such people are in denial. The Inner Critic likes it that way; it's happy for you to think you don't have it. Then it can function freely, constricting your life by imposing its shoulds and shouldn'ts. (Of course, you may not know that your life is constricted. You may have gotten so used to doing what your Inner Critic wants that you have simply been avoiding its emotional punishments.)

Is The Inner Critic Really All That Important?

As you read this book, you may be thinking, "My Inner Critic can't be such a powerful influence in my life. This theory is too simplistic. It reduces everything to one cause."

Thoughts such as these are common among people who have not done Anthetic Inner Critic work. It takes a while to realize, under the guidance of an Anthetic Therapist, how destructive and pervasive the Inner Critic has been in one's life "Before I began doing Anthetic challenging," Beatrice said, "I didn't know about my Inner Critic. But once I learned the challenging skills, I realized it had been programming me negatively all my life. I had no idea how much it was affecting me without my knowledge."

If you think we're exaggerating the importance of this sabotaging agency, our response is this: we only wish there were stronger words we could use.

WHAT IS THE INNER CRITIC?   23

Please reserve judgment about this issue until you finish the book. Read it with an open mind. Experiment with some of the challenges.[8]

QUESTION: I'm still not convinced that I have an Inner Critic. Can you give me more evidence?

ANSWER: The Inner Critic is **defined** here as the source of such emotional punishments as feelings of defectiveness, shame, guilt, and inferiority. If you have ever felt any of these feelings, rest assured that you have an Inner Critic.

However, many people can't become aware of the Inner Critic just by reading a book. But once they learn the Anthetic Dialogue process, they can experience the Inner Critic as an entity. If this book does not convince you of the existence and power of this inner saboteur, we hope it motivates you to attend a workshop or therapy session where you can experience the harsh reality of the Inner Critic for yourself, whereupon you can enjoy the liberating freedom that occurs when you do Anthetic challenging.

What You'll Need to Know

Here's what you'll need to know from this chapter in order to build a solid foundation for learning the skills necessary to disarm your Inner Critic:

☐ You do have an Inner Critic, although it may be hidden from your awareness. Just because you're not aware of it doesn't mean you don't have one.

☐ Your Inner Critic is not just a critic; it's also the source of shoulds and shouldn'ts.

☐ Shoulds are not just rules for living; they get their power from the fact that if you disobey them, your Inner Critic delivers a jolt of emotional punishment.

☐ Your Inner Critic is not a minor nuisance. It has been having a major destructive impact on your life.

☐ Your negative beliefs don't come from you; they come from your Inner Critic. They began as messages which you have bought into; once you realize this, you will be in a better position to buy out of them.

Now that we've explained how Anthetic Therapy defines and describes the Inner Critic, let's take a look in the next chapter at the origins of this sabotaging agency.

NOTES

1. Anthetic Therapy defines the Inner Critic as "the source of those voices that are negative." The Inner Guide, on the other hand, is defined as "the source of those voices that are positive, gentle, caring and loving."

Separating the negative voices from the positive voices is essential, since each must be dealt with by using a different strategy. The ontological question as to whether the two are "really" different is beside the point; the reason for separating them is purely pragmatic. That is, if you accept the above principles of separation, you'll find the work described here much easier to do. *[From p. 16]*

2. Up till now (1999), writers who mentioned the Inner Critic have understood its ability to criticize but not its ability to impose shoulds and inflict emotional punishments if the shoulds are disobeyed. I (Jim) discovered this revolutionary idea by analyzing the Anthetic Dialogue sessions of my clients. *[From p. 16]*

3. Here are Freud's words: The conscience "constantly watches the real ego and measures it by" the ego ideal (1914/1949, p. 52). See also Eidelberg (1968). *[From p. 18]*

4. Most Freudians agree on the following ideas: (a) The superego consists of values imposed by society; (b) The superego is a result of the Oedipus complex; (c) Addressing the superego, while important, is not the central factor in overcoming personal problems; and (d) If the superego is addressed, its harshness must merely be reduced.

Anthetic Therapy holds that (a) The Inner Critic (i.e., superego) may or may not consist of values that come from society; its values may have other sources, too; (b) Although the Oedipus complex is an important determinant of Inner Critic functioning, it is not the only one; there are also pre- and post-oedipal determinants; (c) Addressing the Inner Critic must be the central task of psychotherapy; and (d) It's not enough to simply reduce the Inner Critic's harshness; the client must be taught skills necessary to buy out of every one of the Inner Critic's commands.

Because Freudians believe the superego incorporates the values of society, they hold that criminals or other antisocial individuals lack a superego or have "superego lacunae"—holes in the superego.

AT holds that although the Inner Critic usually incorporates societal values, it may incorporate values that are the opposite. For example, although a criminal may appear to lack an Inner Critic, closer examination reveals that the criminal's Inner Critic simply contains values that are opposed to the caring values often found in society. For example, the criminal usually has Inner Critic shoulds to be tough and strong, to get revenge when wronged, and not to be taken advantage of or conned by anyone.

In addition, AT holds that the Inner Critic is the source of shoulds and their accompanying emotional punishments, a concept not found in psychoanalysis or any other school of therapy (as of 1999).

You can find a survey of Freud's varying meanings of the superego in Sandler (1960) and of the ego ideal in Sandler et al. (1963). *[From p. 18]*

5. The existence of the Inner Critic is inferred from its voice, in the same way that the physicist infers the existence of a subatomic particle from its track in a cloud chamber. In any case, whether the Inner Critic "actually" exists or not depends on the ontological framework you apply. If you apply a physicalist ontology, there is no room for any mentalist item, unless it is reduced to physicalist concepts. In any case, this issue seems beside the point; our clients and group members find that if they *assume* the existence of the Inner Critic, it is easier to challenge their negative self-talk. They report two reasons for this: (a) They now have a stronger focus for their challenging, whereas if they simply challenge dysfunctional beliefs, they do not; and (b) The focus is in the form of an adversary, which makes it easier to mobilize the energy needed for challenging.

It may be useful to consider the ontological status of the Inner Critic as that of a fictional construct (Vaihinger 1935). *[From p. 18]*

6. The repressed unconscious, as defined here (or "subconscious"; we prefer Janet's term to Freud's), is simply a part of your mind of which you are unaware; which nevertheless influences your conscious thoughts, feelings, and behavior; and which has a vested interest in your not becoming aware of it. Special unblocking techniques are required in order to become aware of its contents.

What this means is that for any given feeling, you can never say for sure that you do *not* have it, since it may be unconscious. Likewise, you cannot say for sure that you do not have an Inner Critic, since you may have one without knowing it. *[From p. 19]*

7. Here's how to tell whether you have an Inner Critic. Our clinical experience shows that the Inner Critic is the source of the following feelings. So if you have ever had any of these feelings, you have an Inner Critic:

- feeling mildly (or severely) depressed
- feeling embarrassed
- feeling guilty
- feeling inferior to other people, or "less than"
- feeling and/or expressing judgmentalism
- feeling angry
- feeling as though you want revenge
- feeling as though you're responsible for other people's feelings

- feeling overconcerned about other people's opinions
- feeling worried
- feeling anxiety
- feeling panic
- feeling disempowered
- feeling shame
- feeling defective

When you stop and think about it, anyone who claims not to have had any of these feelings is denying her or his humanness. The Inner Critic, then, appears to be an existential condition of being human—a fact which is mentioned neither by such existentialists as Karl Jaspers and Martin Heidegger, nor such contemporary existential therapists as Medard Boss and Irving Yalom.

It might be asked "How do we know that those feelings have their source in the Inner Critic?" The answer is that Anthetic Dialogue with thousands of clients has revealed the Inner Critic as the source. *[From p. 19]*

8. Edmund Bergler (1962) is one of the few writers to have recognized the power and influence of what we are calling the Inner Critic. "The extent of the power wielded by the Frankenstein which is the superego," he writes, "is still largely unrealized" (p. x). "It is my contention," he declares, "that unconscious conscience, although the key to the theory and therapy of neurosis, has been grossly underestimated" (p. vii). *[From p. 23]*

3
Origins Of The Inner Critic

WHERE DID THE INNER CRITIC COME FROM? You'll need to know this so you can understand it better and recognize the negative messages it gives you. In fact, you'll need as much information about this internal saboteur as you can get.

The Inner Critic began to be installed in the first few months of life. Let's begin our examination of this process by talking about the primary self and secondary self.

The Primary Self

To understand the primary self, think of the newborn baby. It's practically all primary self.[1] The baby is mostly a bundle of unfocused energies—bursting with vitality and aliveness.[2]

The baby has not yet learned to channel its energies in such a way that it can cope with the world. It learns this task as its parents (and others) teach it the rules for getting along in our culture.

The result of this process is the creation of the secondary self—a structure whose purpose is to focus and channel the energies of the primary self.[3]

Of course, it's not that there are two separate selves inside a person; the terms primary and secondary self are just useful ways of referring to primary structure and secondary structure. The two structures are always intermingled.

The Secondary Self

The secondary self mediates between the unfocused energies of the primary self and the world. The secondary self consists of structures called "schemas"—or programs—that help the child match its own desires to what the world offers.[4]

For example, at some point you learned a schema for getting a job. The schema would include your desire for money, your knowledge that jobs are ways of acquiring money, your knowledge of the training and preparation needed to get a job, and your awareness of how to locate and apply for a job.[5]

Secondary self structure is built up as the child learns things about the world. The schemas of the secondary self channel the energies of the primary self so those energies are not scattered aimlessly but instead are deployed in focused ways on specific projects. This focusing is accomplished as the child learns the skills not only for getting a job but also for such projects as obtaining a driver's license, ordering a meal in a restaurant, and acquiring an education.

If all goes well, the schemas will include programs for living a responsible and principled life. For example, schemas will be learned for overcoming self-centeredness, empathizing with others, engaging in caring behavior, and postponing immediate gratification for the sake of working hard to achieve future goals.

The Natural Self: Primary Self Plus Secondary Self

Your natural self is pretty much who you are before you get any negative programming. Your natural self is made up of your primary self and secondary self. It's an important part of you: it contains all the vital energies of the primary self plus the structure of the secondary self which you use to deploy those energies.[6]

Unfortunately, your natural self was subject to a process of distortion while you were growing up —with the result that you will be using schemas that are not 100% functional in getting what you want. These dysfunctional schemas are responsible for every psychological problem you now have.

Dysfunctional Learning

The dysfunctional schemas in the present resulted from dysfunctional learning in the past. Perhaps you learned that the way to get along in the world was by being "tough," by dominating others, by displaying no weakness. Perhaps you learned the opposite: to get along meant being "tender" —sensitive and caring, complying with others' wishes, being a GLK (a Good Little Kid).

Possibly you learned to be dependent on others for feeling good, for support, or for approval. Or perhaps you learned that the thing to do was to become self-sufficient: scaling down your needs, not depending on anybody except yourself, being somewhat (or a lot) withdrawn.[7]

Each of these response patterns was learned. Because of its complexity, each is what we call a "superschema," containing a set of schematic elements. We've found there are four basic superschemas, or types: Tough, Tender, Dependent, and Self-sufficient.

If you are flexible (which is the ideal), you might be able to deploy elements from each of these four superschemas whenever you wish. For example, sometimes you will choose to be tough, sometimes you will choose to be tender, sometimes you will choose to be dependent, and sometimes you will choose to be self-sufficient.

If you have experienced dysfunctional learning, however, chances are you'll be "crystallized" by being limited to one or perhaps two of the superschemas. The corollary of this is that you'll have behavior gaps, in that you will be emotionally blocked from using the other superschemas.

In other words, if you have experienced dysfunctional learning in childood, you will tend to pursue a superschema rigidly. Each rigid superschema then becomes the blueprint for a reactive way of life. And each dysfunctional superschematic element is locked in place by the Inner Critic.

Let's take a look now at the negative programming you might have received in childhood—the kind that lends itself so readily to dysfunctional learning.

What You Needed As A Child

When you were growing up, you needed certain things in order to develop a functional natural-self structure. For example:

■ You needed opportunities to achieve autonomy by separating from your parents, and you needed encouragement from your parents in order to successfully undertake this process.

■ You needed opportunities to achieve competence through making your own mistakes, and you needed to be let alone by your parents so you could make them. The more your parents did things for you, the less chance you had of learning to do them on your own.

■ You needed to discover your uniqueness, your abilities, and your particular gifts and talents, and you needed affirmation of these things by your parents—even if what you wanted was different from what your parents wanted for you.

■ You needed a certain amount of guidance from your parents. You especially needed to know about the world and its resources, along with the goals that were possible to achieve, and you needed to know the steps you could take to achieve those goals.

■ You needed enough love from your parents so you could learn to value yourself, so you could soothe and reassure yourself when necessary—and, most important, so you could love and accept yourself unconditionally. You needed to know that your parents (and other adults) thought you were OK, acceptable, and lovable just as you were.

Now, if all the above processes had happened perfectly, you would have come to believe three things:

First, that it was OK for you to be a separate self and to have your own values and goals, even if they were different from those of your parents;

Second, that while some of your behaviors might be inapproproriate at times, none of them was evil, wicked, or blameworthy; and

Third, that all your thoughts and feelings were OK to have—every single one of them.

If you got messages that encouraged you to adopt these three beliefs, you would easily be able to create the secondary self structure you needed, and your natural self would be running things.

As a result, you would be able to live an effective, satisfying, and happy life. The primary energies, channelled and focused by the secondary self structure, would be permitted optimal deployment, consistent with the constraints and requirements of the external world.

This, as we say, is what would happen if you had received 100% perfect parenting and support—not only from your parents but from other people who were influential in your early years.

Negative Programming

But few if any children get 100% perfect parenting. So if you're like most people, what you got was less-than-perfect (LTP) parenting. This LTP parenting was the occasion of your dysfunctional learning, and the more of this learning you engaged in, the more your secondary self structure was negatively affected.

The LTP parenting you got is what we call negative programming. Each time you bought into it (that is, each time you learned to accept it), it produced reactivity in your self-structure.

Reactivity

As used here the term reactivity does not mean "reacting to." It is simply a more accurate replacement for such pejorative terms as "mental illness," "immaturity," "neurosis," and "pathology." Those terms, we maintain, have acquired a few Inner Criticky barnacles over the years and need to be declared obsolete.

"Reactive" refers to that part of a person that is dominated by Inner Critic functioning. Reactive people (i.e., people to the extent that they are reactive) function "in their machinery" or "from their stuff."[8]

We all have some reactivity. No one is without it, although some people deny they have it.

Emotional Punishments

Most of your reactivity was created in response to the emotional punishments you received, which you then incorporated into your Inner Critic. Here are some examples of emotional punishments and the messages that may have produced them:[9]

■ **Defectiveness and Shame Messages.** Defectiveness and

shame have to do with being "bad" or "evil" or otherwise not-OK. Among the parental messages producing these punishing feelings are:

• "Shame on you! You ought to be ashamed of yourself!" This punishment is often inflicted for such behaviors as getting your clothes dirty, fidgeting instead of sitting still, walking around naked, touching yourself "down there," slouching in your chair, spilling your milk, and making bubbles in your glass with a straw.

• "You were an accident." "I wish I'd never had you, I wish you'd never been born." Messages such as these are designed to punish you for simply existing.

■ **Humiliation Messages.** Humiliation, an intense form of shame, occurs often in the classroom: when a child is scolded for not reciting properly, is made fun of by other children, is defeated in a fistfight and made to say "Uncle," or is not promoted to the next grade.

■ **Inferiority Messages.** Inferiority messages occur when your "defectiveness" is compared with someone else's supposed superiority. A typical parental message is "Why can't you be more like so-and-so?" (e.g., "Why can't you be neat like your sister/brother/friend?").

■ **Guilt Slinging.** A guilt-slinging message is one designed to install guilt feelings. Some parents seem to be quite ingenious at this, as with the mother who said, "Of course, you can do whatever you want, but remember: you're breaking your mother's heart."

■ **Magnified Fear Messages.** Did your parents threaten you with the "bogeyman"? Did they talk about all the scary things that could happen to you—especially if you were to separate from them? Were you afraid of death because you prayed, "If I should die before I wake...?"

All these seemingly normal events can install magnified fear messages in your Inner Critic.

Prototypes:
It Wasn't Just Your Family Of Origin

Much negative programming came from your parents (or parental figures), but some didn't. It came from your brothers, sisters, and other relatives (who may have teased you and laughed at you), teachers (who may have scolded you or otherwise humiliated you in front of the class), playmates (who didn't want to play with you, or who picked you last when it was time to choose up teams), neighbors, religious authorities, and other significant people in your life.

So your family of origin was not the only source of reactive programming. There were other sources. It's useful to think of all these sources as prototypes. A prototype is any source of reactive programming you experienced, usually as a child. It can be a person or a situation. When you mentally go back in the past to unearth, explore, and unlearn these programming messages, you are doing what Anthetic Therapy calls prototype work.

Reactivity Is Learned

It's important to repeat that the negative experiences you had as a child didn't automatically and inevitably produce reactivity. You may have had some negative experiences that had very little impact. On the other hand, something that seemed very slight may have had a great impact.

The difference is in what you brought to the experience. There are at least three elements in your contribution: First, there was your interpretation of what happened. Second were the elements that got installed in your Inner Critic. Third were whatever life-decisions you made in response to the experience.[10] All three of these elements (and perhaps more) made up the learning you took from the experience.

If a parent died, for example, you may have interpreted this as a personal rejection—which then got incorporated into the matrix of your Inner Critic, along with the meaning, "I wasn't valuable enough for him or her to go on living for." Your Inner Critic may generalize this to the belief that no one will ever find you valuable enough to stay with you. And your final life-decision might be to keep to yourself and avoid intimacy.

Seemingly neutral events can also have a negative impact. For example, Brenda was the first-born child in her family. A few years after her birth, her mother had a second child, whereupon Brenda concluded: "I must be of little value, because if my mother had been satisfied with me, she wouldn't have wanted to have another child." What got incorporated in Brenda's Inner Critic was the message, "You are somehow defective." Based on this message,

Brenda's life-decision was to settle for less: for example, she stayed in a low-paying job because she thought she didn't deserve a better one.

In addition to the specific events that happened in childhood, there are some things built into the parent-child relationship that in themselves either cause or encourage reactivity. For example, as a young child you were weak, often helpless, ignorant, and unskilled—and you lived among giants, who were powerful and wise (in everything, you thought). Little wonder that you decided that you were inferior, and little wonder that you jumped to the conclusion that you might in some way be defective or flawed because you couldn't measure up to the giants.

Learning and Unlearning Are Key Concepts

As you can see, Anthetic Therapy is based solidly on a learning model, not a trauma model. That is, early childhood traumas have a negative impact only if dysfunctional learning results from them.

In addition, AT holds that learning is not just cognitive and intellectual; learning may be emotional, and it may be somatic, too. The body learns, as well as the emotions and the intellect.

What this points to is a way of overcoming personal problems: What was learned in the past can be unlearned in the present.[11]

The Black Hole

I (Jim) was working with Ted, a 30-year-old attorney, directing him in Anthetic Dialogue, when he enacted a new figure in one of the empty chairs. He described the figure as very young, in pain, needy, and wanting love. "It's like a black hole," he said. "It's never satisfied; no amount of love is ever enough for it." From that time on AT had a new name for this kind of needy child figure: the Black Hole.

Astronomically speaking, a black hole is a region of apparently infinite gravity that sucks in and swallows up all matter that comes within its gravitational pull. The Black Hole in a person is that part that yearns for love. It's a terrible emptiness and neediness that wants to be filled but can't ever be satisfied.

Everyone seems to have a Black Hole, but it can become stronger in some people if certain things happened while they were growing up. For example, your Black Hole will become more needy if your parents ever threatened to abandon you—or actually did abandon you. Or if you were "underbonded"—not given enough affection, love, or touching. "Overbonding" can also make a Black Hole worse. A lot of love, affection, or touching can make the child yearn for it, especially if it is suddenly withdrawn as the child grows older.[12] In any case, you'll have a Black Hole no matter what happens—even if you got exactly the right amount of love.

Adults often cover it over and deny it. This happens especially with men, because of their shoulds to be mature, tough, and self-sufficient.

In any case, the Black Hole seems to be necessary if you are to experience closeness; its energies cause you to fall in love, to seek intimacy, and to want to merge with another person. The important thing is not to eliminate it (which no one can do) but to work with it so it doesn't dominate your life. Otherwise, it may drive you to make relationship decisions you will later regret.[13]

The Inner Critic and The Black Hole

The inner figure we have been calling the Inner Critic is separate from the one we call the Black Hole, although the two are closely related. For example, your Inner Critic can intensify the power of your Black Hole by giving you commands to try to fill your emptiness with love and approval from other people—telling you that you won't be able to survive without these commodities, and commanding you to pretzelize yourself to avoid others' disapproval and anger.

The Black Hole produces what we call primary pain (that is, feelings of abandonment); the Inner Critic produces secondary pain (feelings of self-condemnation).[14]

Are Parents To Blame?

We hope we have made it clear that there is no way at all for parents to win the game of perfect parenting. As a result of "normal" growing up, we all wound up with some reactivity in our secondary self- structure. And it's not necessarily attributable to dysfunctional parenting.

In any case, most of the time parents were sincerely trying to do their best, operating at whatever level of consciousness and knowledge they had. Many of them truly thought they were doing the right things. They were, of course, confused and misinformed about how to raise children. They were bewildered by what they were told by various friends, relatives, and experts—whose advice often conflicted with each other.

Like all of us, parents are fallible human beings—sometimes irrational and vindictive, sometimes loving; sometimes hostile and critical, sometimes supportive. And like all of us, they were to some extent reactive, especially in their parenting. But we must have received *some* love while we were growing up; infants who get no love at all simply die.

So in the case of most parents, we cannot really blame them. They were not evil people; they just didn't know any better.

Coping With Parental Guilt

If you're a parent, the chances are good that your guilt has been triggered as a result of reading the foregoing paragraphs. We want to reassure you that it's physically impossible to raise a child in such a way that it will be totally free from reactivity. There's no way. And if you feel guilty about what you've done (or not done), there are Anthetic challenging skills you can learn so you can get released (see Chapter 9).

Results Of Negative Programming

To say that no parent functions perfectly is to say that every parent, to some extent, engages in dysfunctional parenting. Such parenting would not be so bad, except that children who are raised in dysfunctional environments often come to believe that dysfunctionality is the right way to live; that criticism and harsh punishments are simply forms of love and caring; that constant conflict and dramatic episodes are perfectly normal; that detachment and aloofness are appropriate ways of relating. And that they themselves are the problem, not their dysfunctional parents.

The child usually doesn't think, "They treat me that way because they don't know how to be good parents." Instead, he or she thinks, "They treat me that way because there must be something wrong with me. My parents are right. Nothing I do is good enough. I am bad for being me. So I'd better stop being me and start being what Mom and Dad want me to be. Then I can be good. Then they might love me. Or at least not criticize me so much."

The Illusion Of A Perfect Childhood

"I had a good childhood," Leonard told me (Jim). "But I still have problems. Doesn't that destroy your theory?"

Leonard had consulted me because of his anxiety. I had always maintained that no one ever had a perfect childhood. It just wasn't possible. But maybe I was wrong.

When I worked with Leonard, I asked him to do Anthetic Dialogue, speaking to his father, imagined as sitting in an empty chair. As he did this work, Leonard discovered a curious feeling.

"Dad," he said, "I *had* to see you as a perfect father, and I had to see my childhood as OK."

"Because?" I said.

"Because I couldn't see you as bad. I wanted to be like you. I knew I *was* like you, and if you were bad, then *I* was bad. So I couldn't see any imperfections in you."

As Leonard dialogued with his father, then gradually came to get free from his Inner Critic, he saw that his low self-esteem came from the fact that his father was withdrawn and self-centered and unable to express love. "I thought he loved me, because he gave me material things," Leonard said. "My former therapist told me that was his way of expressing his love. But I see now that I didn't want the *things* he gave me; I wanted him to love me. I wanted him to say just once that I had done a good job doing something. He couldn't bring himself to do that.

"I guess my childhood wasn't so perfect after all," he concluded.

QUESTION: But don't some people have very good childhoods?
ANSWER: Yes, of course. But even with the best possible childhood, there will still be some dysfunctional learning, which gets stored in the Inner Critic, creating reactivity and adversely affecting your life. There's no way to avoid it.

Unfortunately, because parents feel guilty about the way they raised their children, they are apt to deny any dysfunctionality in their parenting. But if you check with your siblings, you may get some clues as to the negative influences that occurred while you were growing up.

And sometimes when you ask parents about your childhood, they will say something revealing. Some of our clients report incidents like that of the mother in a recent TV episode of *Mama's Family*. Mama was responding to her adult son, who had complained about not getting enough emotional support while he was growing up. "You're telling us we didn't give you enough emotional support?" she said. "Hell, we praised to the high heavens every dumb, stupid, idiotic thing you ever did!"[15]

The Inner Critic Is Formed

It appears that when you were born, your Inner Critic began as a kind of framework, a matrix, that was empty of content.[16] Shortly after your birth, this matrix began filling up. Into it was poured all the shoulds that occurred as a result of the dysfunctional learning described above, along with the threats of emotional punishment if you were to disobey the shoulds.

Now that you're an adult, your Inner Critic is filled with those shoulds, together with the ability to zap you whenever you disobey them.

What You'll Need to Know

Here's what you'll need to know from this chapter in order to build a solid foundation for learning the Anthetic challenging skills:

☐ Your reactivity has its source, not necessarily in traumatic events, but in the dysfunctional learnings you underwent in the past, mostly during your childhood. These learnings were installed in your Inner Critic.

☐ Because reactivity was learned, it can be unlearned.

In the next chapter we'll explain how your Inner Critic, once formed in childhood, continues to threaten you with punishment, oppressing you, constricting your life, and taking away your rights to feel, think, and behave.

NOTES

1. The Anthetic concept of the primary self is much like the Freudian concept of primary process. The latter is a mode of functioning of the psyche that is characterized by an urgency for tension reduction without regard for external reality. See Freud (1900/1955, p. 601; 1915/1957, pp. 186f). *[From p. 27]*

2. The newborn, of course, is not *all* unfocused primary energy; it comes equipped with some built-in secondary structure. *[From p. 27]*

3. Secondary self structure is like the Freudian concept of secondary process, characterized by delay of gratification of needs and wishes (Freud 1915/1957, pp. 186f; 1900/1955 p. 601). It attempts to control primary self energies by channelling and focusing them so as to match them to the environment, thereby satisfying the primary needs. *[From p. 27]*

4. The concept of the schema is taken from Piaget (1926) and Bartlett (1932). The scrupulously correct plural is "schemata" (accent on the first syllable). *[From p. 28]*

5. Strictly speaking, I'm talking about "goal schemas," a concept I (Jim) originated to refer to a configuration of motives, impulses, desires, feelings, cognitions, perceptions, and scripts, all leading to one or more goals. The usual meaning of schema in Cognitive-Behavioral Therapy has to do with cognitions and perceptions only. *[From p. 28]*

6. The primary self is like the concept of Natural Child in Transactional Analysis. The secondary self is something like the TA concept of script, provided one distinguishes between what might be called a driven script and a free script. Anthetics holds that the secondary self is partly free, partly driven (i.e., partly "machinery").

Berne describes two forms in which the Child can occur: "The *adapted* Child is manifested by behavior which is inferentially under the dominance of the Parental influence, such as compliance or withdrawal. The *natural* Child is manifested by autonomous forms of behavior such as rebelliousness or self-indulgence" (1961, pp. 77f). The Anthetic concept of primary self is distinguished from the TA concept of Natural Child in that (a) not all rebelliousness is seen as autonomous; some of it is reactive and (b) the Natural Child appears to consist of primary self plus secondary self. *[From p. 28]*

7. Those familiar with the work of Karen Horney will recognize here the three types she describes: moving against, moving toward, and moving away from. Anthetic Therapy adds one more type—dependent—and provides a psychodynamically-based theoretical context for Horney's ideas. AT holds that the rigidity of the types is not accidental; it comes from the driving force of the Inner Critic, which locks the type-elements solidly in place and submerges their polar opposites. *[From p. 29]*

8. The term "stuff" is equivalent to "machinery" or "reactivity." *[From p. 31]*

9. The brief list of punishments imposed by prototype people is taken from a much larger list that will be presented in detail in a later book. Moreover, most of the punishments mentioned here are inflicted via verbal messages; there are, of course, nonverbal punishments and influences, too. For information on prenatal and perinatal influences, which are, of course, intrinsically nonverbal, see Grof (1985), Janov & Holden (1975), Ridgway (1987), and Verny (1981, 1987). *[From p. 31]*

10. For an excellent book on decisions and redecisions, see Goulding & Goulding (1979). *[From p. 33]*

11. For more information on the prototype work needed for unlearning, see Kathy's article (K. J. Elliott, 1995). *[From p. 34]*

12. It is not uncommon for parents to withdraw love as the child gets older. The mother may withdraw love when the child becomes more autonomous around the age of 5; the father may withdraw love from his daughter when she begins to show signs of being a sexual female around the age of 13. *[From p. 35]*

13. As an adult you may make bad relationship choices; for example, choosing as life partners only people who do not value you. *[From p. 35]*

14. The trauma resolution process in Anthetic Therapy helps the client express pain (and other feelings) as fully as possible, thus reducing the "charge" on the Black Hole. To this is added a cognitive-behavioral step: eliciting and challenging dysfunctional beliefs, together with enacting new behaviors. This process results in reducing the energy of the Black Hole and diminishing its ability to compulsively drive behavior. *[From p. 35]*

15. Some people may even create some of the shoulds in their own Inner Critic. One client said, "My parents were so permissive that I figured I'd better set up my own standards, and I'd better set them pretty high so I wouldn't make any mistakes." *[From p. 38]*

16. The Inner Critic is an Anthetic archetype, as is the Black Hole and a number of other inner figures. Anthetic Therapy derives its archetypes from the Anthetic Dialogue process, not from accounts of dreams, religions, and myths. In addition, AT holds that the archetype *is* the inner figure that appears in Anthetic Dialogue. What Jung called the archetype is known in Anthetic Therapy as the archetypal matrix. Jung's commitment to Kantian dualism caused him to see the archetype as a noumenon which was represented in experience by symbols and images, which is why Jungians focus on these phenomena. Kantian dualism prevented Jung from seeing the archetype as an inner figure. *[From p. 38]*

4

How The Inner Critic Functions

ONCE INSTALLED, YOUR INNER CRITIC serves as an internal controller of your thoughts, feelings, and behavior. Having absorbed the programming messages from Mom and Dad (and others), it now serves as a portable Mom and Dad, standing ready to zap you with its twinges and jolts of pain whenever you transgress.

The result is that a big shift, starting in childhood, gradually occurs in your life. Whereas before you were concerned with living from your natural self, now you are concerned more and more with living from your reactive self, which was created in response to your Inner Critic. In this chapter we will see how this process works.

The Blueprint And Its Shoulds

The Inner Critic functions by creating a blueprint that serves as a master plan setting forth the way it wants to coerce you into being.[1] The specifications of the blueprint are imperative shoulds—shoulds imposed by the Inner Critic.[2]

Imperative shoulds are sometimes felt as "oughts" or "supposed-to's"—and they can also be "shouldn'ts" and "oughtn'ts";

but for the sake of convenience, we'll refer to all these items as "shoulds."[3]

These Inner Critic shoulds are powerful commands that set the standards you are supposed to meet. The Inner Critic demands that you mold yourself into a model of perfection. In the service of this goal, your shoulds tell you what is and is not acceptable in your thinking, feeling, and behaving. Once implanted, the shoulds function like post-hypnotic suggestions; that is, they control your life, but you may not be aware of them.

It's important to realize that imperative shoulds are not innocuous "rules for living." Their power is backed by the threat of emotional punishments if you disobey them. That is, the shoulds are locked in place by the Inner Critic, which is why it's so difficult to change yourself through sheer willpower, without disarming your Inner Critic first.

It's also important to realize that your shoulds tell you that you no longer have certain rights. For example, if your Inner Critic imposes a should to put other people first, this means that you don't have the right to put yourself first.

Because of the brainwashing you received from your Inner Critic, all this seems to you to be a perfectly normal and appropriate way to live. The shoulds appear to you to be reasonable and desirable rules that are to be obeyed without ever questioning them. If you're like most people, you will not realize that they are the very things that are blocking you, limiting you, constricting your options, and in general sabotaging your effectiveness and happiness.

Imperative Shoulds Vs. Wants

It's important to distinguish between imperative shoulds (i.e., Inner Critic shoulds) and simple ordinary wants. It's a subtle but important distinction. There's one infallible way to tell the difference—-and only one.

If you don't obey an imperative should, you'll feel a twinge (or jolt) of pain, which will be experienced as one or more of the emotional punishments to be described in Chapter 5: feelings of defectiveness, shame, guilt, inferiority or magnified fear.

If, on the other hand, you don't get a want, you'll just feel disappointed. Maybe even sad. And maybe even grief-stricken, if, for example, someone close to you has died.

In any case, if you don't get the want, you believe that you are still a good person. There's no guilt, no feelings of defectiveness, no shame, and no feelings of inferiority. No belief that you are bad.[4]

Shoulds and Wants For The Same Thing

One reason we want you to be clear about the distinction between wants and imperative shoulds is that you may have an imperative should and a want for the same thing. In order to do Anthetic challenging of shoulds, you must be able to separate the two; otherwise, your Inner Critic will be able to confuse you.

Here's an example to illustrate the distinction. I (Jim) may have a want for a piece of chocolate cake right now. If I don't get it, I'm not at all a bad person; I'm just disappointed. My self-esteem is not at stake.

But suppose I have a should to make this book absolutely perfect—with no flaws whatever. Then if anybody were to point out a flaw, my Inner Critic would pounce. I'd feel a twinge of pain each time I thought of the flaw. "How could I have been so careless!", I might well exclaim. "What a dumb thing I did!"

My self-esteem would be lowered. I might feel depressed as I contemplated the rising number of flaws pointed out by my critics. I would begin to feel pretty discouraged. Perhaps guilty. Certainly defective. And ashamed to have been found out. And inferior to others in the field, whom I would believe to be much more competent than I.

But side by side with that should to make the book perfect, there might be a want to create a truly good (or even perfect) book. Or as close to perfect as possible.

Here, then, is a should and a want for the same thing.

This makes the understanding of shoulds tricky: a want can (and often does) exist side by side with the should. The problem is that the should can then masquerade as a simple want. If that's happening, you may say, as one of our clients did, "I don't want to challenge my should to be sensitive and caring; what's wrong with being sensitive and caring?"

In this case, the want must be disentangled from the should, and each must be expressed separately. For example: "I *want* to be sensitive and caring. That comes from my natural self. At the same time I have a *should* to be sensitive and caring. That comes from my Inner Critic. Since I don't want to be driven by my Inner Critic, I'll work on my should, realizing that I will still have the want. I will then be sensitive and caring because I want to be, not because I'm driven to be."

Imperative Shoulds Vs. Recipe Shoulds

Another important distinction is that between imperative shoulds and what we call recipe shoulds. An imperative should prescribes what you must do or how you must be in order to meet the Inner Critic's standards for being "a worthy person." If you don't meet these standards, you are what the Inner Critic calls an unworthy person, whereupon you'll feel the pain that occurs when the Inner Critic pounces with one of the five emotional punishments to be described in the next chapter.

A recipe should, on the other hand, is one that tells you what to do in order to achieve a certain result. For example: "If you want to bake a good cake, you should use two eggs." There's no issue of self-esteem involved. Your badness or goodness is not at stake. A recipe should is just an "If X, then Y" statement. Very objective. No self-condemnation.

This distinction is important because when people first learn about shoulds, the information is seized on by the Inner Critic as grist for its mill. People become so sensitized to the word "should" that whenever they use it, their Inner Critic pounces.

"I shouldn't say should!" is what they say, and they have simply added a new should to their already burdened life: not to say the word "should."[5]

But of course, as you will see, it's perfectly okay to use the word "should" any time you want.

You Need To Know The Context

"I should go back to school and get my degree," said Nancy, a member of one of our groups.

"Aha!," exclaimed Charles. "A should!"

"Well, I guess it is one," Nancy responded. "What should I have said?"

HOW THE INNER CRITIC FUNCTIONS   45

"Aha again!" exclaimed Charles smugly. "Another should!"

"I don't know what I'm supposed to do here," wailed Nancy.

"Still another," Charles added, folding his arms and beaming.

People like Charles are not uncommon in therapy and self-help groups, and sometimes you'll even find them among the therapists who lead such groups. Driven by their Inner Critic, they like to pounce on other people who don't say the right words.

But apart from Charles's reactivity, the point we want to make here is that, all by itself, the statement "I should go back to school" may or may not be a "shouldy" statement. It's not clear whether it's:

- "I should go back to school and get my degree; otherwise, I'm a terrible person" or
- "I should go back to school and get my degree so I can get a good job."

The first statement is an imperative should; the second is a recipe should.

So you need to know the context in order to tell which kind of should it is. That is, you need to know what would happen if the should is disobeyed.[6]

Aren't Some Imperative Shoulds Okay?

Your Inner Critic would like you to think that there are some imperative shoulds that are okay to have as guides to your life. Of course, it wants to survive, to stay in control.

Remember: we are defining imperative shoulds as commands originating in your Inner Critic. If you don't obey them, your Inner Critic inflicts psychological suffering. So anyone who argues in favor of using imperative shoulds as guides to living is arguing in favor of psychological suffering; i.e., torture.

If anyone knowingly chooses to live by torture, we can see no way of persuading them to live otherwise. It's up to each person to make this choice, and we can't force anyone to avoid unhappiness and suffering. What we can do, however, is show them, as fully as possible, all the negative consequences of choosing torture, and that's what we're going to do in Chapter 7.

When I (Jim) mentioned these ideas in a lecture recently, one woman said, "Oh, I wouldn't call it torture. That's going too far."

"I would call it torture," I replied, "because that is exactly what it is. Most people, though, are not in touch with the torture—because they follow the commands of the Inner Critic. So they may never feel this torture, and they may say exactly the kind of thing you have said: 'It's not really torture.' But if they were ever to step outside of a limited range of behavior, they'd feel the torture immediately."

The Electric Fence

I (Jim) grew up on a farm, and some of the farmers were in the process of replacing their rail fences with electric fences. The cows were astonished. Before, there was an obviously impenetrable fence made of split logs. Now there was only a single strand of barbed wire, strung on shiny white insulators. How easy it must be to break through!

And one by one, the cows tried it. As each cow's nose touched the single strand, she got a 12-volt jolt of electricity, whereupon she realized there was more to this than met the eye. From then on, she steered clear of this barbed-wire strand. And after a while, all the cows learned this lesson.

Whereupon the farmer turned off the electricity. And the fence worked just as well.

Though not exact, the analogy is close enough. Each of us is imprisoned within an electric fence made up of shoulds. In many places in the fence, the current has been turned off—or the voltage is a lot weaker than it was in childhood. But we think it will still give us a strong jolt.

And, of course, sometimes it does—if we are not armed with methods for draining the electric fence of its energy. Which is what this book will give you.

What's important about this analogy is that most people never feel the twinge of pain connected with the shoulds because they never try to break through the fence that pens them in. They just go on doing the same old routine things day after day, appearing well-adjusted, seeming to get along okay, but wondering why life at one time seemed so full of exciting possibilities but now is dull and gray. Like the cows, they might say, "Let's just stay in the middle of the pasture, under this nice tree. We like it here."

But others are willing to listen to a voice inside that wants something more out of life. They're willing to try to break through their fences, even if the other cows look down their long noses at them for being different.

These are the people who are willing to work on their shoulds, because they value inner freedom above all other values.

The Judgmentalism Of The Inner Critic

To recapitulate: the Inner Critic functions via shoulds. The shoulds are commands, and if you don't obey them, the Inner Critic will give you a twinge (or jolt) of pain. The pain is usually felt as "feeling that I am unworthy or bad: guilty, defective, shameful, inferior." These feelings result from the judgmentalism of the Inner Critic, inflicted through one or more of the emotional punishments to be discussed in the next chapter.

An emotional punishment inflicted by the Inner Critic can be a mild sort of thing—a mere twinge, hardly felt unless you are looking for it. Or it can be very bad indeed—it can be a feeling of devastation and deep despair.

In any case, the negative feelings you experience result from the Inner Critic's judgmentalism. That is, when your Inner Critic delivers a negative message, the major portion of the message consists of a judgmental attack. This judgmentalism will be some sort of putdown, disparagement, or devaluation.[7]

What makes the judgmentalism so powerful is that it is often combined with a neutral factual statement in such a way that the whole message seems factual. So when the Inner Critic says, "You are stupid," you might be tempted to say, "That's the truth; I *am* stupid." That is, you might take what is really a feeling, or emotional expression, and treat it as if it were a factual statement, something to be believed in the way you would believe someone who said, "The earth is the third planet from the sun."

But the emotional attack of the Inner Critic is not factual. It's just the expression of a feeling. It's like an expression of anger—for example, "I'm mad at Bob"—which says nothing whatever about Bob but tells only of the feelings of the speaker.

Judgments vs. Judgmentalism

Judgmentalism is defined here as any disparagement, putdown, or devaluation. It includes language or nonverbal behavior that is humiliating or belittling. It must be distinguished from a judgment, which is simply an assessment.

For example, suppose Typist A can type 40 words per minute. This makes him a faster typist than Typist B, who can type only 30 words per minute. To say "A is a better typist than B" is a judgment. But it is not judgmental, because there is no disparagement—simply an objective assessment and comparison.

If, on the other hand, you say, "I can't believe Typist B is such a lousy typist!," that's judgmental.

The reason for keeping this distinction in mind is that many people use the word "judgment" when they really mean "a judgmental statement."[8]

It's important to understand that *judgments* are perfectly okay, even necessary; it's *judgmentalism* that creates problems. To be specific, we're referring here to the judgmental messages that come from your Inner Critic.

Important Points in This Chapter

Here's what you'll need to know from this chapter in order to build a solid foundation for challenging your Inner Critic:

☐ The difference between a want and an imperative should.

☐ The difference between an imperative should and a recipe should.

☐ The difference between "judgmentalism" and "a judgment."

☐ The fact that imperative shoulds are simply commands combined with expressions of judgmentalism, not factual statements.

In the next chapter, we'll explore the five kinds of emotional punishment inflicted by your Inner Critic when you disobey its shoulds.

NOTES

1. The blueprint is the same as Freud's ego ideal—a set of standards the superego uses by which to measure the ego. *[From p. 48]*

HOW THE INNER CRITIC FUNCTIONS 49

2. The idea of shoulds comes from Karen Horney, who calls them coercive inner dictates and taboos (1950, Chapter 3).

Shoulds are roughly equivalent to the "drivers" mentioned in Transactional Analysis, which are defined as "negative restrictive messages" (Woollams & Brown 1979, pp. 155f). Anthetics identifies many more than the five listed in TA.

Unlike Rational Emotive Behavior Therapy, Anthetics distinguishes between shoulds (which prescribe emotional punishment when you don't obey them) and musts (something you want badly—but which are just strongly-held wants). Since REBT does not use the concepts of the Inner Critic or shoulds, it cannot account for the source of the "awfulism" it describes. *[From p. 41]*

3. Albert Ellis prefers the term "must" to "should." One problem with Ellis's term, however, is that you can't use it to talk unambiguously about shoulds referring to past events. For example, if you use Anthetic language, your meaning is clear when you say "I should have saved enough money for a down payment on a house." In Ellis's language this becomes "I must have saved enough money for a down payment on a house," a sentence which in ordinary usage simply means "I probably did save the money." *[From p. 42]*

4. Some people think the difference between a should and a want is that the should is externally imposed, while a want comes from within. However, both wants and shoulds come from within. *[From p. 43]*

5. For more information on shoulds, see Jim's article (Elliott 1995). *[From p. 44]*

6. If a recipe should is not obeyed, there's no psychological pain; if an imperative should (i.e., an Inner Critic should) is not obeyed, the Inner Critic pounces, inflicting one or more of the emotional punishments to be described in the next chapter. *[From p. 45]*

7. It might bear repeating to say that, contrary to what most writers and lecturers maintain, "a judgment" is not the same as "judgmentalism." A judgment is simply an assessment or evaluation: e.g., "X-therapy is better than Y-therapy." Judgmentalism is a disparaging remark; e.g., "Y-therapy is a con game." *[From p. 47]*

8. Many writers believe that "judgmentalism" means "evaluation." This position leads them to urge the avoidance of evaluating anything. For example, McKay & Fanning (1987) recommend that people abstain from: (a) judging anyone's behavior as good or bad; (b) evaluating as good or bad or right or wrong anything one reads, sees on TV, or observes in the street (including assaults, terrorist bombings, and political corruption); and (c) comparing people on any dimension (e.g., intelligence) where one person is judged to be better and another person is judged to be worse. *[From p. 48]*

5

The Five Emotional Punishments Inflicted by Your Inner Critic

WE HOPE YOU'VE GATHERED BY NOW that your Inner Critic is in no sense a benevolent figure.[1] It is instead the source of most of the psychological pain you experience. This psychological pain consists of five emotional punishments that the Inner Critic inflicts when you disobey its shoulds. Let's take a look at these punishments one by one.

Punishment #1
Feeling
Defective

The Inner Critic messages that produce feelings of defectiveness are of two kinds:

Messages of imperfection: "You are flawed, imperfect, faulty, inadequate, deficient, and blemished" and

Messages of evilness: "You are evil, sinful, and wicked." Your Inner Critic may also call you nasty or say you have a dirty or filthy mind.

Both kinds of messages, if you believe them, will make you feel

THE FIVE EMOTIONAL PUNISHMENTS 51

defective. This feeling can be captured in one sentence: "There's something wrong with me." (Feeling evil means "There's something *morally* wrong with me.")

None of these things are true. They are simply Inner Critic messages you have bought into.

Now let's take a look at some things you might feel defective about:

■ **A body part:** a large nose or ears, pimples, being over- or underweight, wearing braces on your teeth, being very tall or short; or having very small or very large breasts, a small penis, bow legs, or a receding or jutting chin.

■ **Thoughts and feelings:** e.g., feeling anger or feeling hurt or having sexual feelings and fantasies (i.e., "impure thoughts").

■ **Illness or disability:** having a medical condition or disease; for example, a cardiac problem, venereal disease, or AIDS. Having a disability may also be the occasion for feeling defective: for example, wearing a hearing aid or glasses or having an artificial limb.

■ **Engaging in certain sexual practices:** e.g., creative sex, masturbation, or even conventional sexual intercourse.

■ **Engaging in such natural functions as** defecation and urination. Menstruation may also be seen as a defect.

■ **Performance defectiveness:** e.g., impotence, frigidity, difficulty in engaging in small talk, not being able to speak English well, stammering, being inarticulate, or having a mental block while giving a speech.

■ **So-called childishness:** Defectiveness is often felt about one's immaturity or lack of strength. The Inner Critic message in this case is "You should be an adult, but you're not an adult. You're just a child, a boy or girl pretending to be an adult." Men are especially vulnerable to Inner Critic shouldn'ts having to do with being weak, passive, cowardly, fragile, submissive, meek, unassertive, soft, chicken, wimpish, shy, effeminate, and sissyish.

■ **Mental problems:** Another kind of defectiveness is reflected in such terms as having psychological problems (or just "problems") or being mentally ill, neurotic, crazy, insane, unbalanced, disturbed, or emotionally unstable. People who have anxiety or panic attacks often think they're going crazy, partly because they feel out of control and partly because they think nobody else has these feelings (which is definitely not true), but mostly because their Inner Critics are condemning them for being defective.

It's important to note that the above feelings of defectiveness seem "realistic"; that is, if you have them, you may think the feelings represent "real" badness of some kind or other. We want to tell you as emphatically as we can that this is not so. They are just feelings, not facts. They have their source in your Inner Critic, and if you believe you are bad or evil, it's just that you have bought into into what your Inner Critic has been telling you. That's all that's been happening.

It's also important to note that defectiveness is not the same as shame. Feelings of shame occur only when you perceive your "defectiveness" as being actually or potentially revealed to others.

<u>Punishment #2</u>

Shame

As long as nobody knows about your "defectiveness," it can be a secret, and no actual shame will be involved. But if you are (or might be) observed by someone, your secret defectiveness is out in the open, and shame becomes added to it. Embarrassment is a mild form of shame; mortification and humiliation are more severe varieties.

Here are some examples of "defective" behaviors or conditions that your Inner Critic might condemn as shameful if they were to be observed by someone: walking around with your zipper unzipped, forgetting someone's name, changing your hearing aid battery, needing a haircut, taking heart medication, having a spot on your clothing, mispronouncing a word, and having your slip show. You may also feel shame when someone can hear your stomach gurgling, and you may even apologize for this totally involuntary and natural happening.

Blushing is a good clue to shame; if you were alone and you exhibited some "defective" behavior, you probably wouldn't blush.

<u>Punishment #3</u>

Guilt Feelings

Guilt feelings may be as minor as a slight twinge, or they may be experienced as a heavy, oppressive, pervasive sense of having done something terribly wrong.

To understand guilt feelings, it's important to separate "being guilty" from "feeling guilty." Being guilty means you have broken a law. Feeling guilty, on the other hand, is just a feeling. "Feelingful guilt" is not "factual guilt."

Guilt feelings are not to be trusted; they are merely a form of psychological pain generated by your Inner Critic when it says "You have transgressed, and you are a bad person for having done that."

If I drive a couple of miles over the speed limit, I may *be* guilty, but I may not *feel* guilty. Similarly, I may feel guilty when I am not in fact guilty (e.g., when I say No to someone's request); that is, when I have not committed a crime. So guilt and guilt feelings are independent of each other; each can occur without the other, even though they often occur together.

What we'll be talking about here is feelingful guilt, not factual guilt.

Disadvantages Of Guilt and Shame

In order to disarm your Inner Critic and reduce (or end) your psychological suffering, it's vitally important that you become convinced of the harmful effects of such suffering. It will certainly be obvious to many people that suffering is not a good thing, but for those who think mental anguish might lead to some positive results, here are a few reasons that will, we hope, persuade them otherwise:

■ **Guilt feelings are not reliable guides to factual guilt.** This has been mentioned above but is worth mentioning again. Sometimes you feel guilty about something you know quite well is not a crime or transgression. For example:

- If someone asks to borrow money from you, and you say No, you might feel guilty, even though you haven't committed a crime.
- People are often taught by religious authorities to feel guilty about simply having sexual feelings. Most people know these are not crimes but instead are perfectly normal, no matter how unusual.
- Others feel guilty about assertive and constructive behaviors: asking for a raise, winning money in the lottery, being chosen over others for a promotion, being singled out for special praise, turning down an applicant for a job, or evaluating an employee's performance.

To repeat: You can feel guilty without being guilty, and that's why guilt feelings are unreliable.

■ **Guilt feelings may program you to do dangerous things.** Ellen reported that while waiting for traffic to clear so she could turn left, the car behind her started honking its horn. She felt guilty. The crime: holding up traffic. Driven by her feeling, she began her turn too soon. An approaching motorcycle slammed into the side of her car. The motorcyclist was not injured, fortunately, but his bike was damaged, and Ellen's insurance company paid the bill (and raised her rates). She got a ticket. It could have been much worse, and it sometimes is. And all because of guilt feelings.

■ **Guilt feelings may drive you to punish yourself for any success you achieve.** Your Inner Critic may tell you that you didn't deserve the success, and it will demand that you atone for your audacity in overstepping your bounds. For example, you may unconsciously punish yourself by having an accident, making mistakes, procrastinating, or losing interest in what you are doing.

If you hit it big in the lottery, you can feel so guilty that you must atone by giving away all the money you won—or losing it through what appear to be bad decisions but which in fact are modes of atonement. Russian writer Fyodor Dostoyevsky felt so burdened by guilt that he found relief only through gambling—and losing. Writes Freud : "He never rested until he had lost everything. For him gambling was a method of self-punishment..." (1928/1964, p. 191).[2]

Some people go out of their way to unconsciously search for people (even mates) and situations that will punish them, becoming what Bergler (1962) calls "injustice collectors."[3] What seems like a poor choice of partner often is the correct choice from the standpoint of your Inner Critic, which requires that you experience a certain quota of suffering to atone for the guilt feelings it inflicts. So you are punished twice over.

■ **Guilt feelings are disempowering.** Not only must you atone for any success you have achieved in the past, you can even atone in advance. That is, you can protect yourself against feeling both guilt and shame by giving away your personal power, thus ensuring that you won't transgress by getting too big for your britches.

For example, being self-effacing will ward off almost all guilt. If you never make requests of others, you'll avoid feeling guilty about "burdening" them or "intruding on" them. You might buy something you don't really want because if you said No, you'd be guilty of hurting the salesperson's feelings. You might associate with people you don't like because you'd feel guilty about hurting their feelings if you refused to be with them. You might find yourself unable to end a telephone conversation, too, so you listen on and on, even if it's only a sales pitch you're hearing.

You may be afraid to carefully count the change you get back after paying for something because it would be a reflection on the other person's honesty. You may find it difficult to tell an employee what to do, to check that employee's work, or to reprimand or fire someone who is not working properly.

All these are labelled "crimes" by your Inner Critic, who wants you to be a GLK (Good Little Kid) at all times.

One of my (Jim) clients, Harry, married his first wife because he couldn't tell her he didn't want to go through with the marriage. It would devastate her, he said, and he would feel too guilty. After five miserable years, they got divorced, and she was devastated anyway.

In relationships, guilt feelings cause you to pretzelize yourself—twist yourself into a pretzel to avoid offending others. For instance, you can't say when you want to be alone, and you can't say No, because you'll hurt someone's feelings. The result of pretzelizing is that you feel trapped in the relationship. Smothered. Suffocated.[4] And inevitably angry.

So then you've got to get free. But you can't just say you want to leave, because that would *really* hurt the other person's feelings. So instead, you start complaining and feeling judgmental and picking fights to set the stage for leaving. And then you explode with anger. You say "That's the last straw!" And only then can you leave without feeling guilty.

Guilt and shame may also disempower people by blocking them from excelling. Those who have a vision of achieving excellence in their fields, perhaps even making important contributions, may find an emotional barrier to this mission. The barrier appears when they buy into the Inner Critic's message that if they became better than others, they would be elitist, arrogant, and conceited.[5]

In addition, we may feel guilty if we make a lot of money. We may feel flawed if we show off and attract attention to ourselves. We may feel shame if we achieve success of any kind. And so superiority becomes a crime, while averageness and mediocrity are glorified. Abraham Maslow writes of the Jonah complex: fear of one's own greatness. "We fear our highest possibilities," he declares. "We are generally afraid to become that which we can glimpse in our most perfect moments,...under conditions of greatest courage" (1971, p. 35).

All this results in a tragic loss for our culture—a loss of vitality that occurs because the Inner Critic prevents people from living a life informed by greatness of spirit and nobility of purpose.

Not only individuals but whole nations may be negatively affected by a kind of national Inner Critic. A nation may be so guilt- and shame-ridden that it suffers from a failure of nerve that prevents it from acting forcefully when such force is appropriate; for example in carrying out a war that is fought to resist aggression.

All the above consequences are disempowerments, and they occur when you trust your feelings of guilt.

■ **Shame makes you pretend to be what you're not.** The shame of being found ignorant makes people confabulate answers even when they don't know what they're talking about. The shame of losing makes them cheat. The shame of being thought weak makes them arrogant, insensitive, and domineering. Shame makes people engage in superficial chit-chat and avoid the intensity of honest and direct communication, because of their fear that they'll be unmasked.

The shame involved in saying "I love you" makes men hard-hearted and uncaring; whatever love they feel is blocked from expression because they have bought into their Inner Critic's message that expressing love is mushy, feminine, and unmanly.

■ **Guilt feelings and shame will undermine your self-esteem by blocking you from loving yourself.** How can you love someone (yourself) who is so defective, shameful, and guilty?

■ **Guilt and shame prevent you from having pleasure.** Think for a moment of the guilt you feel (or once felt) at having those unusual sexual thoughts and fantasies. Or perhaps the guilt you feel at the thought of enjoying yourself in any way. Note the messages you get from your Inner Critic that having pleasure would be trivial, frivolous, unproductive, and a waste of time.

If your life seems dull and unhappy (or if you're depressed), it means you aren't having enough pleasure, and the reason is probably the anti-pleasure messages coming from your Inner Critic.

■ **Guilt and shame feelings will also make you vulnerable to manipulation by others.** To the extent that you are driven by guilt feelings, you'll be easy prey for your counterpart: the guilt-slinger.

Guilt-slingers will try to make you feel bad (i.e., by triggering your Inner Critic) for not measuring up to their standards.

Here are some examples from guilt-slinging parents: "After all we've done for you, don't you think you owe us something?" Or: "It's your decision, but think of the pain you're causing us—and we won't be around much longer." (For a great many people, statements like these sound perfectly normal.)

■ **Each of the emotional punishments described here makes you vulnerable to using drugs and alcohol as anesthetics.** Drugs and alcohol can put your Inner Critic to sleep, thereby easing the pain felt by your devalued self. Temporarily. When your Inner Critic is medicated, you can feel good. Other parts of your personality can emerge—perhaps a Playful Child. After a while, of course, drugs and alcohol don't make you feel good any more; you take them just for maintenance—to get back to "normal." Finally, you take them simply for the oblivion they bring.

■ **Each emotional punishment can also make you vulnerable to using food to comfort your devalued self.** Since this comfort will frequently be needed, the result is overeating. Food seems to numb the pain, so when your Inner Critic pounces, you may eat too much. If you're a person who binges on food, you might take a look at what your Inner Critic was saying (and what you were feeling) just before the binge.

Inner Critic Propaganda About Guilt and Shame Feelings

As you might imagine, your Inner Critic has a stake in your continuing to believe its messages. As long as you are a True Believer in its ability to give you useful guidance, it can remain in control. But as soon as you start to buy out of what it says, its power is lessened. So in order to maintain its position as your guiding star, your Inner Critic will load you up with all the propaganda at its disposal. This, of course, will not sound to you like propaganda at all. It will sound like "perfectly good sense" and "it just seems normal" and "that's the way things really are."

We want to tell you, however, that the propaganda is just that. It's not good sense at all. If you believe it, it's something that destroys your happiness and effectiveness. It's something to be challenged.

In Chapter 14 you'll find an extensive description of Inner Critic propaganda. Here are some examples of this propaganda as it refers to guilt and shame, along with some suggested countering statements:

PROPAGANDA: Using guilt feelings and shame to guide your life is proof that you're conscientious, caring, "good," responsible, moral, etc. Without such a guide, you'd be irresponsible, uncaring, bad, and immoral, just like those people who have no guilt feelings at all and can get away with anything they want.
COUNTER: I don't need to be punished by guilt feelings in order to be morally good. I can be morally good simply by choosing moral goodness as a value—I can choose to be conscientious, caring, and responsible.

PROPAGANDA: Having guilt feelings and shame keeps you in line. Such feelings help you become a good person by maintaining self-control. They prevent you from running amok. Without them, God knows what you'd do. If you didn't have guilt feelings and shame to restrain you, you might do anything. You might rob banks and cheat people. You might hurt or offend others.
COUNTER: I don't need punishment to keep myself "in line." I can choose freely to be a good person, to not rob banks, to not cheat people. Moreover, if I'm driven by guilt, I might find myself doing destructive things simply in order to get punished. I might also find myself being judgmental toward others, which will block my ability to love them and care about them.

PROPAGANDA: You wouldn't know how to behave without guilt feelings and shame to guide you. You'd be in limbo. It would be too uncomfortable. If you didn't use guilt feelings, how would you live your life? You'd have no guidance at all.
COUNTER: If I gave up my guilt and shame as guides, I might feel in limbo for a while, but I could rely on my Inner Guide for guidance. I could figure out how to live a good life without using self-punishment as a deterrent.

Your Inner Guide

Your Inner Guide is a positive and gentle inner figure that often

THE FIVE EMOTIONAL PUNISHMENTS   59

gets covered over by the domineering and negative Inner Critic. Whereas the Inner Critic stands ready to inflict emotional punishment if you don't obey, the Inner Guide stands ready to offer you unconditional love and acceptance, along with its gentle and caring guidance. Whereas the Inner Critic is your negative conscience, the Inner Guide is your positive conscience.

For example, your Inner Critic will say, "Look both ways before you cross the street; if you don't, you're a stupid idiot." Your Inner Guide would say, "I care about you and I don't want you to get hurt, so it would be a good idea if you looked both ways before you cross the street so you won't get hit by a car. But if you don't look both ways, you're still okay."[6]

The voice of the Inner Guide tells us we should drive on the right side of the road, not because we would be bad, guilty, or otherwise devalued if we didn't—but simply because it makes sense within the context of the traffic rules. Your Inner Guide will tell you: "It's important to drive on the right side (in the U.S., anyway) because I don't want you to get in any accidents. I care about you."

Whereas the Inner Critic often appears in Anthetic Dialogue as a diabolical figure, the Inner Guide appears as a positive spiritual figure.

QUESTION: Is the Inner Guide like a "spirit guide" that occultists talk about?

ANSWER: No. The term "Inner Guide" is just a name for the positive conscience. It has nothing to do with occultism.

The Payoffs
For Feeling Guilt and Shame

Why are people so addicted to their Inner Critics? Partly because they believe the above propaganda messages. But also because of the following powerful payoffs:

■ Feeling guilty sets up a game you think you can win if you try hard enough. First, your Inner Critic tells you that you're bad. Then it gives you the illusion that you can buy your way out of the pain and suffering of your badness through confession, atonement, and reparation. Usually, you can't. You'll still feel guilty. But you'll keep trying, thinking that some day you'll make it.

■ Guilt and shame can "protect" you by holding you back from doing scary things—for example, making requests, becoming closer to someone, getting promoted, applying for a new job, beginning a new project. Because you like to be protected from overstepping your bounds, you'll value your Inner Critic.

■ Guilt makes you feel self-righteous. Not only does it prop up your self-image of being a highly moral person, it also permits you to be judgmental toward others—which compensates for your own feeling of devaluation. Of course, your partner won't like your judgmentalism very much, and you'll experience some bitter arguments.

Some Questions And Challenges

We hope the above discussion has persuaded you that shame and guilt feelings are dysfunctional as guides to behavior. But perhaps not. We realize that what we are proposing here is a big shift in your thinking. We want to give you as much support as possible in deciding to make this shift, because if you think that shame and guilt feelings are in any sense useful, you will not see them as material to be challenged, and your Inner Critic will have a strong grip on your life.

In order to challenge your Inner Critic, you must be firmly convinced that emotional pain, suffering, and anguish are not desirable, and you must see that the five emotional punishments (especially guilt and shame) are examples of that suffering. To help you arrive at this position, here are some questions asked by our clients, along with our answers:

QUESTION: Aren't guilt feelings useful in serving as warning signals? Won't they help us tell right from wrong?

ANSWER: Even if guilt feelings did not add to your mental anguish, there's a good argument against using them as signals pointing to wrong behavior: they are notoriously unreliable. If you're like most people, you may (and often will) feel guilty about something which is in no sense a crime or transgression. So if you use guilt feelings as warning signals, you're making a mistake, because you just can't trust them.

But, keeping this in mind, you might say you still want to use them as signals. Remember that they're a form of suffering. If you want to use your own suffering as a warning signal, you're welcome to do that, of course.

THE FIVE EMOTIONAL PUNISHMENTS 61

However, choosing to use guilt feelings as guides to behavior (in the form of warning signals) is like trying to lose weight by putting poison in your food. The poison makes you feel bad when you eat the food, so you won't be likely to eat so much of it. You might say, "Well, I'm using just a little bit of poison," but it's still poison, and it's still destructive to your system. Like poison, a lot of guilt is more destructive than a little guilt—but a little guilt is still poison.

QUESTION: But if I don't use guilt feelings as warnings, how will I know when I'm doing something unethical? Don't we need some internal guide for our behavior?

ANSWER: Yes, indeed we do. The question is whether that internal source of guidance is to be a harsh, punitive, perfectionistic Inner Critic—or whether it is to be a loving, caring figure—your Inner Guide.

The more your Inner Critic's power is reduced, the more chance there is for this new source of guidance to emerge.

QUESTION: But my Inner Guide, if I have one, doesn't seem strong enough to give me guidance. Don't I need the strength of my Inner Critic?

ANSWER: If your Inner Guide seems weak, it's only because it has been eclipsed by your Inner Critic. As you reduce the voltage of your Inner Critic, your Inner Guide will have a chance to emerge in all its power.

QUESTION: If I feel guilty, doesn't it show that I'm concerned about others and care about them? If I stepped on someone's toes and didn't feel guilty, I'd think I was callous and uncaring.

ANSWER: The assumption here is that guilt feelings are manifestations of sensitivity and caring. But that's not true. Certainly, if I care about you, I will not choose to step on your toes or otherwise injure you. I can make this choice driven by a fear of guilt, or I can make it freely, simply because I have adopted caring as a value, and because I have chosen to care about you. And because, if I stepped on your toes, and you felt pain, I would empathize with you—I would feel your pain—and I would not want you to feel that pain, because my sense of self is bound up with yours.

QUESTION: Simple caring and empathy don't seem to be strong enough. Won't guilt feelings add to the power of my commitment to be caring?

ANSWER: At first glance, they may appear to. It's certainly true that if I were to feel guilty about hurting you, I would be very, very careful not to hurt you in any way whatever. But there would actually be a great net loss in my ability to be caring, because I would feel that I had to walk around on eggshells to avoid upsetting you. Sooner or later I would feel resentment about this, followed by anger, judgmentalism, and vindictiveness (what we will call the JAV triad in Chapter 17). These JAV feelings will not only block my ability to be truly loving, they will more than outweigh any caring that guilt feelings might punitively enforce over the short run.

QUESTION: But aren't some guilt feelings normal, natural, valid, legitimate, and/or appropriate?

ANSWER: Questions like this are usually attempts to place guilt feelings in a special category: "Normal—not to be worked on." The assumption is that if they are normal, natural, valid, legitimate, and appropriate, they just are what they are: "terminal feelings"—not to be processed (i.e., not to be seen as clues to Inner Critic functioning).

But if you are committed to inner freedom (i.e., freedom from oppression by your Inner Critic), you will see all guilt feelings as "material to work on." That is, you'll see them as forms of punishment and suffering. Then you'll want to work on them no matter whether they are normal or abnormal, natural or unnatural, valid or invalid, legitimate or illegitimate, appropriate or inappropriate—whatever those words might mean.

QUESTION: Aren't guilt feelings inevitable? Aren't they universal?

ANSWER: They may be inevitable, and they may even be universal. The only issue we're addressing here, however, is whether they are useful guides to behavior. Our contention is that they are not.

QUESTION: But if something is universal, how can you call it pathological?

ANSWER: First of all, Anthetic Therapy doesn't use the term "pathological." It uses the term "reactive." But even more important is a hidden assumption in questions like this. The assumption is that there's a sharp demarcation between "healthy" people and "pathological" people and that the "healthy" ones have little or no reactivity.

AT holds that every one of us (saints, spiritual gurus, and therapists included) have some reactivity. In other words, having reactivity, to a greater or lesser extent, is universal.

QUESTION: Isn't it good to feel guilty if I knowingly betray a confidence or deliberately injure someone out of sheer malice?
ANSWER: If you want to live a life based on mental suffering, it's okay to use guilt feelings as guides to behavior. But then you might expect a certain amount of psychological pain and suffering in your life, along with the other problems mentioned in this book, and you won't be too surprised when they occur. Maybe you won't even complain about them, knowing that through your belief in healthy guilt, you have chosen to have them.

QUESTION: Isn't civilization built on shame and guilt feelings?
ANSWER: Sure, civilization is built on shame and guilt feelings, because civilization is built on a sadomasochistic morality. Look where it got us: cruelty, war, torture, revenge. How about a civilization built on love and caring, instead?

QUESTION: If you don't have guilt feelings, doesn't that mean you're a psychopath?
ANSWER: A psychopath doesn't have caring feelings toward others. A psychopath is so self-centered that he or she can't empathize with other people. We believe that as you reduce the power of your guilt feelings, you must add love and caring as values in your life, along with the ability to be empathic. In any case, the Inner Critic, as we shall see later, is what prevents us from expressing love and caring.

QUESTION: Maybe guilt feelings and shame are bad for me. But aren't they useful for others? Won't they prevent others from committing crimes?
ANSWER: A case can be made that the fear of experiencing guilt and shame will prevent some people from committing crimes. These are people who, unless they fear inner punishment, will not choose to be caring.

We have two responses to this question. First, if such people read this book, they will find here the strongest possible recommendation to add love and caring behavior to their inner freedom—and a warning that destructive things happen to people who achieve inner freedom without also valuing love and caring (see Chapter 17 for more on this).

Some of the newer therapies do in fact help people overcome their guilt feelings, so a certain number of people will get free from guilt whether they read this book or not. But if such therapies do not also encourage love and caring behavior, their adherents may report the achievement of a certain amount of inner freedom but be puzzled by the fact that their relationships are not very satisfying. Love and caring are necessary for good relationships.

Second, all the negativity we have seen in our clients has come from the fact that the clients are guided by an Inner Critic-based conscience. Once the Inner Critic is disarmed, the natural love and caring that exist in everyone can well up and be expressed.

QUESTION: But aren't there such things as wrongdoing and immorality?

ANSWER: Yes, of course. When you don't conform to a moral standard, that's immorality. Moral standards are absolutely necessary, both for the welfare of society as a whole and for the welfare of each individual.

The question is whether morality should come from the Inner Critic or the Inner Guide. Sadomasochistic morality comes from the Inner Critic. It's harsh, punitive, repressive, and perfectionistic. Of utmost importance, it inevitably leads to rebellion, revenge, sadism, and destructiveness. Anthetic morality, originating in the Inner Guide, is gentle and empathic. It leads to love and caring.

QUESTION: Granted that guilt feelings are dysfunctional. What about remorse or regret? Are these okay?

ANSWER: The Inner Critic is a slippery character and will try to smuggle in its punishment wherever it can. If you won't buy guilt from it, it will try to sell you the same article under such names as remorse or regret.

To tell whether these terms are merely synonyms for guilt feelings, use the following criterion: When you have these feelings, do you feel bad about yourself—as though there's something wrong with you or defective about you? If so, it's one of the Inner Critic's emotional punishments in disguise.

But if your answer is a firm, unequivocal No, then remorse or regret simply means sorrowful disappointment; e.g., "I wish I hadn't done that." It's a simple wish not to have done something. The Inner Critic is not involved.

QUESTION: Are you saying, then, that I should eliminate all guilt feelings and shame?
ANSWER: Not if you do it through willpower or "thought-stopping." If you think you have eliminated them using these methods, those feelings would probably just be driven underground, where they would cause even more trouble, because then you wouldn't be aware of them.

The goal here is to reduce your psychological suffering, which includes guilt feelings and shame, but only through challenging your Inner Critic. This leaves you with the *capacity* to feel guilt and shame but eliminates their negative impact on your life, because you are no longer using these feelings as guides to behavior.

Why do we recommend that you continue to have the capacity to feel guilt and shame? Because only then will you be able to empathize with others who also have these feelings.

QUESTION: Are you arguing for moral relativism?
ANSWER: Absolutely not, if by moral relativism you mean morality based on arbitrary choices having their source in transitory impulses, feelings, and whims. Nor are we saying that right and wrong should be different for different societies or different people. The argument here is for a firm, substantial, principled morality that is based on such rock-solid values as inner freedom, love, responsibility, and genuine caring for others. These are absolute values, in the sense of being uncompromising and universal.

Many Experts Are Unaware of The Inner Critic

Once people see that guilt and shame are forms of mental suffering, few would be inclined to say anything good on their behalf. Yet, strangely enough, some writers in the field of recovery and psychotherapy have not yet become aware of the power, pervasiveness, and destructiveness of the Inner Critic. The result is that these experts contend that certain forms of guilt and shame are actually healthy—that is, good for you.

Although such writers have helped hundreds of thousands of people, Anthetic Inner Critic theory is such a new development that it has not yet been incorporated in their books and articles. And so they see some forms of shame and guilt as useful.[7]

Shame is said to prevent us from getting carried away. It's supposed to keep us grounded, to warn us that we are limited in our powers, and to remind us that we don't know it all and that we are not God.

Remember: when such writers talk about guilt and shame, they are talking about psychological pain. Therapists who recommend any form of guilt and shame are recommending suffering and anguish—the very things, in our opinion, they should be helping their clients to reduce.

One writer declared that shame at being sexually impotent is good because it teaches us that we cannot achieve an erection through sheer willpower![8]

Rollo May (1939) described guilt as "a positive constructive emotion...a perception of the difference between what a thing is and what it ought to be."

In later works, May spoke favorably of "ontological guilt," a concept apparently derived from German philosopher Martin Heidegger. This kind of guilt comes in three varieties: (1) guilt at giving up some of one's potentialities; (2) guilt at failing to understand others and meet their needs; and (3) guilt at being separated from nature (May 1958, pp. 54f).

Abraham Maslow was another who argued in favor of guilt, calling it "justified self-disapproval" when it results from "a turning off the path to self-actualization." He continues: "[I]t is good, even *necessary*, for a person's development to have intrinsic guilt when he deserves to. It is not just a symptom to be avoided at any cost but is rather an inner guide for growth toward actualization of the real self, and of its potentialities" (1962, p. 182).

Few writers are as direct as George Bach and Scott Peck, who actually recommend self-punishment. Bach suggests that you deal with guilt by punishing yourself. "This may sound foolish or harsh," he explains, "but the 'twerp' [his term for the Inner Critic] will punish you unless you do so yourself" (1985, p. 173).

Peck actually argues for self-hatred. The fault of "evil people," he declares, may be "that they do not hate the sinful part of themselves." "The central sin at the root of the scapegoating behavior of those I call evil," he continues, "is the failure to be displeasing to oneself—a failure of self-hatred" (1983, pp. 74f).

We're All Guiltaholics And Shameaholics

If you know about Alcoholics Anonymous, you know how difficult it is for an alcoholic to become aware of the destructiveness of his addiction. We maintain that the same is true of people who argue in favor of guilt and shame as useful feelings. Like alcoholics, they're also addicted, but to guilt and shame. We call them guiltaholics and shameaholics. In fact, our clinical work has convinced us that we are all guiltaholics to some extent—we seem to want a "fix" of guilt. We are shameaholics, too. To rationalize our addictions, we may hold the belief that both guilt feelings and shame are good for us. We have difficulty seeing that both these emotions are dangerous and destructive. That is, we are in denial, just like any alcoholic prior to recovery.

In this chapter we have talked at great length about the dangers and disadvantages of guilt feelings and shame, just as we would tell you about the dangers of any addiction, whether it be to drugs or alcohol. We do this because we know that you might be thinking that guilt is good for you, just as an alcoholic thinks that booze is a necessary part of his life.

Guilt feelings and shame are nothing but suffering, and anyone who buys into suffering—even a little of it—is buying into something destructive, something that creates reactive living, and something that blocks genuine love and caring.

We do not need shame to let us know that we are not God; we know that already. We do not need shame to let us know that we are limited; we know that, too. We men do not need shame to teach us that we cannot use sheer willpower to have an erection. We know all these things perfectly well without shame.[9]

Challenging The Experts About Feelings of Guilt and Shame

To summarize: If you want to challenge your Inner Critic, you'll need to realize the uselessness of guilt and shame as guides to behavior. If you have believed the experts who say that guilt and shame are good for you, you've got to challenge those experts.

It's easy to see what they've been thinking: "We see guilt and shame in our clients, and we know we've got to reduce it so they will reduce their suffering. But if we remove all of it, why, they might do anything. Better to leave them with some guilt and shame so they'll continue to conform and be caring." As though people can't be loving and caring on their own.

So not only must you counter your Inner Critic, you've also got to counter any propaganda you've received from "the experts" that guilt feelings and shame are good for you.

How can you do this? By realizing the following:

First, guilt feelings and shame are the material of pain and suffering.

Second, anybody who tries to tell you that pain and suffering are good for you is not acting in your best interests. Such a person is trying to sell you a belief system that is oppressive and disempowering.

QUESTION: But isn't there some positive value in suffering?
ANSWER: Your Inner Critic would sure like you to think so.

QUESTION: Come on, now. Can't you learn from suffering?
ANSWER: Hopefully, you can learn one thing from psychological suffering: how to reduce it.

<u>Punishment #4</u>
Feeling Inferior

Your Inner Critic loves to compare you negatively with others. Not only does it say you're defective, it tells you that you are more defective than others and therefore ought to feel inferior to them. It says that no one else has those bizarre thoughts, feelings, and anxieties that you have. It tells you that others are powerful and effective, while you are helpless and ineffective. Moreover, adds your Inner Critic, your greater defectiveness or evilness makes you less worthy than they.

According to your Inner Critic, everyone else is pretty normal, but *you* are somehow abnormal. Others are successful, but you are a failure. Others are much further along in their financial, emotional, or spiritual development; you are a laggard. Others are paragons of maturity and wisdom; you are immature.

Things seem to come easily to others; they don't have to struggle much or work hard to get what they want, but you do. Unlike you, they rarely feel nervous, anxious, or inadequate. They never have any of those strange fantasies that cross your mind from time to time. Most other people seem to be doing fine; you're the only one with those serious problems.

In short, your Inner Critic tells you that others are sane, successful, and "together." They are, in some basic way, "better" than you, and you are "less than" or inferior to them.

This means that, because you are not their equal, they have rights that you don't have. It also means that their feelings are more important than your feelings. Finally, it means that what others want is more important than what you want.

Of course, none of this is true. It's simply the disempowerment you feel when you buy into the messages of your Inner Critic.

<u>Punishment #5</u>
Magnified Fear

Your Inner Critic will take any little fear or concern you have and blow it way up into such things as panic, anxiety, and constant worry. In its mistaken zeal to protect you, your Inner Critic will warn you not to try anything new because nothing you do will turn out right. In addition, it will declare that you are so defective that you won't be able to handle any problems that might come up. On top of that, it will tell you that the negative outcome it predicts will be catastrophic, terrible, and devastating. Here are some of its predictions:

- ■ If you go to the party, you'll have an awful time.
- ■ If you go to the singles group, you won't meet anyone worthwhile.
- ■ If you don't get the job, you'll go bankrupt and have to go on welfare.
- ■ If you fly in an airplane, it will crash.
- ■ If you make a request or say what you don't like, a disaster will occur.
- ■ If you leave an abusive spouse, you'll never find another partner who is any better.

Each of these may seem like a given fact, but each is probably a factoid—a pseudo-fact concocted by your Inner Critic to make you feel so scared that you'll stay within the constricting boundaries defined by the electric fence discussed in the last chapter.

The Emotional Punishments In Action

To understand the distinctions among the five emotional punishments inflicted by your Inner Critic, imagine yourself spilling a glass of water in two possible situations. First, you're home alone and you knock the glass over. Chances are your Inner Critic will pounce and tell you what a klutz you are. That will produce a feeling of simple defectiveness, but no one has seen what happened, so it is not yet shame.

Now suppose your boss has invited you and your spouse to dinner at an expensive restaurant. Imagine that top executives from your firm are also present. And now you knock over that glass of water as before and get the tablecloth all wet. The result this time is defectiveness plus shame. Shame means that your defectiveness is there for all those important people to see.

Now imagine that at the restaurant, you spill your glass of water not on the tablecloth but on your boss's lap. In this case, guilt is added to your emotional punishments.

And as you look around the table, and you notice the other diners in the restaurant, you see that no one else has spilled any water. Feelings of inferiority will then be added to your burden of psychological suffering.

Finally, you reflect on what this episode might mean. You thought your boss had invited you to dinner to announce your new promotion. Fat chance of getting it now, your Inner Critic whispers in your ear, and you are beset with magnified fear—not only that you won't get promoted but that you might be terminated in the downsizing program that (you imagine) will begin soon.

In each of the above cases, you may think your feelings are realistic. In each case, however, your Inner Critic is the source of the feeling, and the feeling is not necessarily to be trusted.

Triggering

It may appear that other people are responsible for any emotional punishments you feel—that what they say or do "produces" or "creates" these feelings in you. This is not true. It is instead the mechanisms inside you, set up by your Inner Critic, that are the primary cause. This is so important that it deserves some discussion.

Suppose your friend forgets to call you, and you feel hurt and rejected. Does this external event *cause* your negative feelings? Yes, of course. You wouldn't have felt hurt had your friend not forgotten. But although the external event can be a cause, it is not the *primary* cause.

The primary cause is your machinery, which simply got triggered by the external event. The external event pokes your Inner Critic, which then sends a jolt of punishment to your natural self, telling you something like the following: "Your friend doesn't value you, since he forgot. Since he doesn't value you, you must be defective." (Of course, there's more going on than that, but space limitations prevent us from going into it.)[10]

As we mentioned before, it's as though you were sown with land mines, and when an external event (e.g., criticism, a loss, a failure) occurs, it triggers one of those land mines, which then explodes, causing hurt, anger, lowered self-esteem, and depression, caused by one or more of the punishments.

Armed with skills to challenge your Inner Critic, you can dismantle the land mines one by one, so you can feel good about yourself no matter what external thing happens.

The concept of triggering permits you to take responsibility for your feelings instead of blaming them on others. At the same time, it includes the concept of causality, which seems intuitively correct.

The more you realize that the source of negative feelings is your Inner Critic, the more you'll be able to focus your psychological work on the right place. And the less you'll feel like a victim, at the mercy of some villain. You will have taken back the power you had given away to people or events.

Summary:
The Five Punishments

The five emotional punishments described in this chapter add up to most of the psychological pain and mental anguish that people suffer from.[11] At an early age, we decided to live from an Inner Critic-backed philosophy. By doing that, we began to invite psychological pain and mental anguish into our lives.

How can you reduce this mental anguish? Only when you make a value shift to an Anthetic way of life. That way of life begins when you decide to value inner freedom above all other values.

What You'll Need to Know

Here's what you'll need to know from this chapter in order to learn to challenge your Inner Critic:

☐ The five emotional punishments are completely useless as guides to behavior. Since they are forms of mental suffering and anguish, they are not constructive in any way whatever—no matter what the experts say.

☐ Each emotional punishment is not a terminal element. Instead, it's a clue to the fact that your Inner Critic is pouncing, attempting to constrict your life through its shoulds and shouldn'ts. The mechanism that drives each emotional punishment can be dismantled by doing the Anthetic challenging that will be described in later chapters.

The next chapter will explain how reactive self-structure is created in response to the Inner Critic's constricting influence.

NOTES

1. The Inner Critic is non-benevolent by definition. That is, AT defines Inner Critic messages as those that impose shoulds, inflict punishment when the shoulds are disobeyed, and predict disaster for your undertakings. On the other hand, any benevolent messages that you receive come from your Inner Guide; again, this is by definition.

Unlike material objects, inner figures can be demarcated and defined according to the purposes of the demarcator. These definitions, however, are not arbitrary. For example, AT demarcates inner figures according to two criteria: (a) the general purpose of the inner figure, and (b) the kind of work needed to work with the figure.

Moreover, the two sources of messages described in this book must be kept separate so you don't begin to think that your Inner Critic is suddenly having a change of heart and becoming helpful and loving. When that seems to happen, it is simply that your Inner Critic is being *replaced by* your Inner Guide. This way of thinking keeps everything straight, maintains the integrity of each inner figure, and makes inner figure work much easier and more effective. *[From p. 50]*

2. For more information on gambling as self-punishment, see Bergler (1957). *[From p. 54]*

3. Injustice collectors, writes Bergler, are psychic masochists who "unconsciously approach human relationships in a way that makes refusal, rejection or disappointment inevitable" (1962, pp. 85f). Collecting injustices, we have found, gives people a "buffered" kind of permission to act vindictively, which they would ordinarily be unable to do—and, of course, would not even need to do—were it not for the guilt they felt as a result of Inner Critic oppression. *[From p. 54]*

4. If you blame your partner for suffocating you, it may be that all along, you've simply disempowered yourself in response to your own imperative shoulds, and that's why you feel suffocated. *[From p. 55]*

5. People who have strong Inner Critic shoulds not to think they are better than others will be judgmental toward those who present themselves as being better than others. Such judgmental people believe they are better than and superior to others by virtue of their belief that it's wrong to be better and superior.

It appears to be a general rule that your own judgmentalism is a clue to your Inner Critic shoulds. That is, whatever judgmentalism you feel toward others is the same judgmentalism that your Inner Critic would inflict on you, were you to disobey its shoulds. (Note that this does not mean that if you are judgmental toward others, it's about something that you yourself have. If you obey your Inner Critic's shoulds, you might not have it.) *[From p. 55]*

6. Your conscience may be Inner Critic based or Inner Guide based. *[From p. 59]*

7. Among the recovery writers who propose the concept of healthy guilt and/or shame are Bradshaw (1988), Friel & Friel (1988), Kaufman (1989), Mellody (1989), Wegscheider-Cruse (1985), and Whitfield (1987). *[From p. 66]*

8. Kurtz (1981) made the comment about shame and erections. *[From p. 66]*

9. When recovery writers talk about the usefulness of shame, they appear to be conflating that emotion with humility. Humility is a corrective for arrogance, self-righteousness, and grandiosity. These three character traits are indeed destructive. However, they come from living a reactive life based on counterfeit buffers. The traits can be overcome not by doses of emotional punishment in the form of "healthy" shame but by Inner Critic work, since the Inner Critic is the internal agency that demands the buffers and, consequently, creates the arrogance, self-righteousness, and grandiosity. *[From p. 67]*

10. Those familiar with Albert Ellis's A-B-C sequence will recognize the connections between our theory and his. In Ellis's school of therapy, "A" is the Activating event; "C" is the Consequence. Most people believe that A causes C directly. Ellis points out correctly that B is the Belief that is the true cause. Anthetic Therapy agrees but adds that Ellis leaves out the Inner Critic (the source of B) as an intervening variable. Not having the Inner Critic as a concept, Ellis is unable to account for the source of emotional punishment (which he labels "awfulism") and the fact that awfulism results from disobeying the shoulds. *[From p. 71]*

11. Some of our colleagues argue that such items as defectiveness, inferiority, and not belonging are not really emotions but cognitions. Our response is that they are what we call Janus words—terms with dual meanings: one emotional, the other cognitive. (Janus was a Roman god with two faces; he could look both ways).

For example, if I am a short person, I can *be* inferior (in height) or I can *feel* inferior (because of my inferior height). I can *be* defective or *feel* defective. Note also that the term *guilty*, as mentioned in this chapter, is another Janus term. *[From p. 71]*

6

How Your Inner Critic Creates Reactivity

BACKED BY THE POWER OF ITS FIVE emotional punishments, the Inner Critic spreads its influence over the personality like an octopus, creating suffering wherever it goes.

No longer will you be free to fully release the energies of your natural self. Instead, you will be more and more concerned with constricting yourself by developing maneuvers to avoid the punishment threatened by your Inner Critic. Internal scripts for these maneuvers will become crystallized into what we call the reactive self structure.

From The Natural Self To The Devalued Self

The first step in the process of creating reactive self structure occurs when your perfectly good natural self gets converted, in your eyes, into a devalued self.[1] Gradually, large sections of your natural self become pejoratized until many of the thoughts, feelings, and behaviors of your natural self seem to you bad: defective, evil, inferior, shameful, or guilty.[2]

It's important to realize that this is not a real conversion. Instead, it's as though the Inner Critic has placed an overlay of pejoratism over your natural self—an overlay that dulls the natural self's brightness, dims its happy spirit, and turns down its bright flame to a mere flicker.

Because of this overlay, you now see large parts of your natural self as undesirable and bad; that is, not OK. In addition, the devalued self is seen as The Enemy: dangerous, disgusting, unpredictable, uncontrollable, and likely to burst forth in any unguarded moment.

The truly sad part of this process is that it all seems to you to be normal, valid, and realistic. You will probably not be conscious of this process, nor will you be aware that its source is your Inner Critic. You'll just think there are parts of yourself you don't like, parts you need to keep under control, parts that need to be kept submerged. Perhaps you will be so successful at submerging them that you're not aware of them at all.

But the truth is that those parts of your natural self are all perfectly good. You see them as bad only because of the overlay that acts as a filter between you and your good natural self.

As you grew up, the overlay was gradually put in place. As your outer critics criticized you, you internalized their messages, incorporating them into your Inner Critic. The Inner Critic then became the ongoing source of your self-disparagement, self-constrictedness, and self-disempowerment.

As a result of this process, you mistakenly concluded: "There must be something wrong with me; I'm not good enough just as I am."

This conclusion did not seem to be a hypothesis or theory; it took on the force of truth, as solid as any scientific fact. There was no question about it: you were bad. "It was like something God had said," one of our clients declared. "It was not to be questioned."

Reactive Self-Structure Is Created

As a reaction to the threat of punishment by the Inner Critic, your reactive self structure was gradually created. This reactive self structure, or reactive self, consists of two parts:
- The compensatory self
- The protective self

Each "self" was created as a way of coping with primary and secondary pain. Strictly speaking, each of these is not a self but a self-structure—a pattern of feelings, thoughts, decisions, and impulses that are responsible for the major reactive themes in your life.

The Compensatory Self And Its Buffers

Your Inner Critic not only condemns you for not living up to its standards, it also offers what seems to be a way out. What the Inner Critic says is, "You are indeed worthless, you are not good enough as you are, and you deserve to feel bad. But there are ways you can compensate for your badness so you can feel OK again. For example, you could get a job that pays well and that carries with it a lot of prestige. As long as you hold this job, you will feel OK."

This job is an example of what we call a buffer.[3] It's an achievement that temporarily buys off the Inner Critic and prevents it from pouncing. If you feel good because of a buffer, you will continue to feel good as long as the buffer is in place.[4]

Based on years of work with clients and workshop participants, we've been able to identify the following kinds of buffers:

■ **Signs of prosperity and success, both material and intangible:** owning an expensive automobile, living in an expensive house, wearing fine clothing, collecting rare paintings; dining at expensive restaurants; being seen at the opera or concert; owning a successful business; having money in the bank or in investments.

■ **An increase in income:** getting a raise, winning money at gambling or on the stock market; inheriting money.

■ **External emotional supplies:** being loved, getting approval, receiving praise and support, being listened to and attended to, being cared for.

■ **Personal accomplishments:** winning an argument, a game, an election, or a contest of any kind; having the last word; getting an article or story published, acquiring a college degree, getting a job, being promoted, being effective, choosing the shortest line at the bank or grocery store, not letting anyone pass you or cut in front of you on the highway.

■ **Physical attributes:** having a youthful appearance (e.g., a full head of hair); being attractive, healthy, and of standard appearance and physical ability.

■ **Personal traits and attributes:** having a good memory,

having a high IQ, being considerate of others, being strong and self-sufficient, having knowledge or expertise in certain areas, appearing to be mentally healthy, well-balanced, sane, and normal.

■ **Interpersonal accomplishments:** having well-behaved, healthy, and successful children; having prestigious friends and colleagues or business associates; having relatives (including parents) of whom one is proud.

■ **Power:** Power can be a buffer not only for political leaders, military officers, spouse abusers, criminals, racists, and business executives, but also for anyone who acquires control over other people. Buffering power may be sought in a marriage, in a friendship, or in a debate or argument. Loss of power means loss of a buffer, which is why the aforesaid items are so vigorously pursued and maintained. The power-buffered person sees others not as subjects like himself or herself but as objects to be converted, exploited, oppressed, dominated, or kept in their place.

Disobedience on the part of the controlled person is not a little thing; it is a threat to the power-buffered person's ability to stave off the Inner Critic, which is why disobedience is punished so severely and fanatically, either by verbal or physical abuse. (When power is used as a buffer, we call it reactive power. When, on the other hand, power is used in a caring and loving way, it is called Anthetic power.)

■ **Revenge:** You may have a craving for a revenge-buffer if someone injures you, either physically or psychologically. Examples of such injury are: if someone takes advantage of you, steals something from you, doesn't pay back money you have lent, seduces your wife or girlfriend, or takes over what you think of as your country. In any of these cases, your Inner Critic may pounce until you get even.[5]

Comments on Buffers

As long as the buffer prescribed by your Inner Critic is in place, the emotional punishment will be held in abeyance, and you'll feel pretty good. You will have compensated for your supposed badness.

Unfortunately, buffers have two characteristics that prevent their use as permanent compensators. For one thing, the effects of any buffer tend to wear off quickly. If you get promoted, for example, and use that as a buffer, you'll feel good for a while, but then you'll begin to feel unhappy (and perhaps depressed), and you'll need another promotion to continue feeling good.

Apparently, the Inner Critic can be bought off for a short time, but then it gets used to the buffer and demands another—and often better—one. It's like a junkie needing stronger and stronger fixes.

The second characteristic of buffers is that their existence is precarious. Suppose I use my job as a buffer. Then if I should get fired, I may be plunged into a depression. Similarly, if I retire, my self-esteem may plummet; I may feel unhappy and depressed and puzzled as to why I should be having these feelings, exactly when I expected to start enjoying life.

Other losses, such the loss of a chess game, an election, or a reputation may debuffer me, as may the loss of someone's love or approval or the loss of a spouse (through death, divorce, or abandonment). If I don't get recognized or complimented for something I do, if someone insults me, or if someone criticizes me—I may also be debuffered. If I become disabled or disfigured, if I get older and lose my youthful appearance, I will also be debuffered and experience lowered self-esteem and possibly depression.

It's well known that a loss will trigger depression, but it's not well known why. This is the reason: it does so only if what is lost is a buffer.[6] And this is the reason that achievements and material possessions sometimes do and sometimes don't bring happiness: they will not make you happy (in the long run) if they are buffers, meant to buy off the Inner Critic through compensation. On the other hand, they will make you happy if they simply satisfy the needs and desires of your natural self.

Of course, nothing is intrinsically a buffer, but almost anything can be used as one. That is, anything can be used to compensate for the worthlessness felt by the devalued self.

Judgmentalism As A Buffer

Judgmentalism includes put-downs, disparagements, ridicule, blame, faultfinding, and pejorative criticism. It is so common in our society that it seems normal and unremarkable. It is the ordinary, everyday method most parents use in their attempts to discipline their children. It is also the ordinary, everyday way most couples have of relating to each other. Yet judgmentalism is a form of verbal abuse that is destructive not only to children but also to couple relationships.

In every case, judgmentalism is directly connected to Inner Critic functioning, because what your Inner Critic condemns you for is the same thing that you condemn other people for. For example, if your Inner Critic would punish you if you were to become irresponsible, you would condemn other people who appeared to you to be irresponsible.

Note that this is not simply projection of a personal quality or trait. In other words, you do not condemn others for what exists in yourself, since in the case above, you would never permit irresponsibility to exist in your life. Instead, you condemn in others what your Inner Critic would condemn in you, if that trait or quality would ever appear.

But that's only one dynamic that keeps judgmentalism locked in place. Here's another one: The judgmental person uses blame as a buffer. He or she says "As long as I can blame someone, I'm not such a bad person. I'm better than the person I feel judgmental toward, and so I have an alibi to use in fending off my Inner Critic.

"Take that superiority-buffer away from me, and my Inner Critic would swoop down like a marauding dragon, and I would be shattered." For many judgmental people, the subjective value of their blaming someone is so great that they wouldn't dream of working to reduce it.

Addiction To Buffers

As you might imagine, buffers can be highly addictive. There are two reasons for this, each complementary to the other. First of all, the buffer is a support for self-esteem; without it, self-esteem vanishes. Second, if the buffer is lost, the Inner Critic pounces, with all the pain of the five emotional punishments.

For example, if you are buffered by holding an opinion or belief, you will fight tenaciously if your position is threatened by contradictory evidence.[7] In fact, you will have difficulty seeing that there is any merit whatever in the other person's position. (People may accuse you of having a closed mind; you will see yourself as simply a person who knows the truth.)

If your partner leaves you, you will almost certainly feel the immense pain of debuffering, and you may quickly look for a new partner as a means of getting rebuffered. If you lose all your money at gambling, you may borrow money so you can return to the gambling table to try to get your buffer back.

Unfortunately, because they are props to self-esteem and not what is really wanted by the natural self, buffers are not very satisfying. They can be thought of as symbolic goals: things you want for their symbolic value in compensating, not for their real value in satisfying the needs of your natural self.

Natural-Self Pleasures

What is the alternative to relying on a buffer? It's what might be called a natural-self pleasure—a simple pleasure that is pursued for itself and liked for what it is, not because it props up self-esteem. Among the things most commonly serving as natural-self pleasures are tasty food, pleasurable sex, absorbing work, good music, and genuine contact with other people. Each of these is satisfying in itself. (Each, however, can also be used as a buffer in addition to its function as a simple pleasure.)

How do you tell a buffer from a natural-self pleasure? First—and most important—if you fail to obtain the buffer, you will experience low self-esteem and depression. Your Inner Critic will pounce, inflicting one or more of its five emotional punishments: feeling that you're defective, inferior, shameful, or guilty—or feeling anxious. (If you have one of these feelings, all you need do is ask when you began to feel it, then look for the buffer that collapsed.)

On the other hand, if you don't get a natural-self pleasure, you just feel disappointed or sad—but you'll still believe you're a good person. Issues of self-esteem or self-worth are not involved.

The second way of distinguishing a buffer from a natural-self (non-buffering) pleasure is that if you are addicted to the buffer, you will pursue it compulsively. It will be difficult or impossible to cut down on it or give it up altogether, because your Inner Critic might pounce.

A third way is that if addiction to the buffer is present, you will need more and more of it in order to feel good. Any satisfaction will be short-lived. If you find that your pleasures don't give you much lasting satisfaction, chances are good that they are simply buffers—symbolic goals that are empty of genuine satisfaction.

Is It Okay To Use Buffers?

As we mentioned previously, the Inner Critic has a propensity to use everything as grist for its mill, and it may tell you that you're bad for enjoying a buffer. But there's nothing "bad" about using buffers to have good feelings, even if those good feelings are precarious and temporary.

What leads to low self-esteem and depression is not the use of buffers; it's an inordinate reliance on them—that is, an addiction to them—coupled with the belief that buffering is the only way to feel good.

In other words, you will inevitably use buffers, and you should not necessarily pass up opportunities to use them to enjoy good feelings. What makes you vulnerable is not the use of buffers but the addiction to them. You must realize that the effects of buffers are fleeting and that buffers have a tendency to fail. If you are fully aware of this, you can feel free to feel good whenever you acquire a buffer.

Buffer Training

It's common to think that reactivity is caused only by negative childhood programming, but it can also be caused by positive programming. An example of this is what we call buffer training, which begins in early childhood and occurs whenever you are praised for good behavior. It continues in school: getting a good report card, doing school projects well, being on the honor roll, being a cheerleader, or becoming a good athlete. Buffer training also includes being praised for taking care of Mom and/or Dad, putting other people's feelings first, and being very nice and polite—at the expense of your own needs.[8]

As your accomplishments mount, you feel better and better about yourself, and you see these accomplishments as the main source of your self-esteem. As long as you continue to collect them, you'll continue to have high self-esteem. The danger, of course, is that when an accomplishment ceases, your debuffered reactive self will feel depressed.

Waiting For Buffers

Buffers can be goals for the future that seem like carrots dangled in front of you. If you focus on them, you may overlook here-and-now pleasures and keep putting your life on hold while waiting for future happiness. "I may not be very happy now," you say, "but I will be happy—When I graduate from school, get married, make enough money, become financially independent, lose enough weight, become famous, and so on and so on." That is, when I get my buffer.

Buffers And Shoulds

Each of your buffers is locked in place by a should. For example, suppose your Inner Critic says, "You should be financially successful, drive a late-model car, and live in an expensive home." Each of these items becomes a buffer, a symbolic goal, prescribed by the should. As long as you do what the should commands, you'll feel OK. But if your buffers collapse—if you lose your money, your car, or your home—your self-esteem will drop, and you'll probably feel depressed. Your shoulds get their power from the fact that they prescribe the buffers needed to avoid feeling bad.

So if a buffer fails and you feel depressed, you can use this as a learning experience. The first step is to ask "What shoulds was I having that I didn't obey?" The second step is to use one of the releasing statements to be described in Chapter 9.

Buffers And Pride

Although pride may seem a worthy goal, it may have some drawbacks. Because pride is a buffer, it can be an obstacle to your growth. Consider carefully the concept of pride as used in these examples:
- "I'm proud of my kids."
- "I'm proud to be a German."
- "I'm proud of my ability to make money."

In each of these cases, there's a great possibility that "I'm proud of" means "I'm buffered by." The way to tell, of course, is to imagine how you'd feel if you didn't get (or have) the thing you were proud of: for example, suppose your kids were not turning out well, suppose Germany not only loses a war but commits unspeakable atrocities, and suppose you lost your ability to make money (for example, through disability).

If you were to feel bad in these cases, or if your self-esteem were to be lowered—then your pride is reactive and is a clue to your buffers.

Reactive vs. Anthetic Self-Esteem

Self-esteem is best defined as how you feel about yourself. If you feel good about yourself and loving toward yourself, you have high self-esteem. If you feel bad about yourself and judgmental toward yourself, you have low self-esteem.[9]

If your self-esteem is based on your accomplishments, whether external (e.g., money, possessions, popularity) or internal (e.g., competence, rationality, or courage) it is self-esteem based on buffers. It will be what we call reactive self-esteem, always at the mercy of circumstances.

That is, you could lose any of your buffers at any time—not only your money but also your competence—because you don't always have 100% control over a buffer. And when you lose a buffer, your reactive self-esteem will drop. Relying on buffers means giving away your power to feel good, putting it in the hands of people and circumstances.

Unfortunately, most writers on the subject of self-esteem have been talking about the reactive kind. Coopersmith, for example, defines self-esteem as the extent to which the individual believes himself to be capable, significant, successful, and worthy (1967, pp. 4f). Maslow proposes two sources of self-esteem: (1) strength, achievement, adequacy, mastery, and competence and (2) reputation, prestige, status, fame, glory, dominance, recognition, importance, dignity, and appreciation (1970, p. 45).

Nathaniel Branden declares that self-esteem depends on competence, rationality, honesty, and integrity (1987, pp. 6 & 151).[10]

What these writers are talking about is conditional self-esteem, because it's based on buffers. Such self-esteem suffers from the precariousness and fragility that buffers are subject to.

However, there's a different kind of self-esteem—one that's more solidly based. This kind of self-esteem comes when you reclaim your power to feel good about yourself. It comes not from getting buffered but from challenging your Inner Critic, disarming it, and permitting self-acceptance, self-love, and self-nurturing to grow. When you do this, you'll experience *unconditional* self-esteem—you'll feel good about yourself no matter what happens.

The Protective Self

The protective self is used to cope with the pain of the devalued self, partly by blocking off awareness of feelings, partly by blocking off direct contact with other people. It leads you to unconsciously choose friends who won't challenge you and thereby disconfirm your buffers. The protective self builds walls not only to keep feelings out of awareness but also to keep others from getting too close. Closeness means that your cover might be blown; people might find out what you're really like, and if they did (your Inner Critic says), they'd reject you. So your protective self defends you against the pain of rejection and any other uncomfortable feelings.

The walls you put up are probably doing a good job of shielding your inner life. While they were built to protect you as a child, the net effect they have on your adult life is simply to wall you in, preventing you from enjoying genuine intimacy and closeness.

Another purpose of the protective self structure is to ensure that the natural self energies will not emerge into consciousness, since they are now seen as devalued (and in some cases dangerous).

The protective self is also concerned with control:

■ control of yourself so that no submerged energies will bubble up to disturb your equilibrium, and

■ control of others so they will support (or at least not disconfirm) your self-image.

The protective self structure tries to create a machinelike state of controlled predictability. To do this, it must make you rigid and unyielding—or perhaps so yielding that you conform to whatever outside influences affect you.

The protective self is the part of you that says "I don't really need therapy," "I don't want to talk about my feelings," "I don't want to get close to people," and "I don't need to change."

The protective self is also the part of you that wants to blame others for your problems, the part that rejects feedback without considering it, the part that responds tangentially to questions, the part that dislikes directness and honesty in others, and the part that needs to keep people at a distance.

The Protective Self As A Suit of Armor

It's as though you had put on a suit of protective armor, which in childhood worked quite well in warding off danger. But your adult self no longer needs the armor, which has simply become an impediment to happy and creative living. Your adult self, unfortunately, may think the armor is a natural and necessary part of you.

In any case, your Inner Critic keeps the armor locked in place by warning you of the dangers that would befall you if you were to remove even a small part of it.

The Forgetting Process

As you grew up, you gradually created reactive self structure in response to your Inner Critic, and at the same time you gradually forgot how it happened. By the time you became an adult, you may have forgotten the process completely. This forgetting usually happens in two stages:

First, because it was so painful, you may have blanked out your awareness of the Inner Critic's voice. All you felt was the pain of feeling worthless. You wound up thinking that your badness was as solid a truth as any scientific fact.

Second, you may then have blanked out and submerged your *awareness* of feeling worthless. Not only might you have split off these feelings from consciousness, you also may have installed such effective buffers that today you rarely feel any negative feelings. If this happened to you, you may be saying, "But I really don't have an Inner Critic. All these ideas don't apply to me! I don't think I'm so bad! I really like and accept myself!"

But although you may not be aware of your Inner Critic, or aware of what got submerged, you are probably fully conscious of the final effects of the submergence. These effects are described in detail in Chapter 7; among them are:

■ Any negative feeling; e.g., anger, fear, anxiety, depression

- Puzzling behavior that does not seem like you
- "Mistakes," apparent accidents, important things you forget
- Depression
- Lack of motivation
- Procrastination

Each of these is the surface result of the deeper processes driven by your Inner Critic. Each may seem puzzling to you only because you can't see the connections it has to the mechanism that drives it. If you are unaware of this connection, you won't know what to do about the surface problems except use willpower to try to make them go away. Which doesn't work very well.

Trying to Keep The Lid on

In the forgetting process, almost all feelings may be submerged—positives along with negatives—since any feeling can become a reminder of pain and threatens to unlock a Pandora's box of submerged elements. (This is often expressed by the protective self as: "Why open up a whole can of worms? Let sleeping dogs lie. You can't change what happened in the past; it's over and done with.")[11] The result is some degree of inner numbness.

Pseudo-positive feelings may then be used to cover up the numbness, a process we call "frosting the garbage." For example, you may say "Life is wonderful; I am always happy," when underneath you are feeling terrible.

Numbing always results in behavior gaps and disempowerments: People report things like "I don't feel it when others put me down," "I can't get in touch with my anger" (often in the case of women), and "I won't permit myself to cry or feel pain" (often in the case of men).

Frozen Feelings

The feelings that have been numbed in response to the Inner Critic are usually stored in the body musculature as stiffness, tightness, or other muscle tensions. Wilhelm Reich (1972) refers to these muscular tensions as character armor. This muscular tightness may lead to a number of physical problems: e.g., stomach ulcers, headaches, and backaches.

Machinery

It's useful to think of your reactivity as being like a robot inside you that's calling most of the shots in your life. That robot is what we call "machinery." The word was chosen because when you're "in your machinery," you tend to act like a machine. You may even use machine metaphors to describe what's happening; e.g., "Somebody pushed my buttons" or "You really turn me off."

When you get in a heated argument, when you feel defensive, when you feel hurt, angry, or depressed—you are in your machinery. Being in your machinery means being reactive, being driven, being a victim of your Inner Critic. It means functioning like a machine—in kneejerk reactions—not like a free person.

To have machinery is like being an electric typewriter. Someone pushes your buttons, and you have to respond; you have no choice. You must function in a predetermined way.

Perhaps you have learned to respond to your Inner Critic by adopting a rebellious stance. You may think you're being free, but you may find that your rebelliousness is just as driven as any behavior you're rebelling against. Someone may simply have pushed your "Reb" button, and your machinery has no choice but to rebel.

In other words, if you ever feel compelled to do something, that's your machinery. If you ever feel addicted to a person, to being loved, to approval, or to anger, that's machinery, too. If you ever feel that you cannot possibly do something (like give a lecture, or supervise employees, or make a request), when it's well within your power to do it, it's your machinery that's running your personality.

If you think other people have the power to make you feel bad psychologically, that's your machinery, too. And if you feel compelled to explain, defend, and justify yourself—that's also your machinery, clanking away.

Machinery runs your life without your knowledge. It locks you into certain behavior patterns.

And then makes you think you freely chose them.

The Reactive Self As A Player Piano

Eric Berne compared the person to a pianist who sits in front of his piano, thinking he's playing it, when all along it's a player piano,

HOW YOUR INNER CREATES REACTIVITY 89

operated by a paper roll that has been punched out in childhood by his parents. "The music pours forth," he wrote, "in a pattern that he cannot change, at times melancholy, at times gay, now jarring, and now full of melody. *** He is under the illusion that the music is his own.... Sometimes, during the pauses, he rises to take a bow or a boo from his friends and relatives, who also believe that he is playing his own tune" (1973, pp. 244f).

We all have some player piano in us, some machinery, along with a non-machinery part that's free. The good news is that the more you work on your Inner Critic, the more free you can become. You yourself will be playing the piano instead of following the prepunched piano roll.

But if you do not do this liberative work, your machinery runs you—without, of course, your awareness. So a lot of the time, when you think you're acting according to your own free will (and taking pride in being free), you may not be. It's the robot inside you that's doing the acting, and you're just getting taken along for a ride, whether you like it or not.

Machinery Masquerades

Machinery not only masquerades as freedom, it assumes a mask of normality. It says:

■ It's valid to feel bad after a failure

■ It's just natural to get angry when someone does something offensive

■ It's perfectly normal to feel uncomfortable if someone praises you[12]

Machinery creates a number of "ego-syntonic" problems. Ego-syntonic means that the problems don't look like problems; they appear to you as normal, legitimate, valid, and appropriate ways of behaving, thinking, and feeling. You see these things simply as part of your personality—as "terminal elements" with no deeper mechanisms driving them. Some of these ego-syntonic items are your most cherished values, beliefs, behaviors, and ways of relating—but they may be the very things that are sabotaging your happiness, all unbeknownst to you.

The Results Of Machinery Are Puzzling

Remember: everyone has machinery, and most people are unaware of their machinery. It feels normal to them. All they're aware of are the problems they have that result from the machinery, and they're quite puzzled by those problems.

Any puzzling behavior, any uncomfortable thought, or any negative feeling may seem to come from out of the blue. It just seems to happen.

We want to assure you that these things seem mysterious simply because they have their source in your machinery, hidden away in your subconscious mind.

Machinery As Stuff

The terms "machinery," "stuff," and "reactivity" are equivalent and interchangeable. "Stuff" is the more common term and is used to refer to any negative mood or feeling: judgmentalism, anger, depression, or anxiety—or feeling upset, prideful, indignant, resentful, self-centered, arrogant, jealous, embarrassed, or ashamed. Each of these is a form of stuff. And each negative feeling is a clue that can be tracked back to your Inner Critic. (Exceptions to this, of course, are negative feelings that have biological causes.)

Machinery Resists Recognition and Change

Because machinery wants to survive, it will resist change. It got installed at an early age in response to your Inner Critic, and it's been around a long time. It's not about to give up without a fight.

So as you read this book, you may sense that your machinery isn't liking the ideas presented here. It wants to survive. It might feel offended. It might be indignant and angry. It might make you feel superior to these ideas, and it might make you feel contemptuous toward them.

Our purpose in this book is to show you a way of getting free so you can make some new and more positive changes in your life. The changes, says your machinery, are strange and unfamiliar. Freedom is scary. Better not seek it. Why not stop reading, close the book, and continue in your old ways.

That, of course, is simply your machinery, trying to keep you enslaved.

Machinery Resists Willpower

The connection between machinery and willpower is complex. First, machinery gives rise to willpower. Here's how that happens: Because your machinery cuts you off from the energies in your natural self, it leaves you with no choice but to use the energy of willpower if you want to change.

But then, when you apply the willpower, machinery resists like crazy. You might think you just need even more willpower, but your machinery resists that willpower, too, sabotaging your efforts. And even if willpower works, there's a price: you'll lose the spontaneity, creativity, playfulness, and ability to love that come only when the natural self can be accessed and expressed.

Reactivity As A Trance State

When people recover from reactivity, and they look back on their former way of being, they sometimes report that they had been going through large portions of their lives as sleepwalkers. They were functioning on automatic, run by mechanisms in their subconscious. In a very important sense, they were hypnotized and entranced, put under a spell cast by the Inner Critic.

People in a hypnotic trance will not be aware of that trance. They will think of themselves as making free decisions. This can be illustrated by the story of Joe, a medical student who attended a demonstration of hypnosis as part of his training. Joe volunteered to be a subject, and he was hypnotized. He was given the following suggestion by the hypnotist: "Shortly after you wake up, I'll light a cigarette, and that will be a signal for you to take off your shirt, fold it up neatly, and put it on the lectern. And you won't remember having received this suggestion."

And that's exactly what happened. Joe was brought out of the hypnotic trance, the hypnotist lit a cigarette, and Joe dutifully removed his shirt, folded it, and placed it on the lectern.

Now comes the interesting part. The students asked Joe why he did this strange thing. He replied: "Well, I've been interested for a long time in the various ways that people react to unexpected situations. So it occurred to me that it would be interesting to observe the class's reaction to what I did. Since I was willing to be the subject so you could learn about hypnosis, I decided to use you as subjects for *my* experiment."[13]

Stories like this are common in the annals of hypnosis. The point of the story is that (1) Joe's behavior was dictated by subconscious forces, since he did not know the real reasons for his behavior, although those reasons were evident to everyone else, and (2) Joe had to concoct a cover story to explain what he did in terms of a conscious decision. (He would probably be debuffered if he thought someone else had control over his actions. Can you see the should?)

Like Joe, we are all hypnotized to some extent—which is to say that we function via a series of quotidian trance states. The hypnotic-like messages that we began receiving in childhood became stored in the Inner Critic, and the result is that we have learned automatic, trance-like ways of behaving, feeling, and thinking. And then we have forgotten the messages.

So we are left with the effects, which we call our personality, with all its reactivity, and we don't know about the deeper forces that program this reactivity, nor do we know that we function in a trancelike state part of the time—until, that is, we do the work necessary to break out of each trance.[14]

What You'll Need to Know

You'll need to know three things from this chapter to build a solid foundation for learning the Anthetic challenging skills:
- ☐ The difference between buffers and natural-self pleasures.
- ☐ The difference between reactive and Anthetic self-esteem.
- ☐ The concepts of stuff, reactivity, and machinery.

Whether you call it machinery, reactivity, or just plain stuff, the results of Inner Critic functioning affect practically all aspects of your personality, as we shall see in the next chapter.

NOTES

1. Freud thought the superego oppressed the ego; Anthetic Therapy holds that the Inner Critic oppresses elements of the natural self (Freud's "ego") together with elements of the reactive self. *[From p. 75]*

2. The verb "pejoratize" is Jim's coinage. It's taken from the adjective "pejorative," referring to a description that is disparaging or belittling. *[From p. 75]*

3. The concept of buffering is a modification of Alfred Adler's notion of compensation. Adler believed each person begins life from a position of inferiority and then strives to compensate by moving to a position of superiority. The feeling of inferiority, he says, is simply "a stimulant to healthy normal striving and development. It becomes a pathological condition only when the sense of inadequacy overwhelms the individual, and so far from stimulating him to useful activity, makes him depressed and incapable of development" (1969, p. 31). For more information on Adler's theory of compensation, see Ansbacher & Ansbacher (1964).

For Adlerians, buffering would be seen as healthy if it led to useful activity in terms of *Gemeinschaftsgefühl*, or, literally, "community feeling." For Anthetic Therapy, buffers are unhealthy if their acquisition is driven and if they are addictively relied on for good feelings and high self-esteem. Whether or not they lead to *Gemeinschaftsgefühlisch* activity is irrelevant. AT also holds that feelings of inferiority are always forms of suffering which must be reduced by challenging the Inner Critic.

While Anthetic Therapy makes compensation a central concept, Adlerian psychology has largely ignored it. "[O]ver the years," write Ansbacher & Ansbacher, "inferiority feeling and compensation lost their primary importance for Adler" (in Adler 1973, p. 50). Textbooks on Adlerian technique usually do not include methods for helping people recognize the crucially important process of compensatory buffering and its consequences. *[From p. 78]*

4. Some of Albert Ellis's irrational beliefs are commands to acquire buffers; for example, "It's a dire necessity to be loved and approved of" and "One should be thoroughly competent" (1962). Anthetic Therapy holds that the direness and compulsiveness of such irrational beliefs comes from the fact that if the buffers were to collapse, the Inner Critic would pounce with its punishments, resulting in the "awfulism" that Ellis mentions. In other words, awfulism is not a terminal (unexplained) element; it comes from the Inner Critic. *[From p. 78]*

5. When they feel debuffered, national populations, ethnic groups, and aggrieved political leaders may start a war to correct an injustice by rebuffering themselves. Germans, for example, were debuffered when they lost World War I, especially since they thought they were about to win it. Once the patriotic

trappings are removed from rebuffering processes, they can be seen for what they are.

If some men do not get deference from women, they may feel debuffered and seek revenge. If some whites do not get deference from racial minorities, they may seek revenge for the same reason. When children are debuffered, they may, out of revenge, grow up to become criminals in order to get rebuffered. When grown-up criminals are debuffered, they may torture and kill as a way of getting "buffering justice." Among the clues to all these attempts at rebuffering are such phrases as saving face, preserving our country's honor, and not letting anyone make a fool out of me or us.

Without a strong Inner Critic, no one would deliberately oppress minorities, commit a serious crime, start a war of aggression, or engage in terrorism. *[From p. 78]*

6. For more information on buffers and depression, see Jim's article, *Compensatory Buffers, Depression, and Irrational Beliefs* (Elliott 1992a). *[From p. 79]*

7. A major reason that marital conflicts are so difficult to resolve is that each person is defending buffers. *[From p. 80]*

8. If your parents say "You were never a problem to us while you were growing up," you probably had a lot of buffer training that made you into a GLK—a Good Little Kid. *[From p. 82]*

9. Strictly speaking, of course, feeling judgmental toward yourself means buying into your Inner Critic's judgmentalism toward you. *[From p. 84]*

10. Branden further declares: "Sometimes people confuse the whole subject of self-esteem by declaring that everyone should have good self-esteem regardless of anything he or she does or fails to do. This is utterly impossible. They are confusing self-esteem, which necessarily depends on certain conditions, with self-acceptance, which can be unconditional (1987, p. 67)."

Anthetic Therapy, on the contrary, holds that self-esteem is simply how you feel about yourself. Esteeming oneself highly means valuing oneself and having positive feelings for oneself. Reactive self-esteem is conditional and comes from buffers; Anthetic self-esteem is unconditional and comes from self-acceptance and self-love. *[From p. 84]*

11. It's true, of course, that you can't change the past. However, if you can unearth the dysfunctional beliefs you learned in the past, you can change *them*, and that will then enable you to change the future. *[From p. 87]*

12. An article in *Psychology Today* reported on a study which showed that people who received praise tended to feel uneasy. Researchers concluded that "a compliment often makes the recipient feel suspicious, embarrassed, defensive and cynical" (Campbell 1974). They didn't know about the Inner Critic as an

intervening variable. *[From p. 89]*

13. The story of Joe is adapted from Laughlin (1970). *[From p. 92]*

14. When Eastern philosophers talk about the ego, they are referring to what Anthetic Therapy calls the reactive self.

Wilber, for example, declares that many advocates of Eastern approaches maintain "that the ego itself is the very source of all suffering in the world...." (1977, p. 21). Buddhists contend that desire of any kind is a source of suffering. AT, however, holds that only the desires of the reactive self cause suffering. The natural self is never the source of psychological suffering. The Zen master who simply "chops wood and draws water" appears to be functioning from the natural self, although he may have shoulds to live a simple life by chopping wood and drawing water. Zen Buddhists who have attended our workshops have Zen-imposed shoulds; e.g., be spontaneous, live in the present, don't think of yourself as "I." (These are not simple rules; if the shoulds are disobeyed, the individual's Inner Critic pounces.)

Moreover, the judgmentalism that appears in some of the Zen stories is an indication of "Zen shoulds" that are imposed by the Zen ideology. (We define an ideology as a philosophy that does not explicitly teach the self-correcting procedures of critical thinking about its own ideas, theories, and principles.) *[From p. 92]*

7

Consequences Of Living by Inner Critic Shoulds

BEING GUIDED BY YOUR INNER CRITIC means being guided by shoulds. That is, you do what you *should* do, because if you don't, your Inner Critic will deliver a jolt of emotional punishment.

Now, you might think that's not such a big deal. Why not simply avoid the punishment by obeying your shoulds?

We want to assure you in no uncertain terms that if you follow this strategy, there is a price to pay, and it's a heavy one. For one thing, you'll have to settle for suboptimal living. You'll have a life that is less fulfilling than one you might have. And so you'll have a vague sense of discontent and dissatisfaction.

In addition, you may experience a certain amount of anger and judgmentalism toward others. Because of this, your relationships will not be as satisfying as they could be. You may have arguments with your partner, and you won't know what causes them. Or you may be so distant that you never have arguments.

These are the results of living by imperative shoulds.

It could be, however, that you have gotten so used to living with your reactive self that it has come to appear natural and normal. Each of your reactive character traits or behavior patterns will seem ego-syntonic, and you'll invoke the Popeye Principle by saying "That's just the way I am." (The comic strip character Popeye often said "I yam what I yam and that's all I yam.")

In addition, your Inner Critic's propaganda may work so well that you have come to see constrictedness not as destructive but as protective. Your reactive self will feel like a safe and familiar place; you will come to like it, even cherish it. On the other hand, your natural self will seem dangerous, vulnerable, and unfamiliar; you will come to dislike it and fear it.

But we know that we may have not convinced you yet. So the purpose of this chapter is first to list some of the advantages of being guided by your Inner Critic (there are only a few) and then to compare them with some of the disadvantages (there are a lot).

In order to challenge your Inner Critic, you'll need to be thoroughly convinced of how destructive it is.

The following lists come from the experiences of thousands of people who have learned to disarm their Inner Critics. As you read the items, you may want to check off the ones that apply to you.

Advantages of Living An Inner Critic-Driven Life

Here are some of the things our clients have told us:
- ☐ "My Inner Critic makes me do the things that are needed, so those things get done."
- ☐ "I feel good when I obey my shoulds."
- ☐ "When I obey my shoulds, I feel self-righteous and superior to other people."
- ☐ "My shoulds supply me with motivation; they get me going. If I didn't have them, I might lie around all day."
- ☐ "Obeying my shoulds makes me a good person."
- ☐ "If I weren't guided by shoulds, I wouldn't know how to behave."
- ☐ "I might hurt or offend someone if I weren't guided by shoulds."
- ☐ "Living by shoulds is comfortable and familiar."
- ☐ "Living by shoulds is a sign that I'm a caring person."

Disadvantages Of Living An Inner Critic-Driven Life

Here are some of the disadvantages of guiding your life by shoulds:
- ■ **You'll feel emotional pain whenever you disobey your**

shoulds. Most emotional pain comes from living a life driven by your Inner Critic. Sure, your Inner Critic makes you do needed things—and sure, you'll feel good when you obey your shoulds—but your Inner Critic also inflicts pain and suffering. Who needs pain and suffering?

QUESTION: But I feel emotional pain only once in a while. What's wrong with that?

ANSWER: If you feel emotional pain only once in a while, it means that you have been obeying most of your shoulds—that is, you have enough buffers in place. But using buffers to stave off your Inner Critic's attacks leaves you vulnerable. Buffers are unreliable; sooner or later, they'll collapse. If you lose enough of them, you may find yourself living a life of misery and unhappiness.

■ **You may not have much pleasure in your life.** Your Inner Critic doesn't want you to have pleasure; instead, it wants you to be safely constricted. So any pleasure you contemplate will be labelled frivolous, unproductive, and a waste of time. If by some odd chance you should actually find yourself doing something that gives you pleasure, your Inner Critic will make you feel guilty about it.

■ **You may not be able to experience the pleasure of accepting compliments.** If someone compliments you on something you're wearing, you may say, "Oh, this old thing? I got it on sale." If someone praises you about an achievement, you may say, "I was just lucky." This is what we call praise deflection, and your Inner Critic is behind it; its goal is to safeguard you against the danger of thinking too well of yourself. So it blocks you from experiencing the pleasure of agreeing with someone who gives you a compliment.

■ **You may experience overreactions and mood swings.** Because your Inner Critic will make you dependent on buffers for feeling good, you may feel like you're on an emotional roller coaster as you continually gain and lose external props for your self-esteem.

■ **You may have episodes of depression.** Depression is almost always triggered by some loss, and it's usually the loss of a buffer. Once a buffer is lost, the emotional punishment inflicted by your Inner Critic may cause a depression.

Your Inner Critic may also persuade you that you're responsible for other people's negative feelings, which will probably make you even more depressed. In addition, your Inner Critic may demand that you isolate yourself because of your inferiority to others. Added to this is a negative prediction: "If you let people know what you're really like, they won't like you." All these things are what we call "depression sustainers." (They're discussed in greater detail in Chapter 11.)

■ **You may suffer from quotidian depression.** One form of depression hits you with a bang; you feel lousy, and it takes you a few days or weeks to pull yourself out of it. Another form is what we call quotidian depression (QD). Quotidian means "everyday." Those suffering from QD might well paraphrase the Bob Dylan lyric as, "Been down so long it feels like *normal* to me."

Ralph, for example, told me (Kathy), "I was depressed for years, and I didn't even know it. I couldn't tell I was depressed until I began coming out of it after I started challenging my Inner Critic."

Clues to QD include boredom, lack of zest and excitement, and feeling that life is a series of dull routines. We're here to tell you that life can be a series of exciting adventures—provided your Inner Critic is no longer running things.

■ **You'll be living by other people's rules.** Not knowing what you really want, you may live by traditions and rules you have uncritically adopted from others. It will be difficult to live by your own principles—the ones that take into account the deep feelings, desires, and needs of your natural self. For example, you may choose a job you don't really like because it pays well and you think you should make a lot of money. Or you may follow the traditional occupation of a parent instead of doing what you love.

■ **You may be overly concerned with what other people think.** Your Inner Critic may demand that you give away your power by believing that what other people think is more important than what you think. When you become overconcerned with their reactions, your own needs and wants may be unsatisfied.

■ **Because your Inner Critic makes you do what *it* wants, you may not know what *you* really want.** Not knowing what you want, you won't be able to pursue your own goals. The result: you'll have a certain amount of unhappiness in your life—anywhere from a chronic, low-level feeling of dissatisfaction (QD) to a more or less continual state of misery.

■ **You may need external unifiers.** Because you tend to feel divided within yourself, you may have a tendency to seek out what we call external unifiers. As your submerged elements clamor for expression, you may have a feeling of disunity. You may feel a need to "hold yourself together."

You may try to get unity by organizing your life around a single theme or purpose. You may plunge one-sidedly into work, sex, studies, political action, or religion, for example.

As part of the search for an external unifier, you may find it tempting to become attached to a charismatic guru, therapist, or political figure. If you're a psychotherapist, you may become enmeshed with a therapeutic ideology.

In each case you hope that by submitting to the rules of this external unifier, you yourself will feel unified.

■ **You may have difficulty listening to feedback and criticism.** To the extent that you have a strong Inner Critic, your good feelings about yourself will be undermined by any criticisms someone might make. Any disconfirmation of your self-image will trigger negative feelings: hurt, anger, depression, lowered self-esteem.

For example, whenever you get feedback—whether it's a grade you get in school, a performance evaluation on the job, or a critique of your writing—you may feel debuffered.

You may adopt the belief that all feedback as destructive, a form of "mind-raping" or "taking someone's inventory." Your ego-syntonic feeling might be: "It's just that I hate being evaluated; doesn't everyone?" This may seem realistic to you, until you discover that your feelings come from a mechanism created in response to your Inner Critic.

■ **You may have problems with drugs or alcohol.** You may become addicted to a variety of substances to anesthetize your Inner Critic and dull the pain felt by your natural self. You will, however, think you don't really have a problem; for example, you may think you can quit any time.

■ **You may have overweight problems.** Another way to anesthetize a strong Inner Critic is by eating. In addition, several Inner Critic messages may contribute to an overweight problem; e.g., "Clean up your plate" and "If you're fat, you'll have a good excuse if people don't find you attractive—and you won't have to confront the fear of getting close to anyone."

■ **You may suffer from insomnia.** Most insomnia is caused by your Inner Critic, bombarding you with worries and fears.

CONSEQUENCES OF LIVING BY SHOULDS 101

■ **You may experience a lot of stress.** As your Inner Critic demands that you perform perfectly, as it criticizes and condemns you, as it makes you confused and indecisive—stress is generated. Because stress depresses the immune system, it can lead to a variety of physical ailments—one more consequence of Inner Critic functioning.

■ **You may idealize other people.** You may put other people up on pedestals, idealizing them; that is, attributing a kind of intrinsic superiority to them, with yourself as "less than." [1] Among such "pedestalized" people may be your spouse, your boss, your therapist, the founder of a school of therapy, your guru, a religious authority, a political leader, a medical quack, a medical non-quack, or anyone who has written a book (including the authors of this one).

By failing to think critically about what the idealized person says or writes, you will disempower yourself.

■ **You may find that living your life by shoulds just doesn't work.** Because shoulds are commands, you may find yourself rebelling against them. So they simply won't work.

■ **You may hide your natural self.** The result of all the above factors operating together is what may be called inauthenticity: the failure to be your natural (or "real") self.[2] Because of this inauthenticity, you may have one or more of the following puzzling problems in your relationships.

RELATIONSHIP PROBLEMS

■ **You may be addicted to love.** If you have dire needs for love and approval, that's love addiction. Although a craving for love is addiction to a buffer, it may seem to you to be a legitimate need, something freely chosen. Perhaps you will even take pride in the high value you place on love. However, you could be overvaluing love, and you will become aware of your drivenness only when you feel the discomfort (at first) and panic (ultimately) of not having your addiction satisfied. Discomfort and panic are the withdrawal symptoms of this addiction.

■ **You may pretzelize yourself.** If you are addicted to love and approval, you may try to twist yourself into a pretzel to try to get it. Remember that your Inner Critic has already told you that you are defective, shameful, inferior, and guilty. So you may mistakenly think, "If all I have to offer is my defective self, that's not good enough. I have to offer something extra to get people to like me; I can't just be myself."

This "extra" that you must offer is something that will keep people (or one person) attracted to you: perhaps money, sex, gifts, letting someone live with you, listening to someone's problems and complaints, giving someone a job, or helping someone find a job. It may also include "being nice," not making requests, not challenging what people say, and generally walking around on eggshells.

You may give more than you want to give, and your own needs may go unmet, whereupon you may feel used and taken advantage of. You'll have plenty of resentment and anger, because you know deep down that you must really be defective if you have to give so many things just to get someone to like you and stay with you.

But the anger must be suppressed, because (your Inner Critic tells you) it would surely drive the other person away. So you add one more pretzelization, one more thing you must give: not only do you walk around on eggshells, you also pretend not to be angry.

■ **You may have difficulty being assertive.** Disempowered by your Inner Critic, you may find it difficult to speak your voice in certain situations—especially when it comes to making requests. It may seem to you that there are good reasons for not speaking your voice, and sometimes there are. But many times there aren't. The reasons you give yourself may just be rationalizations proposed by your Inner Critic. For example you may say:

- "I hinted about what I wanted, but it didn't do any good."
- "I didn't want to come right out and say what I wanted, because I didn't want to cause trouble, make a scene, or upset the other person."
- "He (or she) should have *known* what I wanted; isn't it obvious?"

■ **You may be vulnerable to pressure from others.** If you are not grounded in your natural self, you may be too easily influenced by other people's feelings. For example, you may be afraid of hurting people's feelings. Or you may be afraid of their anger.

Not knowing what you really want—and being addicted to approval—you will tend to tune in to other people's signals, not your own. You may be so vulnerable to those signals that you will see others as Jupiter people—giant planets, into whose influence you have swung. The other person seems to project a heavy gravitational field that forces you to silence your voice and adopt a compliant attitude.

Because of your own disempowerment (at the hands of your Inner Critic), these Jupiter people will seem inordinately powerful—when all along they may simply be expressing ordinary assertiveness.

The result is that simple requests coming from others will sound like powerful demands or accusations, and you may have trouble saying No or otherwise setting boundaries.

And so you wind up feeling like a victim, and you have difficulty maintaining your identity in a relationship. Moreover, you feel used and taken advantage of.

NOTE: The above four descriptions refer to what we call the Tender personality type. This type made an early childhood decision to live by shoulds to comply and be self-effacing. The Tough type made a decision to live by shoulds to win and dominate. The Self-sufficient type made a decision to live by shoulds to be independent. The Dependent type made a decision to live by shoulds to be either Tough or Tender in filling her or his Black Hole. Each decision was a way of reducing childhood pain and anxiety. Each decision, if followed rigidly, leads to dysfunctional living.

■ **You may be self-centered.** You may come to believe that self-centeredness is simply being realistic; after all, it's a dog-eat-dog world, isn't it? You probably won't be aware of this self-centeredness, since it will appear perfectly normal and ego-syntonic to you; but you will be puzzled by the fact that others don't seem to like the way you relate to them. (You may think they just have problems with your "strength" and "assertiveness.")

Your self-centeredness will serve as a defensive wall; for example, you may talk about yourself at great length and avoid really listening to other people. Only rarely will you display any genuine interest in others (enough interest, for example, to ask them questions about themselves). You will see conversations as arenas—places where you can display your grandiosity by engaging in competitive "experience matching."[3]

While your self-centeredness may protect you from the pain of genuine contact with others (generated by your Inner Critic), the price you pay for it will be high. Because of your inability to empathize with others, your relationships will be unsatisfying.

■ **You may overvalue power and control.** If you're not addicted to love, you may be addicted to power. These are the Tough types—the ones who take pride in winning, being productive, and being practical and realistic. If you're a Tough type, you may make a lot of money, but you'll wonder why your relationships are so unsatisfying.

■ **You may be addicted to self-sufficiency.** If you're addicted neither to love nor power, you may be addicted to being self-sufficient—not needing anybody or anything. This, too, is bad for relationships.

■ **You may feel suffocated in a relationship.** If you're addicted to self-sufficiency, and you're in a relationship, you'll probably feel trapped, suffocated, or smothered. You may complain that your partner doesn't give you enough space. Because of your disempowerment, you may feel burdened by other people's neediness. You probably won't realize that the real cause of these feelings is not the other person; it's your own disempowerment at the hands of your Inner Critic.

■ **You may not be able to enjoy the pleasure of genuine connectedness with others.** This may not be a problem to you, because you'll think either that you already have connectedness or that it's just human nature to be somewhat distant in relationships. That is, you may think that disconnected relating is normal, and you may see direct, honest communication as impolite, rude, and intrusive. It may scare you. You may believe you just don't like this way of relating. You may try to set up your life so you will be unlikely to be challenged by anyone who wants more honesty and connectedness from you.

For example, you may pick friends who are polite and superficial and avoid those who are direct and honest. If you're in a relationship, and your partner speaks of love, you may fend this love-talk off by humorizing or intellectualizing (responding with humorous or intellectual remarks).[4]

These ways of relating will be protective maneuvers to help you avoid the deeper-than-ordinary communication that leads to genuine connectedness, but you will not be aware of this; they will seem like valued parts of your communication style.[5]

There'll be little danger of your feeling threatened, but you'll miss out on real connectedness. And you'll probably feel lonely without knowing why, even if you seem to have a lot of friends.

■ **You may be judgmental.** Self-disempowered people feel helpless. Because of this, they may think the only way they can exercise power is by being judgmental. A second goal of judgmentalism is the acquisition of a buffer: The judgmental person says, in effect, "You're one-down and inferior; I'm one-up and superior." (Of course, you wouldn't need this buffer if you weren't obeying your Inner Critic.)

Although judgmentalism may feel normal and legitimate, it isn't. It's stuff. And it's a well-known wrecker of relationships.

■ **You may feel angry.** Like judgmentalism, anger may seem perfectly natural and legitimate to you, but we want to assure you that it too may be a clue to Inner Critic functioning. For one thing, the power of an angry expression makes a person feel buffered and one-up.

More important, most anger is caused by what we call a failed trade. This is the case when the anger contains the theme, "It isn't fair!" Such "unfairness anger" is experienced when the individual, driven by the Inner Critic to be a Good Little Kid, discovers that being good does not result in gaining the approval of others, or avoiding their disapproval. The trade is: "I give my goodness; I get back nothing (or only criticism)."[6]

■ **You may have a strong drive for revenge.** You may think that getting revenge is perfectly normal.[7] But getting revenge is just getting a buffer that's needed to stave off the accusations of the Inner Critic. The problem with vengefulness is that it blocks you from enjoying the pleasure of expressing your love for people.

■ **You may experience nervousness and tension in relationships.** You may feel free and relaxed only when you are alone. When you are with people, you may be almost continually on guard—nervous, tense, and hypervigilant. You may see almost every personal interaction as a test or a competition. Will you continue to maintain your self-image? Will you be able to deflect any threat to its most cherished elements? Will you continue to be one up? Will you continue to be in control? Will you continue to maintain your independence? Will others ask too much of you? Criticize you? Not admire you? This may be such a familiar set of concerns that they will feel normal to you.

Because you are always on the alert, always performing, with your Inner Critic looking over your shoulder, no relationship will be easy and relaxed. You may feel forever on trial, sensitive to the slightest need to acquit yourself of some imagined crime. In addition, you may find it difficult to be playful in your work and in your meetings with people. Even more important, you may not permit yourself to have the kind of openness with others that creates the pleasures of genuine connectedness.

■ **You may feel unequal to others in personal power.** Your inferiority to others, says your Inner Critic, means that you do not have the same rights they have. What they want is more important than what you want, and what they think is more important than what you think. You need to fear *them*, but they need not fear you. The result is that you "pedestalize" them (put them up on pedestals) and defer to them, thereby disempowering yourself.

Their feelings of pain, discomfort, and hurt are more important than yours, so you must never antagonize them or make them feel bad. But it's okay for you to feel pain, discomfort, and hurt; after all, your emotional well-being is not as important as theirs. You must not make waves or rock the boat; you must walk on eggshells to avoid upsetting others. They, of course, being superior to you, need not be so careful around you. Or so you think.

■ **You may feel as though you don't belong.** Because of your supposed defectiveness, together with your inferiority and inequality, your Inner Critic proclaims that you are not a full-fledged member of some group (or perhaps the whole human race). Therefore, you don't belong. Your Inner Critic labels you an outsider and prohibits you from going to certain places (e.g., expensive restaurants and luxury hotel lobbies) because, as one of our clients put it, "I'm not normal, so I can't go there. The people there would be offended by my presence."

■ **You may make the wrong choice of life partner.** You may choose life partners who are wrong for you and wonder why. For example, you may be attracted to people who are somehow flawed or (you feel) beneath you: alcoholics, people who can't hold a job, and other birds with broken wings. Or you may choose people who are unavailable or otherwise not ready to make a commitment (perhaps married, involved with someone else, wanting to play the field, or unable to leave their parents). You may also choose a person who is distant, a quality you may at first misconstrue as strength.

Because you have bought into your Inner Critic's message that you are defective, you may think a flawed person is the only kind who will put up with you. In addition, if you choose a flawed person, you'll have something to give that person so he or she will stay with you. (You may not realize that a non-flawed person won't want to be "given" anything but will simply like being with you. But that may feel too precarious.)

You may think you need to give something, because your Inner Critic has told you that all by yourself you're not good enough. So you need to find someone who is needy; then you'll have an edge with them. (Someone who is not needy, your Inner Critic tells you, won't accept your defectiveness.)

Moreover, your Inner Critic may give you the bizarre message that if someone does like you for yourself, their judgment can't be trusted. Look who they're liking—you of all people! Think of what low standards they must have! So you'll avoid people who like you for yourself; you'll see their love as not very valuable. (In addition, you'll probably find them boring.)

But if someone dislikes you, their judgment *can* be trusted, and thus she or he is the person who is valuable enough for you to pursue. Valuable love can come only from someone who has the good sense not to love you very much.[8] On top of this, someone who isn't attracted to you strongly will turn out to be exciting, and pursuing such a person will be challenging and dramatically thrilling, with its emotional ups and downs. It gives you something with which to distract yourself from the quotidian depression you experience because of your strong Inner Critic.

And anyway (with your deep love and strong caring and the help you are prepared to give), you might be able to convert this flawed person (who is perhaps cool and distant) into someone who is not only successful and effective but who really does love you. On top of this, your Inner Critic will tell you that if you give up pursuing him or her, you'll never find another one "as good."

Sure, this is all a Catch-22 situation—one you can't win—but your Inner Critic doesn't care about that; it's just interested in protecting you from the riskiness of giving and receiving genuine love.

■ **You may have sexual problems.** Your Inner Critic can destroy sexual pleasure by causing such problems as impotence and blocked capacity for orgasms. It can give you performance anxiety and a perfectionistic attitude. It may also give you messages of condemnation that will prevent you from developing creative approaches to sex. (As an experiment, you might want to think of a few interesting creative approaches right now, then listen for your Inner Critic's judgmental voice.)

■ **You may have difficulty handling other people's feelings.**

If you don't feel comfortable with your own strong feelings, you'll almost certainly have difficulty confronting those feelings in others. While this will usually appear to you as though you just can't handle others' feelings, the real situation is that you will not be able to handle your own feelings *in response* to others' feelings.

If someone is angry at you, you may think you've done something wrong; you may feel guilty. If someone feels depressed, you may feel compelled to fix them by giving advice. If someone feels hurt and cries, you'll feel disgusted or contemptuous—or (because you have difficulties experiencing your own tears) you'll think they're putting on a phony performance or just wanting attention. All this is Inner Critic stuff, not to be trusted.

In any case, because of your difficulty in coping with other people's intense feelings, you may try to make those feelings go away. The result is, you won't be able to enjoy the closeness you could, because closeness comes when you are able to let other people's feelings be what they are and just listen.

■ **You may have problems with jealousy.** Your jealousy may be triggered if your partner is paying attention to someone else, and you feel excluded or ignored or otherwise deprived of love. This jealousy will be partly due to the loss of the buffering that had been provided by the exclusive attention of your partner. It may be complicated by feelings of shame at your imagining (or realizing) that other people have discovered your defectiveness in not being able to hang on to your partner.

You may also feel helpless at the loss of control over your partner and you may fear the loneliness that you imagine will happen if you were to actually lose your partner to the other person. Your Inner Critic, of course, will probably predict disaster in this area. To this it will add the observation that you are being made a fool of and taken advantage of.

In addition, your Inner Critic may tell you how inferior you are in comparison to the person your partner is interested in—or it might tell you that even though you are superior to that person, your partner is degrading you by being attentive to a person who is your inferior.

■ **You may be unable to enjoy the experience of feeling and expressing love for other people.** What we mean by love here is Anthetic love, which is defined as having warm (or very passionately warm) feelings toward someone, which are expressed solely because it feels good to do so.

Reactive love is different. It's given through a sense of duty, it usually means giving material things, and it requires something in return. People who love reactively (i.e., the way many parents love their children) are calculating with their love because they see it as a commodity, not to be given freely but only if they get back the right response.

Anthetic love, on the other hand, is given simply for the joy and pleasure of expressing it. There is never a demand that it be reciprocated or even appreciated. You can tell the difference between these two kinds of love as follows: the reactive lover says "I love you" and requires the response, "I love you, too." The Anthetic lover says "I love you," and if the other person does not reciprocate, receive it, or appreciate it, the Anthetic lover thinks, "You sure are missing out on the good thing I'm offering. That's too bad, but I'll go on loving you anyway because it feels good."

Much of what passes for love in our society is reactive love. This is so much the case that when we introduce our clients to the concept of Anthetic love, they usually have great difficulty understanding it, let alone practicing it.

In any case, it's the Inner Critic that prevents them from experiencing the joy of expressing this kind of love.

PROBLEMS THAT BLOCK YOUR EFFECTIVENESS

■ **You may have low energy.** The disowned energies of your natural self may seem abnormal, inappropriate, and phony. Because of this, you may keep them submerged—which means that you will have less energy available for motivating yourself to reach your goals. In addition, the act of submergence itself takes a certain amount of energy, further reducing the amount you have available. The result: you may feel passive and lethargic, which you may attribute to a terminal trait of laziness, but which is really caused by your Inner Critic.

■ **You may have difficulties in reaching your goals.** Many of your goals may be compensatory buffers instead of natural-self desires. Because of this, they will be more difficult to achieve, partly because you will be relying on willpower instead of wantpower.

In addition, there'll be more at stake if you pursue buffers: if you fail to reach them, your Inner Critic will pounce. Instead of having a free and easy approach to the achievement of natural-self goals, you'll feel anxiety and stress about the buffering goals—which will tend to block you from achieving them. At the same time, part of you will resist the goals for two reasons: first, they will not be what you really want and second, they will be imposed by your Inner Critic, and your resistance will be caused by a need for autonomy.

■ **You may be overly afraid of taking risks.** Your Inner Critic may tell you never to take any risks, to always play it safe, to stay in the middle of the pasture under the nice tree, along with the other cows. This may result in your missing out on many opportunities, for which, of course, your Inner Critic will punish you.

■ **You may have fear of success.** You probably won't be aware of this directly, but you may experience puzzling avoidances and resistances. You may, for example, find yourself doing well on a project or in a competition, then making some ridiculous mistake just as you are about to complete the project or win the competition. Or you may find yourself taking up one project after another, pursuing it for a time, then losing interest in it. These are the classic symptoms of fear of success, and they're produced not by your laziness or instability but by your Inner Critic.

■ **You may experience stage fright.** You may feel reluctant to give a lecture, teach a class, or present a report at a staff meeting. You may believe these activities are just things you don't like to do, but the truth is that your Inner Critic is telling you to avoid them because it thinks you might fail.

■ **You may be blocked by test anxiety.** When you take a test or exam in school, your mind may be a blank, even though you've studied hard and really know the material. Again, your Inner Critic is the cause of this problem, perhaps "protecting" you from the consequences of passing the test.

■ **You may procrastinate.** Because your Inner Critic is so strong, procrastination may be the only way you can resist it and maintain some autonomy. Or the project you're procrastinating about may have some reactive barnacles attached, which will make it harder to achieve. On the other hand, maybe your procrastination comes from your natural self and is an authentic message that says, "I really don't want this, but I can't say it directly, so I'll encourage you to put it off." In either case, procrastination is a clue to Inner Critic functioning.

■ **Even when you succeed, you may feel like an impostor.** Even if you use willpower to overcome your procrastination, and you ultimately become successful, your Inner Critic won't let you enjoy it much. You may not feel the satisfaction you were hoping for, because you'll be suffering from the impostor syndrome (Clance 1985; Harvey 1985).

You'll secretly believe you are untalented, incompetent, and unqualified for your job. You'll suspect that you achieved your goal (graduation, or fame, or a good job) through someone's mistake, or because someone liked you, or because you were able to fool people into thinking you were better than you actually are—not because of your competence.

When Ned finally got his Ph.D., he had trouble believing that he had really earned it; he had the irrational belief that he was given it by mistake. "But when I realized how dumb the other Ph.D.s were," he said, "I felt I earned it all right, but I believed the Ph.D. wasn't worth a damn." So he was unable to take any pleasure in his accomplishment. As usual, the Inner Critic gets you coming and going.

■ **You may find it difficult to make decisions.** Since you'll be out of touch with what your natural self wants, you'll have trouble making decisions, ranging from what to choose at a cafeteria to whether to marry someone or which career to pursue. As one of our clients remarked, it may feel like "No matter what I decide, it's going to be the wrong thing." Your Inner Critic will take almost everything you plan and cover it with a layer of shoulds, and these shoulds will obscure your real wishes. Guilt, shame, and magnified fear will also play a part in making you indecisive.

■ **When you do make decisions, they may be impulsive and emotional.** You may feel so blocked (by your Inner Critic) from doing systematic decision-making that you decide simply on the basis of reactive emotions—fear and anger, for example. You don't do research. You don't analyze consequences. You just jump right in and hope for the best. Later, you may have a few regrets.

■ **You may be a perfectionist.** Your Inner Critic is never satisfied with anything less than 100%, and sometimes it requires 150% or even 200%. If this is the case, you'll have a perfectionistic tendency that will permit few feelings of satisfaction from your accomplishments. You may need to be a perfect wife or husband, a perfect father or mother, a perfect employee or supervisor, and so on. Your plans must be flawless, your reasoning airtight, your decisions impeccable. Because of your perfectionism, you might not even *begin* some things that would be enjoyable to you (for example, learning to dance). You may not complete projects on time because you won't be satisfied until you have done them perfectly—and you know how long *that* takes.

■ **You may have difficulties with learning.** Being a learner or student, says your Inner Critic, puts you in a one-down position. (You, of course, will think this is just normal; that is, ego-syntonic). The older you are and the more pride you have in the knowledge and skills you've acquired, the more powerful will be the Inner Critic's message that if you were to put yourself in the position of learning from others, you would be a non-expert. (That is, you would lose your buffer.)

Consider the case of Carl. Several years after he had graduated from law school, he decided to take his bar exam but had trouble studying for it. To him, studying was dramatic evidence of his ignorance; it disconfirmed his self-image of being knowledgeable. "I don't want to go back to being a student," he said. "I've had enough of that." So he studied only haphazardly. And he kept taking the exam over and over, never passing it.

Sam wrote novel after novel, none of which was accepted by a publisher. So he published them himself at a cost of thousands of dollars each. But each novel failed to sell more than a few dozen copies. "I don't need to take courses in writing," he said. "I just write whatever comes to mind. Some day, people will discover what a great writer I am." For Sam, taking the time to study fiction techniques would be debuffering; his Inner Critic would pounce.

Going back to school, especially if you are older, may be seen as humiliation. So you won't get the training you need in order to achieve your goals.

■ **You may find it difficult to take orders or follow someone's instructions.** If your job requires that you strictly follow your boss's orders, your power and autonomy buffers may collapse, especially if your boss is younger and/or of a lower social class than yours. If you have this problem, people will say you've got a chip on your shoulder. If so, it was put there by your Inner Critic.

■ **Your creativity may be blocked.** If your work requires creativity (for example, if you are a writer, composer, inventor, or artist), you'll find it difficult to come up with ideas. You may turn to alcohol, which will release your creativity by anesthetizing your Inner Critic—which is why so many writers become alcoholics.

You may also be blocked in coming up with creative ideas for solving personal and business problems; for instance, financing an education, resolving a conflict with someone, or solving a sales problem—all because your Inner Critic has blocked the free flow of

CONSEQUENCES OF LIVING BY SHOULDS   113

ideas from your subconscious mind.

■ **You may have vocational problems.** If you obey your Inner Critic's demands for safety, you may choose a job where you will function below your ability. It will indeed be safe and easy to do, but you'll feel bored. And you probably won't make as much money as you'd like.

Another possibility is that your Inner Critic may tell you to choose a job for the big money. Or solely because it's an uncrowded field. Or mainly for the security it brings. Or because someone in your family is in that field, and you don't want to let that person down by choosing something different.

Because you've bought into any of these Inner Critic messages, you may find yourself in a treadmill job instead of pursuing your life calling.

PROBLEMS THAT BLOCK YOUR GROWTH

■ **You may be out of touch with your feelings.** You may suffer from the fear of contacting and expressing your feelings.[9] Your shoulds may demand that you submerge any unacceptable feelings into your subconscious mind, where they will no longer conflict with the ideal self your Inner Critic is trying to maintain.

Since they are out of awareness, those feelings will take on extra clout; they will be seen as irrational forces that threaten to invade consciousness and disrupt the iron control that holds the fragile reactive self structure in place.[10]

The result is thymophobia: fear of feelings. This is not usually experienced as fear but as dislike or avoidance:

- "I don't like to talk about feelings."
- "I see no point in talking about feelings."
- "I don't seem to have any feelings; most of the time I feel numb."
- "I don't see why some people have to endlessly wallow in feelings."
- "Feelings just complicate things; it's better not to have them."

In some cases, thymophobia will be restricted to certain feelings only: for example, you may find it easy to cry but have trouble expressing anger because anger will seem uncivilized or (since this often applies to women) will make you seem unladylike. Or you may find it easy to express anger but find it difficult to express hurt feelings. You may have so much difficulty in crying, for example, that you don't even see it as a problem—it seems ego-syntonic to you not to have the skill of being able to cry.

Thymophobes not only avoid their own feelings, they don't like to listen while others talk about *their* feelings. They often pejoratize feelingful communication, calling it "sloppy sentimentality," "going on and on interminably about one's most trivial feelings," "being emotionally unstable," or "playing Greenhouse" (Berne 1964, p. 142). Feelings may also be pejoratized by calling them rackets, a term used by some therapists.

QUESTION: But don't some people just wallow in feelings and never get anywhere?

ANSWER: The term wallow, of course, is pejorative and is a clue to Inner Critic functioning. True, it is possible to get stuck in feelings, going around and around without processing them Anthetically. It's also possible for someone to become emotionally hyperexpressive as a defense (for example, a histrionic person who acts out what seem like melodramas in his or her life). But the thymophobe views feelingful talk as bad, weak, childish, immature, and irrational and as evidence of emotional instability. All this is Inner Critic stuff.

■ **You may be reluctant to begin counseling or therapy.** Closely connected with thymophobia is therapophobia—fear of therapy, To be specific, it's fear of exploring one's inner world, especially through depth psychological methods. Therapophobes are reluctant to disturb the fragile homeostatic balance that has been achieved between the Inner Critic and its buffers, and therapy is notorious for its debuffering effects.

One form of therapophobia is fear of an Inner Critic attack following the revelation of submerged material. "Me, go into therapy?" a friend of Jim once asked. "Why should I rake myself over the coals?" Statements such as this are clear signs that an Inner Critic attack would occur if self-exploration were to take place.

To put this another way, therapophobia is experienced as the fear of discovering monsters inside. Because of the Inner Critic, they do seem like monsters, of course, but in reality they are beautiful, playful, and cuddly puppies over which a spell has been cast to make them look like monsters.

Another form of therapophobia results from Inner Critic shoulds

CONSEQUENCES OF LIVING BY SHOULDS   115

to be strong and self-sufficient. An example is the person who says "Why run to a therapist whenever you have a problem? I should be able to solve my problems by myself. I don't need a therapist to hold my hand while I tell my life story." Note the pejorative terms here: "run" and "hold my hand."

■ **You may blame others for your personal problems.** If you suffer from thymophobia and therapophobia, you'll have great difficulty looking inside yourself and taking responsibility for the part you play in your problems. So you may blame others, whom you see as bad and/or flawed.

Blaming others for your personal problems and negative feelings is a power giveaway. It puts your emotions and well-being in the hands of other people. If you find yourself saying any of the following, it may be a clue that you are becoming a self-created victim:

- "I feel suffocated by my partner's dependency."
- "Damned if I do and damned if I don't."
- "I feel trapped."
- "My partner won't let me have my feelings."

All along, of course, you'll be quite unconscious of the fact that you have given away your power at the command of your Inner Critic. It will seem to you that others have taken your power away.

■ **Terminalism may block your growth.** Terminalism is a word Jim coined to refer to the belief in terminal feelings, thoughts, personality traits, and behavior. This is The Popeye Syndrome ("I yam what I yam"), and it's expressed as:

- "I'm just naturally shy."
- "I'm just a nonstop talker; that's just the way I am."
- "It's just my nature to be quiet and withdrawn."

The purpose of such statements is to maintain two things:

- "I am like a material object, with unchangeable qualities. I am not really a human, with changeable qualities." So the position could also be called "object imitation."[11]

- "I don't choose to work on my stuff, so I label it natural, normal, legitimate, valid, appropriate, and something anyone would do under similar circumstances."

To the individual dominated by terminalism, machinery will indeed seem natural and normal; feelings, thoughts, personality traits, and behavior will seem to be terminal elements. The fact that they all have been learned (and can be unlearned) will have been forgotten. Which is just what the Inner Critic wants you to believe.

For example, you may think that the reason you don't get more things done is that you are just plain lazy. This "terminal trait" explanation will make so much sense to you that you won't be able to realize that you're operating from the reactivity generated by your Inner Critic. You won't know that your problem is simply that you're not in touch with the powerful energies of your natural self.

■ **You may try to polish and improve your reactive self.** You may undertake a personal improvement program that is intended not to help you become more open to inner experiencing but whose goal instead is to strengthen your reactive self structure.[12] You may see personal growth as the task of shaping and polishing the reactive elements in your persona, or facade self—the part of your secondary self that is seen by others.

To do this shaping, you may be concerned with "eliminating unwanted thoughts and feelings" by "banishing them." You may seek to "let go of negativity" or "upgrade demands to preferences" or "transcend your negativity," "rise above it," or "put it behind you."

If you do inner child work, you may contaminate your work with Inner Critic oppression. "I was procrastinating," said Norma, "so my previous therapist told me to tell my inner child, 'Look; just buckle down and do what you're supposed to do.'" Her inner child, of course, just dug in its heels and resisted.

Bypassing the Inner Critic this way often results in incorporating oppressive elements into your inner child work. Recovery writers may also unwittingly give advice contaminated by the Inner Critic.[13]

This reactive way of working on yourself may sound attractive but will, in the last analysis, be identical with repression and will consist simply of frosting the garbage. Underneath the frosting, the reactive layers will continue to function—but now out of awareness and therefore more powerful and sneaky.

The elements you have submerged will inevitably have a negative effect on your life, clamoring for attention in disguised ways. You may, for example:
- Banish anger and wonder why your partner complains so much about your criticalness;
- Banish self-doubt and wonder why you get those puzzling attacks of anxiety that seem to come out of the blue;
- Banish guilt and wonder why you have so many accidents,

why you make those mistakes, why you keep putting things off, and why you have so many mysterious failures.

In every case, the supposedly banished energies will struggle to return, coming out "sideways" and threatening to spoil the idealized self-image you are trying to maintain.

So you may think that you need to polish your act even more: What's needed is just a little more willpower, a smidgen more self-discipline, a larger dose of positive thinking.

Moreover, when you are unhappy, you may believe the reason is that you have not yet achieved enough external buffering supports—money, power, love, success, possessions, spiritual development. But no matter how much you achieve, it will not be quite enough.

A Sense of Something You're Missing Out On

The Inner Critic is not cruel simply because it despises you; it thinks it's protecting you. But the kind of protection it gives requires that you constrict yourself. So even though you may *seem* to be functioning well, you may feel that your life is not quite what it could be; it may seem that there's something missing. You may feel an emptiness, you may experience some boredom. You may ask "Is this all there is to life?"

After a while, this state of mind can get to feel quite normal and ego-syntonic, since lots of people appear to share it, and you think "Oh, well, everything is going along pretty much the way it's supposed to. I'm probably expecting too much."

But the truth is that you are indeed missing out on something—the great wonderful gifts that life can offer if it weren't for the oppression of your Inner Critic.

The Price You Pay For Having Reactivity

The purpose of this chapter has been to demonstrate to you, as dramatically and comprehensively as possible, the heavy price you pay for obeying the shoulds imposed by your Inner Critic. We hope by now you are persuaded that your Inner Critic—and the problems it creates—are liabilities, not assets.

What Is To Be Done?

What we are proposing is what we call Anthetic growth—not growth by shaping yourself into the perfect person, but growth that occurs through an ongoing self-acceptance of the submerged and disowned elements in your personality.[14] The general strategy in a program of Anthetic growth is:

First, you must learn the skills necessary to challenge and disarm your Inner Critic and

Second, you must encourage the submerged elements to emerge into consciousness, one after another, where they can be accepted and integrated. The goal is reclaiming the full-humanness of the natural self, not achieving the perfection demanded by the Inner Critic.

As you do this work, as the elements emerge from the shadow part of your psyche, they can play a constructive role in your life and make you a whole person, not a one-sided pseudoperson.

What You'll Need to Know

Here's what you'll need to know from this chapter in order to build a solid foundation for learning the skills necessary to disarm your Inner Critic:

☐ The fact that each of the problems described above is caused by your Inner Critic.

☐ The price you must pay if you buy into what your Inner Critic says.

In the chapters so far, you learned what the Inner Critic is, where it comes from, how it functions, and how it is connected to your personal problems. The next chapter will tell you how to recognize when your Inner Critic is functioning.

NOTES

1. "Emotional superiority" is the term we use to refer to a feeling of being *inherently* more worthy than others. It is based on the reactive use of a real or imagined "factual superiority" as a buffer. A factual superiority might be: "I am a highly competent therapist." An emotional superiority would be: "Because I am a highly competent therapist, I am a 'better' person than other therapists, and I'm therefore entitled to look down on them." *[From p. 101]*

therefore entitled to look down on them." *[From p. 101]*

2. German philosopher Martin Heidegger (1962), in his attempt to awaken us to Being, declared that people are inauthentic when they are fused with the public collectivity of *Das Man* ("one," as in "This is how one is supposed to think, feel, and act"). However, owing to his anti-Cartesian stance, he could not utilize such concepts as disengagement, reflective thought, or the challenging of the Inner Critic as ways of achieving authenticity. *[From p. 101]*

3. Experience matching is what passes for connected conversation at most social gatherings. It occurs when one person talks about an experience, whereupon the listener then talks about a similar (and often competitive) experience. For example, A says, "We went to Europe on our vacation." Instead of asking "How was it?", B says, "Oh, we went to Hawaii on ours."

Competitive experience matching is common in support groups in the guise of "sharing." For example, A says, "I had a terrible childhood. My mother locked me in the closet once." Then B, totally uninterested in A and not caring about A's experience, will say, "You think that was bad? *My* mother locked me in the closet every week!" *[From p. 103]*

4. You may also try to "rescue" people by attempting to make their negative feelings go away. For example, if someone is angry or depressed, you may try to get them to stop having those feelings. This will probably appear to you as an attempt to help them, and you may be surprised when they are not particularly grateful for your efforts. *[From p. 104]*

5. It's common for people who complete one of our Anthetic training workshops to say they thought all along they had good relationships but didn't know what "good relationships" really were until they had learned the Anthetic skills. *[From p. 104]*

6. Anger and other forms of negativity will be the subject of a book that will be published later. *[From p. 105]*

7. Much of the motivation behind delinquency, crime, wars, and other evils in the world can be linked to ego-syntonic attempts to get revenge. *[From p. 105]*

8. Most people know about Groucho Marx's statement: "I wouldn't want to be a member of any club that would accept a person like me." *[From p. 107]*

9. Thymophobia is a term Jim invented ("fear of feelings"), although it seems so obvious that we're sure someone else must have invented it, too. It's closely associated with a term in common use, alexithymia—literally, "absence of words for emotions." Sifneos (1973) coined this term, using it to refer to patients suffering from psychosomatic diseases who had difficulty identifying and describing feelings and who suffered from an impoverished fantasy life. Alexithymia is associated with increased vulnerability to illness (Taylor, Bagby & Parker 1991). *[From p. 113]*

10. Your reactive self may go so far as to insulate you from all feelings, resulting from an Inner Critic command to live a life based solely on logic and reason. *[From p. 113]*

11. Jean-Paul Sartre contended that we are in "bad faith" when we imitate objects (1956a&b). *[From p. 115]*

12. As mentioned previously, reactive self-structure is the same as the Eastern concept of ego. *[From p. 116]*

13. For an example of messages for your inner child that are influenced by your Inner Critic, see Wegscheider-Cruse, who writes, "Tell your inner child it's expected to be honest, that it's expected to begin making major decisions in its own behalf" (1985, p. 101). *[From p. 116]*

14. Anthetic growth is called inclusive growth, because it seeks to include all the elements in the individual's personality—all the angry feelings, sexual feelings, hurt feelings, thoughts, desires, and impulses. Inclusion, of course, just means non-submergence; it doesn't mean acting on the feelings. The Inner Critic, once neutralized, can also be included. In other words, the goal of Anthetic growth is wholeness. Note the similarity to Hegel's concept of *Aufhebung*. *[From p. 118]*

8

Clues to Inner Critic Functioning

ONE OF THE MOST DIFFICULT STEPS in the process of getting free from your Inner Critic is recognizing its messages. When you are in the beginning stages of learning Anthetic challenging, you might find it easy to hear the Inner Critic's voice quite clearly—it's the voice that's telling you how awful you are.

But as you continue to practice Anthetic challenging, your Inner Critic may become more subtle, more difficult to detect. This chapter will offer a description of both the obvious and the subtle clues to Inner Critic messages. (In addition, all the items in Chapter 7 may be used as clues.)

Ego-Syntonic and Ego-Dystonic Clues

If you're like most people, you've become so used to living with your reactive self that it has come to appear natural and normal. You may see constrictedness not as destructive but as protective and comforting—in fact, as "the way things are supposed to be."

Your reactive self will feel like a relatively safe place to live from; you will come to like it. Your natural self will seem dangerous, vulnerable, and unfamiliar; you will come to dislike it.

As mentioned previously, each of your reactive character traits or behavior patterns may seem "ego-syntonic"; that is, you will not see them as problems at all but either as neutral facts of life or even (in some cases) as desirable features of your personality. Therefore, it will be difficult for you to see ego-syntonic items as clues to Inner Critic functioning.

In addition to ego-syntonic clues, you may also have ego-dystonic clues—clues associated with feelings and behavior that you do see as problems. It will probably be easier to see these as clues to your Inner Critic.

Here are a few clues that may seem to you to be ego-dystonic:[1]

■ **Self-condemnatory statements**. It's clearly your Inner Critic talking if you make a direct self-condemnatory remark. For example:
- "What a klutz I am!"
- "How could I have been so stupid!"
- "I guess I put my foot in it that time!"
- "I'm always wrong."
- "I felt like a dork!"
- "I felt so gauche!"

■ **Twinges of defectiveness, evilness, embarrassment, shame, inferiority, guilt, or magnified fear.** One of the skills we teach our clients is "twinge work." We help them get in touch with their feelings so they can recognize the twinges that indicate the Inner Critic is pouncing.

For example, if you feel a twinge when someone zings you, it's almost certainly one of the five emotional punishments inflicted by your Inner Critic: defectiveness, shame, guilt, inferiority, and magnified fear. You may feel these feelings intensely, or you may feel them more diffusely; for example:
- "There's something wrong with me" (This means "I feel defective").
- "I dread what's about to happen" (magnified fear plus a negative prediction).
- "It would be awful if I were to fail." ("I'd feel shame.")

■ **Feelings of discomfort that might not appear at first glance to come from your Inner Critic.** For example:
- "I'd feel awkward about doing that (e.g., applying for a job)."
- "I'd feel silly if I said that."
- "I'd feel weird if I did that."
- "I feel uncomfortable (e.g., about meeting someone)."
- "I feel like I'm a misfit."

CLUES TO INNER CRITIC FUNCTIONING   123

- "They'd laugh at me if I did that."
- "I wouldn't be able to show my face there any more if I did that."
- "I didn't want to make a spectacle of myself."

■ **Obvious Inner Critic language**. It's the Inner Critic talking if you use sentences about yourself containing the following words: sinning; copping out; being irresponsible (if it comes from a should), evil, immoral, wicked, or perverted; engaging in behavior that is dissolute, disgraceful, shameful, shameless, flagrant, depraved, atrocious, scandalous, flawed, or blatant.

Be alert also for such Inner Critic words as purity, appropriate/inappropriate (especially "age-appropriate behavior" and "appropriate and inappropriate feelings").

Moreover, if you say "I'm hard on myself" or "I have impossibly high standards," it's a sure sign of a strong Inner Critic.

■ **"Should" language.** If you use the words "should," "shouldn't," "ought," "oughtn't," or "supposed to"—and they are imperative shoulds (not recipe shoulds; see Chapter 4)—it's a good clue to Inner Critic functioning. The criterion is this: It's Inner Critic stuff if you'd feel bad about yourself were you to disobey the command.

■ **More complex Inner Critic language.** Other possible (but not infallible) clues to Inner Critic functioning are such terms as willpower, self-discipline, self-denial, self-sacrifice, responsibility, duty, and obligation. The latter three terms would not be Inner Critic stuff, of course, if they referred simply to natural-self values or contractual responsibilities.

■ **"Why" attacks.** Examples are: "Why didn't I keep my mouth shut?" and "I don't know why I'm so emotional!" Such statements come directly from shoulds: to keep my mouth shut, to not be emotional.

■ **"Who" attacks.** For example, "Who do I think I am to apply for this job?" When you say "Who do I think I am," that's your Inner Critic talking, trying to "protect" you by making you maintain a low profile and not do any risky things.

■ **Issues about being wrong.** Because the term "wrong" could have two meanings, it's also a possible but not infallible clue to Inner Critic functioning. You can be wrong in the sense of being incorrect about something (which is not Inner Critic stuff), or you could call yourself wrong in the sense of being "bad," defective, or "in the wrong." This latter sense of "wrong" would be the result of

124 DISARMING YOUR INNER CRITIC

an Inner Critic message.

■ **Anger at yourself.** If you sense (or say) that you are angry at yourself, this is an Inner Critic statement; that is, it's your Inner Critic that is angry at you.

■ **Self-discounts.** If you discount yourself in any way, that's your Inner Critic pouncing. Self-discounts often occur in response to praise; for example, it's a self-discount if someone tells you what a wonderful job you did on a project, and you say, "I was just lucky." Self-discounts may also occur when no one is praising you but you happen to have some negative feelings about yourself. The word "just" is often a clue to a self-discount; for example, "I'm just feeling sorry for myself."

■ **Self-critical body language.** If you hit yourself (e.g., striking the side of your head with the heel of your hand or slapping your thigh), or if you talk about hitting yourself (e.g., "I could just kick myself" or "I just need a kick in the pants")—it's your Inner Critic beating up on you. In addition, if you bite your lower lip after saying something, it's almost always a sign that your Inner Critic is chiding you for your audacity.

■ **Victim feelings and beliefs.** If you feel like a victim or you feel trapped, stuck, or blocked, it's a good (but not infallible) clue that your Inner Critic is disempowering you by making you into a self-created victim.[2] You may make such statements as:
- "You painted me into a corner."
- "You put me on the spot."
- "You won't let me have my feelings!"
- "I feel like I'm being punished."
- "You're making me into the bad guy!"
- "You put me in a double bind when you said that."
- "You're not letting me be me."
- "You're burdening me with your problems."
- "You're dragging me down with your negative energy."
- "You're smothering me."
- "I feel cornered."

Although you may be tempted to blame other people for your situation, each of the above statements points to your own power giveaway.

What this means is that your own shoulds (not the other person's "power") are keeping you in the victim position. This is especially the case if you feel like you're in a double bind: "Damned if I do and damned if I don't." Each side of the double bind comes from a should coupled with the fear of what other people will think ("I'll be damned by them"). The way out of this dilemma is to challenge your Inner Critic about each side of the double bind, then get in touch with what your natural self wants.[3]

■ **Responsibility language.** If you hold someone else responsible for your feelings or behavior, it's a good clue that your Inner Critic is disempowering you. Examples: "You made me angry"; "You hurt my feelings"; "You made a fool of me"; or "You humiliated me." (Note that these are victim statements, too.)

In each case, your Inner Critic has externalized your own shoulds and self-condemnation, projecting them on others, who you now see as their source. To take back your power, you'll need to challenge your Inner Critic.

■ **Confusion and indecisiveness.** If you feel confused, indecisive, or ambivalent, your Inner Critic may be influencing you by imposing shoulds that obscure what you really want. For example, if you say, "I can't seem to decide," "I don't know how to respond," or "What am I supposed to do here?", you may really be saying "I don't know what should to obey."

■ **"Buts."** Take a look at these sentences: "The spirit is willing, but the flesh is weak." "I want to play, but I know I should work." "I want to be closer to my partner, but I'm afraid." Each "but" is an important clue to Inner Critic oppression and should therefore not be replaced by "and" as gestalt therapists recommend. It's almost a certainty that the second side of the "but" statement is produced by a should or a magnified fear.

■ **Feeling worried or anxious.** If you are worried or you feel anxiety, dread, or a sense of foreboding, it's almost always the result of your Inner Critic, which is predicting disaster and catastrophe for you.

■ **Inability to forgive yourself.** If you find yourself saying, "I can never forgive myself for such-and-such," it's a sure sign of an Inner Critic attack.

Ego-Syntonic Clues

These, you'll recall, are clues that do not seem to be connected with your problems; in fact, you may believe they are pretty good things. However, if you temporarily bracket that belief (i.e., put it out of play), you can use ego-syntonic items as clues, and you may be surprised when you see exactly how your Inner Critic, in the guise of a good friend, has been mechanically programming your life.

■ **Self-respect issues.** If you say you wouldn't like or respect yourself if you were to do something, this is a clue to a message from your Inner Critic, in the form of a warning not to overstep the limits it has set. In each warning you'll find a should or shouldn't.

For example, Wally said, "I wouldn't respect myself if I used language like that." Translation: His Inner Critic was telling him, "You shouldn't use such language."

Barry said "I'd hate myself if I didn't enter that contest." His Inner Critic was commanding him to enter the contest.

The term "self-respect" often means "what I have when I follow the commands of my Inner Critic," in which case it is another name for buffered self-esteem. Or, on the other hand, it can refer to self-love, self-care, and self-nurturing, as in, "I respect myself enough to make sure I stay healthy." In this case there is no Inner Critic stuff involved.

Similarly, the term "dignity" can refer to reactive feelings of superiority and aloofness—or it can refer to healthy feelings of self-worth.

■ **"Lowering yourself" issues.** If you talk about not wanting to lower yourself or stoop to something, it's your Inner Critic saying it would condemn you for such behavior (even though the behavior might be perfectly reasonable—a fact which you would not be able to see as long as your Inner Critic was pejoratizing it). Examples of this clue are: "I decided not to lower myself to his level," "I wouldn't stoop to using such tactics," or "It would be demeaning of me to do that." In each case, Inner Critic shoulds are operating, constricting your options.

■ **Pride issues.** In rare cases, pride can be healthy; for example, pride can simply mean taking pleasure in the exercise of your abilities (even if you might not do a good job). More commonly, pride is reactive; that is, what you are proud of is a buffer. In the latter case, pride points directly to a should: That is, if you are proud of something, you have a should to have it, be it, or do it—and, as always, the should prescribes the buffer.

You can identify reactive pride by two criteria:
- Would you feel bad about yourself if what you were proud of failed in some way?

- Would you feel defensive and angry if someone criticized you about the issue?

For example, you may be proud of your sense of humor, your intellect, your advanced stage of spiritual development, your possessions, your well-behaved children, your good memory, or your skill in picking winners in the stock market.

Imagine that you have one of the above items, and then imagine that you have lost it. If you'd just feel disappointed but still believe you're a good person, it probably wasn't a buffer. If, on the other hand, you'd feel bad about yourself—depressed, self-condemnatory, or as though your self-worth had been lowered—the odds are it was a buffer.[4] Reactive pride is pride about buffers.

■ **Judgmentalism.** As indicated in Chapter 7, any judgmentalism you feel toward others is a clue to Inner Critic functioning. That is, your judgmentalism toward others will be the same as your Inner Critic's judgmentalism toward you.

In my Thursday group, I (Jim) announced that next month we would not be meeting on the third Thursday of the month, because of the Christmas holidays. In the group session a week after this announcement, Mark asked, "Dr. Elliott, are we meeting on the Thursday before Christmas?"

Violet said, "What's the matter with you? Didn't you hear Dr. Elliott say we wouldn't be meeting then?"

"I guess I forgot," Mark said.

Our on-the-spot analysis of this incident revealed that Violet's buffer was her excellent memory, a buffer which rarely collapsed. When it did, however, later in the life of the group, and she forgot something, her Inner Critic pounced on her natural self, just as it did on Mark. She was able to get released by taking back her right to forget things, and her judgmentalism was eliminated on this issue.

Here are some examples of using judgmentalism as a clue: If you say, "It turns my stomach when I see a wimp," it's a clue that you have a should to be tough and strong. If you say, "I despise people who are strong and controlling," you may have a should not to be assertive.

■ **Feeling put off.** "I feel put off by the self-promotion in your brochures," a colleague said. It turned out his Inner Critic command was, "Don't ever promote yourself."

When we gave a copy of the manuscript of this book to another colleague, he said, "I'm put off by the self-confident attitude you display in this manuscript. It's almost cocky." Can you guess what his Inner Critic was saying?

■ **Feeling hurt or betrayed.** If you feel hurt, betrayed, gypped, swindled, ripped off, taken advantage of, or let down, you may think this is "just normal and natural after what happened," but it's an excellent clue that you have been engaging in what we call negative trading—constricting yourself in the hope that the other person will constrict her- or himself.

The self-constriction is done at the behest of the Inner Critic, who tells you that the way to get along with people is to be a GLK: a Good Little Kid. In the GLK position, you are driven by shoulds to be super good, and your hurt feelings will point directly to those shoulds.

■ **Anger.** Chapter 7 mentions anger as a consequence of Inner Critic functioning. That is, if you feel angry, annoyed, irritated, aggravated, or resentful, it's a possible clue that you have been a GLK in response to imperative shoulds. What you need to do is look for any shoulds you are laboring under and make the appropriate releasing statements mentioned in the next chapter. [5]

■ **Reluctance.** If there's something you might want to do (for example, make a request of an "important" person) but feel you couldn't bring yourself to do it—it's almost certainly your Inner Critic pedestalizing the person and taking away your rights.

■ **Dislikes, aversions, and "I hate" statements.** These are often (but not always) clues to Inner Critic functioning; for example:

• "I hate being the center of attention." (This usually means "I have a should to perform, and I'd feel embarrassed if I didn't perform well.")

• "I hate it when someone cries." ("I feel like I'm supposed to do something about it; in addition *I* shouldn't cry, because it would be a sign of weakness.")

• "I hate supervising people." ("I'd feel guilty at telling people what to do.")

But, of course, "I hate parsnips" probably has nothing to do with the Inner Critic.

■ **A dislike of being labelled.** It may seem natural to you that being labelled (e.g., with a psychologically diagnostic label) will seem to be inherently demeaning, but we want to assure you that it feels demeaning only because of what your Inner Critic says about it.

Once you learn the skills of Anthetic challenging, you'll find that people can label you all they want, and you will no longer assume the self-created victim position that results when you buy into what your Inner Critic says in response to the labelling. That is, being labelled will no longer bother you.

■ **Feeling compelled to explain, justify, or defend yourself.** Having to make "acquittal statements" usually points to a strong Inner Critic that is accusing you of something. When someone criticizes you, your Inner Critic gets triggered, and you have a need to set the record straight.

The key idea here is that you will feel compulsive about defending yourself; your goal will be to desperately maintain your buffer. If you feel irresistibly compelled to explain and defend—especially about minor items and when you're talking to people you don't really care much about—it's your Inner Critic for sure.

■ **Feeling taken advantage of, conned, manipulated, gypped, swindled, ripped off, cheated, or duped.** You'll feel the pain of defectiveness when these things happen, and the pain will trigger your anger—or rage. You may seek revenge in order to regain the buffer you lost. Again, your Inner Critic is telling you that you are defective if someone takes advantage of you.

If, after reading all the above, you are saying to yourself, "It looks like I'm wrong no matter what I do," that too is your Inner Critic talking.

Now that you know how to recognize your Inner Critic's messages, let's take a look in the next chapter at some step-by-step procedures for challenging and disarming this sabotaging influence.

NOTES

1. Any of the clues we've labelled "ego-dystonic" can, of course, be ego-syntonic for some individuals. That is, you'll think it's natural and/or desirable, when all along it's a clue to Inner Critic oppression. *[From p. 122]*

2. This section applies only to self-created victims. Some victims are not self-created; they are victims because of what other people do to them, usually physically. *[From p. 124]*

3. Watzlawick (1990) writes of the "be spontaneous" paradox as a double bind. He declares, for example, that if a wife asks her husband to be spontaneous, he can't possibly comply, since anything he does would be done at her

request. Therefore, the husband will be put in a double bind, which blocks him from doing anything.

We maintain that this would be the case only if he operates from an Inner Critic should, triggered by his wife's request. If he could successfully challenge the should, he could then do whatever he wanted. His behavior, originating from his natural self, would be spontaneous no matter what his wife requested. *[From p. 125]*

4. One reason parents have a strong drive to control their children's behavior is that they (the parents) are buffered by the children's good behavior and become debuffered when children misbehave, make poor choices and decisions, act out sexually, get in trouble with the law, etc. When the buffers are in place, you can tell such parents by the statement, "I'm proud of my children." There's nothing "wrong" in this; it just makes parents vulnerable to decompensation if their children are not perfect, which is often the case, as any parent knows. *[From p. 127]*

5. Using angry feelings as clues to Inner Critic functioning will be described in greater detail in a later book. "Negative trading anger" is one of about five kinds of anger we have discovered. *[From p. 128]*

9

Challenging Methods: Making Releasing Statements

YOU MIGHT THINK THAT A GOOD WAY to disarm your Inner Critic would be to argue with it so as to reverse its messages. Or perhaps try to make it shut up or go away. Not so. Years of clinical experience show that neither of these methods works very well.

■ Arguing with your Inner Critic has two drawbacks: First, it sends the message that what your Inner Critic says is worth debating. It isn't. (You wouldn't debate with a crazy person, would you?) Second, it's difficult if not impossible to actually change your Inner Critic in any way by arguing with it. It's a hopeless task.

■ Trying to make your Inner Critic shut up or go away usually doesn't work, either. Your Inner Critic will fight back strongly. But even if you should seem to win this battle, and the Inner Critic's voice is no longer heard, you'll discover after a while that you have simply driven your Inner Critic underground. From there it will function outside your awareness—now inflicting its negative programming in more subtle and undetectable ways.[1]

How, then, can the Inner Critic be disarmed? By doing Anthetic challenging. Before we explain Anthetic challenging, we want to caution you about two prerequisites that are essential to successful challenging.

FIRST,
*You Must Be Convinced
Of The Destructiveness
Of Your Inner Critic*

If you are not convinced, please take another look at the disadvantages of living a life based on the Inner Critic, described in Chapter 7.

SECOND,
*You Must Be Convinced
Of The Need to Disengage From
Your Inner Critic,
Not Integrate It Into Your Life*

Swiss psychiatrist C. G. Jung is the originator of the concept of integration of psychic elements. Integration implies that each element is necessary and useful, and a place must be found for it in the personality so that its energies can be accessed.

While the integration concept may be constructive with regard to a great many inner figures, clinical experience shows that it's destructive when applied to the Inner Critic. If you believe your Inner Critic is useful and you want to integrate it into your personality, it means that you find emotional punishment useful. The result, of course, is that you will experience emotional punishment—the very thing any good therapist should be teaching you to recover from.

QUESTION: But I don't think the Inner Critic is just the source of punishment; can't it also be the source of positive guidance?

ANSWER: What we're doing here is focusing on the source of all negative beliefs and *defining* it as a negative source. The source of *positive* beliefs is defined as the Inner Guide (mentioned in Chapter 5).

You'll find that it helps to keep things straight by seeing these as two separate sources and by realizing that, although first one and then the other can assume a dominant role in your personality, one cannot be transformed into the other.

Mary came to see me (Jim) complaining of depression. She reported she had just moved to Louisiana from Texas. In Texas she had been in therapy for two years with a psychologist who recommended cultivating a benevolent attitude toward the Inner Critic. "Make friends with it," he had said. "Give it a place in your life; don't reject it; integrate it. You'll need it whenever you need to give yourself a push." She had followed his advice, but her depression hadn't been relieved.

I explained that trying to cultivate a benevolent attitude toward the Inner Critic was like trying to cultivate a benevolent attitude toward someone who was trying to beat you up. "I help people challenge the Inner Critic," I said, "not submit to it." She decided to try Anthetic challenging.

As with some clients, one session was enough to bring about a remarkable change in her mood. "This is awesome," she said.[2] "I'm feeling so much better." After an additional session, her depression had lifted completely, and she was now equipped with the tools necessary to bring herself out of any future depression she might slide into.

Mary's case is an example of a general principle: If you find your Inner Critic useful, if you try to cultivate a benevolent attitude toward it, and if you are committed to integrating your Inner Critic into your personality—you will not be able to neutralize it.

Now let's take a look at the chief method of Anthetic challenging.

MAKING RELEASING STATEMENTS

Making releasing statements (Elliott 1994) is the most powerful method you can use for disarming your Inner Critic. To help you understand this method, let me remind you that the Inner Critic functions by imposing shoulds. These shoulds are not neutral rules but are harsh imperatives backed by the power of the five emotional punishments described in Chapter 5.

The shoulds are commands about what you are supposed to think and feel and how you are supposed to behave. The important thing to know is this: **Each should takes away some of your rights.** The should says **"You do not have the right to think, feel, or behave in certain ways."**

For example:

■ "You should be strong" means that you don't have the right to be weak, to cry, or to be tender.

■ "You should always succeed" means you don't have the right to fail.

■ "You should comply with people's requests" means you don't have the right to do what you want.

> *Making an Anthetic releasing statement means simply taking back whatever rights your Inner Critic has deprived you of. The general form of the releasing statement is: "I have the right to be/do/feel/think _____."*

To illustrate this method, let's use the following sequence, beginning with an event:
1. THE EVENT: Mom and Dad have invited you to spend the holidays with them, but you want to be alone with your spouse. You feel pressured and guilty.
2. IDENTIFY EACH SHOULD AND STATE IT CLEARLY:
"I should go to my parents' for the holidays (or I'm a bad son/daughter)."
3. SEE THE SHOULD AS AN ATTACK ON YOUR RIGHTS.
"I don't have the right to do what *I* want; I have to do what Mom and Dad want."
4. CREATE A RELEASING STATEMENT:
The form is: "I have the right...." For example, "I have the right not to go to Mom and Dad's for the holidays." Note that the releasing statement must use the words of the should, and it must begin with "I have the right to..." or "I have the right not to...."

Here are some comments on this technique:

It's Best if You Use
The Anthetic Dialogue Method

The method used for challenging your Inner Critic is Anthetic Dialogue (AD) (Elliott 1992b). AD is a method for talking to various parts of yourself—your inner figures. When you do Anthetic challenging, you use AD to talk to the inner figure we've been calling your Inner Critic.

To use AD, imagine your Inner Critic occupying the space directly in front of you—perhaps occupying an empty chair opposite you.[3] Speak the challenges out loud to that figure.

Of course, it's more complex than that. Moreover, many people find that any intellectual discussion of Anthetic challenging (such as this one) seems meaningless and ineffective—until they actually do the challenging using AD.

So we recommend that you consult a professional who has been trained in Anthetic Therapy. Unless you go through the experience of Anthetic challenging, what you read here may be meaningless.

It's important to work with a trained therapist, because although the work appears simple, it has many complexities that need to be addressed. Working with an untrained therapist may not release you from your shoulds—and may even add more shoulds to your life.

Disengage From Your Inner Critic

While some people are painfully aware of their Inner Critic as something that speaks with a separate voice, most people are so fused with it that they don't even know it's there. All they know are its effects. They think the Inner Critic's voice is their own voice, and they see its beliefs as their own beliefs.

Therefore, in order to do the challenging work successfully, you must first disengage from your Inner Critic. Disengagement con-consists of simply recognizing your Inner Critic as a separate voice that bombards you with commands. To disengage, it's not necessary (nor is it advisable) to argue, to verbally dispute, or to search for evidence that your Inner Critic is wrong.

For this first step, all you need do is: **One,** identify your Inner Critic and **Two,** realize that it's something separate from you.

Take the case of Betty, a forty-two-year-old real estate broker who consulted me (Jim) for anxiety attacks. "I don't think I have an Inner Critic," she said. "I just have these negative thoughts. They come to me out of nowhere. If they are messages, it seems like they're my messages. It's just me talking, not some Inner Critic."

As Betty learned the skills of Anthetic Dialogue, she was able to visualize her Inner Critic, sitting in the empty chair opposite. "Oh, *that's* what my Inner Critic is!" she said. "I thought all along that was just me, giving myself good advice. I can see now what it is, and I can see that it's been putting me down, threatening me with punishment, telling me I'm bad, and telling me to be afraid."

Now that she knew what it was, Betty could identify the voice each time it spoke. "There goes my Inner Critic again," she could say. She was able more and more to see that her negative thinking was coming from an "outside" source. As she learned to challenge it, her anxiety diminished until finally it was completely gone.

Like many people, Betty had been so fused with her Inner Critic that she couldn't hear it as a separate entity. The result was that it had great destructive power in her life. Once she was able to recognize it, by that very action, she had begun to objectify it and disengage from it—and neutralize some of its power.

If you believe that your negative thoughts are coming from you yourself, it will be a big step forward if, each time you have a negative thought or feeling, you see it as coming from your Inner Critic.[4] To illustrate this method, let's look at the following sequence:

1. EVENT: "I made a serious mistake in typing a report, and I thought 'I'm a hopeless klutz!'"
2. RECOGNITION: "There goes my Inner Critic."
   This may not sound like much progress, but believe me, it is. Your Inner Critic will try its best to hide, and each time you spot it and name it, you'll take another step toward disengaging from it and putting yourself in a good position for challenging.

Remember, naming your Inner Critic consists of converting "I'm a hopeless klutz" into "Something is telling me I'm a hopeless klutz, and I'm believing it. That something is saying '*You're* a hopeless klutz.' That something is my Inner Critic."

Say The Challenging Words Out Loud

Do not say the challenging words mentally. Experience has shown that if you do this "silent challenging," you will not achieve success in getting released. You must say the words out loud—preferably in the presence of someone who understands what you are doing and who can listen and simply agree with you.

For example, when you challenge by saying "I have the right to such-and-such," you'll want the other person to say nothing or perhaps agree by saying, "Yes, that's right."

It's Absolutely Essential That You Adopt A Defiant Attitude

Unless you feel defiant and rebellious toward your Inner Critic, challenging will be difficult. You have been obeying your Inner Critic for years; in order to shake off its oppressiveness, you must now be staunchly and gleefully disobedient.

One way of cultivating a defiant attitude is to express anger at your Inner Critic. Your anger, of course, will probably not silence your Inner Critic. Anger will, however, provide the emotional energy for disengagement.

A second way of expressing your defiance consists of making statements to your Inner Critic that indicate that you are aware of its desire to control you, followed by your determination not to be controlled. For example:

- "I know you're trying to control me, Inner Critic, but I'm not going to let you."
- "I'm going to live my life my way, not yours. I'm no longer going to buy into what you say."

No Verbal Disputing Is Necessary

As we mentioned previously, when you're learning to make releasing statements, it's important not to dispute your Inner Critic's messages with the thought of changing your Inner Critic's mind. When making a releasing statement, it's never effective to argue with your Inner Critic, to try to reverse its statements, or to plead your case in any way whatever.

For example, if your Inner Critic says "You spent too much money!," don't try to get acquitted of this "crime" by saying "You're wrong! I *had* to spend that money!" That's just playing into your Inner Critic's accusation that you did something wrong and you have to get acquitted. You need make no "acquittal statements."[5]

All you need to do is identify the should ("You shouldn't spend too much money") then make the releasing statement: "I have the right to spend too much money."[6]

Here's another example of this method:
1. EVENT: You say to yourself, "I shouldn't whine so much."
2. TRANSLATION: Convert this into a message coming from

your Inner Critic; e.g., "You shouldn't whine so much."
3. WHAT NOT TO DO: Do not say you don't whine, and do not explain why you've been whining.
4. THE ANTHETIC CHALLENGE: "I have the right to whine all I want."

The "What You Call" Technique

If your Inner Critic gives you a really pejorative message, such as "You are a lazy bum," don't challenge by saying "I have the right to be a lazy bum." That may tend to buy into the Inner Critic's condemnation. Instead, you can say, "I have the right to be *what you call* a lazy bum."

The YASNY Technique

Suppose your Inner Critic says, "You shouldn't make Eric feel upset." Your releasing statement will be: "I have the right to make Eric feel upset." The YASNY technique adds the following sentence to this statement: "In fact, You Ain't Seen Nothin' Yet! I have the right to make Eric upset all day long! I have the right to make dozens of people upset! Hundreds! Thousands! My spouse! My kids! My parents! Everyone!"

The "Good Person" Technique

If you want to give extra clout to your releasing statement, you can add the following statement: "and I'm still a good person." For example, suppose your Inner Critic says "You shouldn't call attention to yourself." Your challenge can be: "I have the right to call attention to myself anytime I want, and I'm still a good person."

The "Good Person" technique is not designed to change your Inner Critic's opinion of you, since that's an impossible task. It's designed only to declare and solidify your position, and (most important) to remind yourself of what's really true. Behind every should that your Inner Critic imposes is the implied statement, "if you don't obey this should, you're a bad (in some sense) person."

Note that the releasing statement is the thing that does the work in Anthetic challenging, because it gives you the power to take back your rights. Simply making the "Good Person" statement doesn't work very well (e.g., "If I call attention to myself, I'm a good person").

Making Releasing Extensions

For best results, you should extend your releasing statement to the maximum possible range. For example:

- "I have the right to make hundreds of mistakes—thousands of them—a mistake every minute, a mistake every second—as many mistakes as I need or want."
- "I have the right never *ever* to visit Mom and Dad."
- "I have the right to whine all day long. In fact, you ain't seen nothin' yet."

More Releasing Statements

Here are some more examples of releasing statements that can be used in taking back your rights:

- If your Inner Critic says "You forgot again! You were late again! You failed again!", you can say: "I have the right to forget, to be late, and to fail." If you want to make the extension, you can add, "I have the right to forget, to be late, and to fail 100 times a day; in fact, once a minute."
- If your Inner Critic says "What you did was silly and stupid. You are inadequate, incompetent, and sinful," you can challenge it by saying, "I have the right to be what you call silly, stupid, inadequate, incompetent, and sinful."

A Powerful Method For Overcoming Fear and Anxiety

Sigmund, a college student, was distressed when he got a B on an exam instead of the A he expected. "I'm in a state of panic because I'm going to flunk out of school," he told me (Jim).

Carl was terrified because the thought of suicide kept occurring to him. "I wouldn't ever do it," he said, "but I keep getting the thought of it. I think there's something seriously wrong with me.

With my mind. It's deranged."

Alfred consulted me because he was anxious about going away from home for the first time to a university 400 miles away. "If I'm driving," he said, "and I have an anxiety attack, I have to pull over to a gas station and go in the bathroom till I calm down. I think I'm a mental case. Maybe I should be hospitalized."

Each of the above fears was relieved by a method we call Perfectionism Reframing. What this means is seeing every case of fear as a case of perfectionism.

Sigmund believed his perfectionistic Inner Critic message: "If you don't get an A, you're defective. That is, you're not a perfect student. And you should be a perfect student."

Carl believed his perfectionistic Inner Critic message: "If the thought of suicide occurs to you, you're defective. That is, you're not perfectly mentally healthy. And you should be perfectly mentally healthy."

Alfred believed the following perfectionistic Inner Critic message: "If you have to go to a bathroom to calm down, you're defective. That is, you're not perfectly normal. And you should be perfectly normal."

Of course, there were additional complexities in these cases, but the basic challenging statement for each was the same, once the fear got translated into perfectionism: "I have the right to get a B, to think about suicide, to go to a bathroom to calm down." In each case, the fear was reduced to a tiny and manageable twinge. Ultimately it vanished.

Rights Are Neither Legal, Moral, Nor Action-Producing

Note that the process of taking back your rights occurs only with regard to your Inner Critic. That is, your Inner Critic has been telling you that you do not have certain rights. Declaring your rights is only a method for getting released from your Inner Critic. It has nothing to do with legal rights or moral rights.

Moreover, just because you take back your rights doesn't mean you have to take any action at all. In other words, you may take back your right to leave your partner. What you then decide to do, however, is a totally separate issue.

QUESTION: "I have a should not to tell lies, and you tell me to say 'I have the right to lie to people.' But I don't *want* to lie to people. Why should I take back that right?"

ANSWER: Taking back a right is like buying a fishing license. Just because you buy a fishing license doesn't mean you have to go fishing.[7] And just because you get released from a should doesn't mean you have to engage in the forbidden behavior. But once you get released, you'll be in a position to make a decision freely, not driven by your Inner Critic.

To put this another way, taking back a right is simply taking back your right to choose. From that position, you can then freely choose to do whatever you wish, and if you care about people you won't lie to them.[8]

QUESTION: "You say I have the right to be the way I am, but what if the way I am is destructive to me?"

ANSWER: The work you do in Anthetic challenging is just getting free from your Inner Critic, not stating what is the best way for you to live or the best things for you to do. Once you gain inner freedom, you can decide what you really want—but now your decision will be free, not driven.

Don't Use Your Buffers To Challenge

It may be very tempting to simply try to *reverse* what your Inner Critic says. For example, Brad, a 20-year-old accounting clerk, told me (Jim) he wanted to apply for law school. "I don't think they'd accept me," he told me. "I don't think I'm smart enough to get into law school. I know from your lecture that it's my Inner Critic that has been telling me I'm stupid, and I've been trying to reverse that statement for weeks. I've been saying, 'I'm not stupid; I'm intelligent; I got 138 on an IQ test.'" (That was the buffer he was offering to his Inner Critic.)

"What did your Inner Critic say to that?" I asked.

"It said, 'You probably cheated. Or the test scorer probably made a mistake.'"

"So it didn't work?"

"No," he said glumly. "Nothing I said made the Inner Critic stop."

I asked Brad to try a releasing statement: "I have the right to be what you call stupid."

"You're telling me I should admit to being stupid?"

"Not at all," I replied. "You're just taking back your right; afterwards you can decide how intelligent you are."

"Okay. I have the right to be what you call stupid." Brad let this sink in. "I feel better," he said. "It's true! I don't really have to talk my Inner Critic out of anything, do I? All I have to do is ignore it and take back my rights."

"That's correct," I said. "Don't ever play the game according to the Inner Critic's rules. Just buy out of the game altogether."

Note the difference between making Anthetic releasing statements and debating with your Inner Critic by offering it buffers. Releasing statements take back rights and thereby help you become free from the Inner Critic's judgmentalism. Offering a buffer (e.g., "I'm intelligent") is an attempt to convince the Inner Critic that you are trying to obey its shoulds.

Remember: The buffers you accumulate can fail; properly done, the skills for achieving inner freedom will never fail. These skills put you beyond the reach of the Inner Critic for all time, no matter what happens.

Use The Releasing Statement Exactly As Stated

You may be tempted to change the wording of the releasing statement, as given here, especially if you have a should not to follow directions exactly. If you wish, you can certainly experiment with other forms of releasing statements to see what works best. However, our clinical experience with thousands of people has shown that the statement as described here ("I have the right") has the most power.

Don't Add Anything To Your Releasing Statements

It's important to make your releasing statements simple; for example, if your friend asks to borrow money, and you don't want to lend it (but you feel that you should), you can say, "I have the right to say No to my friend." Do not add anything to this statement. For example, don't say, "I have the right to say No to my friend, because he sometimes says No to me." The truth is, you have the right to say No even if he never says No. Adding a "because" means adding a buffer.

An Additional Aid To Challenging

Just because you make a releasing statement doesn't mean you have to do (or not do) anything. It has nothing to do with your actions or behavior. It's just a statement of disengagement from your Inner Critic.

So you might make an additional de-fusing statement (to be explained later) that will help you with your challenging: "Just because I get released doesn't mean I have to do the thing I am now free to do."

Put Reminders Where You Can See Them

For best results, write your releasing statements on large Post-It slips or 4x6 index cards using a felt-tipped pen. Attach these sheets or cards to your car's dashboard, your bathroom mirror, your refrigerator door, or other places where they'll be conspicuous. The more often you see these reminders, the more they'll be reinforced in your mind.

This is important: If you feel reluctant to put up these reminders, it's a clue that your Inner Critic is fighting back, trying to hang on to its control over you. (Of course, you may not be aware of this, but it's worth working on with your Anthetic Therapist.)

Anthetic Master Affirmations

You can think about each of the releasing statements you make as an Anthetic affirmation—a declaration that affirms your inner freedom. Here's a master affirmation you may want to post on your refrigerator door or bathroom mirror to remind you of a number of rights that you have:

"I have the right to make my own decisions, set my own priorities, establish my own life-style, and be the ultimate judge of my behavior. I have the right to be who I am, whatever that may be.

"I have the right to decide whether or not to meet others' expectations, no matter who they are. I have the right to decide whether I am responsible for solving other people's problems, no matter how severe those problems are and no matter how easily I could solve them. I have the right not to hold myself responsible for other people's negative feelings, no matter how much they try to persuade me that I am.

"Furthermore, I have the right to set standards for all my relationships: I have the right to expect that you will behave toward me in a way that is caring, considerate, and respectful; that you will take my opinions and ideas seriously; and that you will carefully consider any requests I might make. If you are not willing to do this, I have the right to terminate my relationship with you."

In addition, here's a master affirmation that sums up all the others: **"I have the right to be human."**

A Final Word

You might want to make a list of your releasing statements, then make a tape recording of yourself reading them. If you listen to this tape once a day, it will greatly accelerate your progress toward inner freedom.

QUESTION: If I believe I have the right to do all those things listed above, won't I become immoral and irresponsible?

ANSWER: Not at all. You are merely challenging your Inner Critic, not deciding to do immoral and irresponsible things. (In fact, you are not deciding to *do* anything.)

Once you challenge your Inner Critic successfully, you will become moral and responsible from a new place—from your heart, instead of from fear of your Inner Critic's emotional punishments.

Shoulds As Disempowerments

Each should (or shouldn't) that you obey is one more disempowerment. Each releasing statement that you successfully make is one more liberation.

How to Tell
If Challenging
Is Working

You can recognize a successful challenge by the fact that you feel lighter. It will feel as though a burden has been lifted from your shoulders, perhaps one you weren't even aware you had been carrying. You will feel free and released; you may have a floating feeling. One of our clients reported: "Before I made the releasing statement, it was as though I had to hold up the whole world. When I got released, it was like I could let go, and the world would still be there!"

Here are some other indicators of successful challenging:

■ You'll feel more playful.

■ You'll experience more aliveness and greater energy.

■ You'll feel more empowered, more able to assert yourself.

■ You'll feel good; you may smile or laugh, and if anyone is observing you, they may smile and laugh, too, through empathy with your new-found feelings of joy and inner freedom.

■ Your shoulders may relax; you may automatically take a deep breath and relax your whole body. You may feel something even deeper inside you relaxing.

If, on the other hand, your challenging methods are not working well, you will still feel heavy, trapped, pressured, oppressed, burdened, jangly, cynical, and pessimistic. If this is the case, tell your Anthetic Therapist, who will give you more help.

Your Options
Will Increase

As you continue the process of Anthetic challenging, your reactive self will become weaker.[9] At the same time, previously submerged elements of your natural self will emerge into consciousness where they can be integrated. This means that now you have more and more options available to you.

For example, if your Inner Critic has submerged your assertiveness, pejoratizing it as "rude," "intrusive," and "pushy," you will now see that your assertiveness is perfectly normal and natural. You may not always act on it, but it will now be available as an option, whereas before it was disowned and submerged.[10]

More Ways To Gauge Your Ability To Challenge Effectively

Here are two more ways to tell if Anthetic challenging is working.

■ Are you reclaiming previously submerged parts of yourself? Take feelings, for example: Can you welcome *all* your feelings—even the ones you think you shouldn't have?

What about anger, sexual feelings, judgmentalism, loving feelings, jealousy, feeling superior to others, anxiety, shame, and guilt? If your Inner Critic has prohibited you from having these feelings, and you have successfully challenged it (i.e., "I have the right to feel _____"), you should now have the right to feel each of these feelings.

■ With the help of your Anthetic Therapist, do you now have more choices open to you? Are you able to express both anger and love? Can you express both toughness and tenderness? Can you be both emotional and logical? Can you be close to someone without feeling trapped and smothered? Can you be assertive as well as passive?

■ Again, with the help of your Anthetic Therapist, have you been able to reduce your anger and judgmentalism?

Your Believability Score:
Using Percentages To Gauge Your Progress

You may find it useful to use percentages to evaluate the effectiveness of your challenges. After you make each challenge, ask yourself the following question: "When I look at the challenge, what percent do I believe it to be true?" This is your Believability Score. Answers to this question can be evaluated as follows:

100%	Excellent! (Make sure, however, that you're not giving this percentage simply because of a should to look good and make progress).
90-99%	Very good. Each time you make the challenge, you'll probably find that your score will increase rapidly.
40%-89%	Good, but you've got some more work to do. Study chapters 12 through 16.

MAKING RELEASING STATEMENTS 147

1%-39%   Better than zero percent! (Again, study chapters 12-16).

0%   If your score doesn't improve after studying chapters 12-16, you might want to ask your Anthetic Therapist to help you make a basic value shift.

NOTE: If you gave yourself a low percentage, watch out for an Inner Critic attack—based on a should to get a high score.

Here are some challenging statements you can use: "I have the right to get a low score—even a zero! I have the right to never learn the challenging skills" and "Just because I gave myself a low score doesn't mean I'm a bad person."

In the next chapter you'll learn some more ways to challenge your Inner Critic so you can achieve even greater liberation from its enslaving tactics.

NOTES

1. Once you become proficient in using the challenging skills, you'll easily be able to shut your Inner Critic up—either by challenging it or by telling it to shut up. *[From p. 131]*

2. "This is awesome" is a comment often made by clients after they have successfully challenged their Inner Critic. *[From p. 133]*

3. When you challenge your Inner Critic, speak to it as though it was in front of you. Do not imagine it to be peeking over your shoulder; that gives it too much power. *[From p. 134]*

4. By negative feelings, we mean the five emotional punishments (Chapter 5) and related feelings. Calling them negative doesn't mean pejoratizing them; it simply means that they are uncomfortable. *[From p. 136]*

5. Acquittal statements represent attempts to get acquitted; their goal is the acquisition of buffers about "being right." You can often hear them in couple arguments, interviews with politicians, and remarks made by witnesses on the stand, even when they are not accused of a crime. *[From p. 137]*

6. It might be argued that making a releasing statement is a kind of disputing, since it disputes the Inner Critic's command that you have no rights. However, we believe the term *disputing* is best reserved for the offering of evidence that a belief is incorrect. Since the Inner Critic is merely issuing a command (a should), no disputing is needed. That is, you needn't dispute a command, you simply assert your right to disobey it. You need give no reason for this, except

that you choose not to obey.

In addition, you can't dispute a judgmental statement, either, since it is just an emotional expression, not a supposedly factual statement. *[From p. 137]*

7. For the idea of the fishing license, see Eric Berne (1973, p. 123).*[From p. 141]*

8. Caring is one of the Anthetic values recommended in Chapter 17. *[From p. 141]*

9. Recall that your reactive self is the equivalent of the Eastern concept of ego, and that spiritual growth, according to many Eastern philosophies, requires the weakening of the ego. *[From p. 145]*

10. The process of Anthetic growth moves progressively forward in three stages:

Stage I. Submergence. Elements in your inner world have become disowned and submerged because they have been pejoratized by your Inner Critic. You are totally unaware of these elements, although you can observe clues to their existence in the puzzling personal problems you have. Because certain elements are submerged, they are no longer available as options, and your personality is to some extent impoverished. This stage includes once-conscious elements which have been repressed, together with submerged elements that never were conscious.

Stage II. Emergence. Elements have begun to emerge and are being integrated into consciousness. They are now owned and accepted because your Anthetic challenging has removed the pejorative overlay from them. (To put this another way, you now accept and welcome them because you have "slots" for them.) You are now free to choose whether or not to actualize these elements.

Stage III. Actualization. Stage II elements, formerly merely in consciouness, may now become actualized in behavior through your conscious choice.

This three-stage process is an important factor in Anthetic individuation. See Jim's book *Personal Growth through Interaction* (Elliott 1976) for more comments on this concept. See also Mahrer (1989, pp. 6f) and Wolinsky (1991, p. 85). *[From p. 146]*

10

Eleven More Challenging Methods

IN ITS MISGUIDED ATTEMPTS to keep you in line, your Inner Critic will not only take away your rights, it will also disempower you in other ways. In this chapter we're going to describe these additional attempts at disempowerment and explain how to challenge them.

-1-
The De-fusing Method

Your Inner Critic often functions by fusing together two things that are really separate and independent of each other, making you think they are one single thing. These "fusions" must be de-fused. The most common fusion is a conceptual fusion.

■ **De-fusing conceptual fusions.** Because your Inner Critic likes rigidity, it will try to fuse together in your mind ideas that do not belong together. For example, your Inner Critic may try to persuade you that if someone is angry at you, it means that you are defective or bad or that something is wrong with you. In this case, the two items that are fused are "someone is angry at me" and "I am defective." The two, of course, do not necessarily (or ever) go together—except in the eyes of your Inner Critic.

To overcome a conceptual fusion, we recommend using the "Just Because" (JB) challenge Jim created (Elliott 1991). The form

of the challenge is: "Just because X, doesn't mean Y." Here are some examples:
- "Just because someone is angry at me doesn't mean I'm a bad person."
- "Just because someone criticizes me doesn't mean I've done something wrong."
- "Just because I *feel* useless, inadequate, helpless, or unworthy doesn't mean I *am* useless, inadequate, helpless, or unworthy."
- "Just because I don't have a partner doesn't mean there's something wrong with me."
- "Just because someone doesn't approve of me doesn't mean I'm wrong, bad, worthless, defective, or inadequate."
- "Just because I'm not perfect doesn't mean I'm a bad person."
- "Just because I don't call Mom every day doesn't mean I'm a bad son or daughter."

■ **The "Even Though" Alternative.** An alternative to the "Just Because" challenge is the "Even Though" challenge: "Even though X, that doesn't mean Y." For example, "Even though I do something for myself, that doesn't mean I'm selfish."

Adding The JB Challenge To Your Releasing Statements

If you add the "Just Because" challenge to your releasing statements, it will give them more power. For example: "I have the right to be late to my appointment; Just Because I'm late doesn't mean I'm a bad person." After a while, you'll see that the JB challenge is an implicit part of every releasing statement, whether you speak the JB part or not.

QUESTION: Is the JB challenge a form of disputing?
ANSWER: In a very broad sense, yes. But no evidence is needed, and it's not necessary to argue with your Inner Critic. All you need to do is realize that the fused items are really quite separate. The Inner Critic, of course, may continue to believe the fusion, but you yourself have bought out of it.

■ **De-fusing the T-self from a buffer.** It's useful to think of yourself as composed of two parts:
- An essential self, which may also be called a Transcendental

Self (T-self)[1], together with
- All the other elements that go into making up "yourself," including your body, your thoughts, your feelings, your behavior, and so on.

Among these other elements are buffers. When we are reactively buffered (Chapter 6), it means we are fused with the buffer. Such a fusion is evident when people say things like, "I am my work" or "I am my body."

When we use our performance, status, or behavior to prop up our self-esteem—and we think we *are* our performance, status, or behavior—we become fused with buffers. This fusion means that we have bought into the position that our value really does depend on having (and, of course, being) the buffer.

The Inner Critic encourages this T-self fusion to further its goal of protecting you by making you machinelike. Here's an example of a disengaging challenge:

THE EVENT: You find yourself feeling good because of a success-buffer, and then your buffer collapses. You feel depressed because you believe you are now of little worth.

THE CHALLENGE: "The essential me is separate. I am not my thoughts, feelings, behavior, body, life situation, or possessions. My worth as a human being has nothing to do with how much money I make, how spiritual I am, the things I own, how popular I am, or my skills and abilities."

■ **Disengaging the present from the past.** Your Inner Critic, in its desperate attempts to protect you, tries to lay down rigid rules for your thoughts, feelings, and behavior. In order to construct this rigid protective structure, the Inner Critic places great value on your first learnings—the ones experienced in childhood.

Your Inner Critic then takes these learnings and generalizes them. For example, if, as a child, you were frightened by a dog, your Inner Critic will tell you that all dogs are dangerous and should be avoided. (You may not be aware of this process; all you may know is that you just don't like dogs.)

To put this another way, the Inner Critic fuses the past (the dog that frightened you) with the present (any dog you might now encounter as an adult).

The Inner Critic can take any prototype situation you experienced in the past and fuse it with a similar experience in the pre-

nced in the past and fuse it with a similar experience in the present. For example, when you were a child, your Inner Critic may have noticed the pain you experienced when you were criticized by your parents. It may then have programmed you to avoid that pain by becoming a Good Little Kid (GLK). If you were very good, Mom and Dad wouldn't scold you; they would bestow love and approval.

Your Inner Critic set this up as a program: *Do what people want, and it's guaranteed that they will like you.* It worked in the past, and now you try to apply it in the present, because to your Inner Critic, past and present are fused.

However, when you continue your old GLK programming in the present, you discover that it doesn't work. You may not receive love and approval; instead, you may be painfully astonished to discover that people will not appreciate your good behavior and may, in fact, take advantage of you. The truth is, if you are an adult, being a GLK means being disempowered. Yet you continue GLK behavior because your Inner Critic has fused the past with the present.[2]

Here's how to challenge this kind of fusion:

1. EVENT: Vera reported feeling hopeless about her 5-year-old marriage. "I keep trying to please Chip," she said, "but nothing I do is good enough. I give up satisfying my own needs and do whatever he wants. But no matter how hard I try, I don't get any appreciation."

2. CHALLENGES:

■ "Just Because I learned to bend over backward to please people in the past doesn't mean it's going to work in the present."

■ "I'm seeing a person in the present (e.g., my spouse) through a filter from the past (e.g., a Daddy filter). I need to identify the filter and set it aside, so I can see the other person more accurately."

-2-
Challenging
Negative Comparisons

In one of our groups, Terrie said to Marcia: "As I watch you work, I feel awful. I should be happy when I see you get free, but I'm not. I compare myself with you, and I feel hopeless. I'll never learn to work on myself the way you do."

The Inner Critic loves to compare us negatively with others; it does this (so it thinks) in order to shape us into "good" people. Here's how to challenge this:

1. EVENT: Someone is further ahead than I am; someone is making faster progress than I am. I feel discouraged.

2. CHALLENGES:
- "I have the right to move at my own pace—even if it's slower than that of others."
- "Just because I'm not as advanced as others doesn't mean I'm a bad person."

-3-
Challenging Perfectionistic Demands

In its attempt to shape you into a "good" person, your Inner Critic will drive you mercilessly to be perfect. You must achieve a score or grade of 100% (or more!). Less than perfect, even 99.99999%, doesn't count. There are no allowances for mistakes.

1. EVENT: Your Inner Critic tells you that you goofed, and that you're grossly incompetent—and you believe it.

2. CHALLENGES:
- "I have the right to make mistakes."
- "Just because I make mistakes doesn't mean I'm a bad person."

-4-
Declaring Your Importance

One way your Inner Critic disempowers you is by persuading you that other people's needs, feelings, and ideas are more important than yours. Since your Inner Critic wants you to believe that other people are superior to you, it wants you to defer to them.[3]

When you buy into this message that others are more important than you, you may be driven by the assumptions indicated in the following example:

1. EVENT: A salesperson calls you on the telephone, and you find yourself frozen. Out of politeness, you've got to listen; you can't say goodbye and hang up. You feel more and more uncomfortable, because you don't want to hurt the caller's feelings. Your assumptions are:

"I should be polite."
"I've got to protect the caller's feelings."
"His/her feelings are more important than mine."

Now let's take another event: someone wants to borrow money from you. You don't want to lend it, but you don't want to hurt the other person's feelings, so you lend the money. Your assumptions are:

"His/her need is more important than mine."
"His/her feelings are more important than mine."
"I'd be rude if I didn't lend the money."

2. CHALLENGES:

■ "I have the right to be what you call rude."

■ "*My* bad feelings (if I don't do what I want) are more important than your bad feelings (if I do). I'm tired of putting other people's feelings ahead of mine. I have the right to stop giving away my power that way."

■ "What I want is as important as what you want; I have the right to ask for it and try to get it, even if you feel hurt."

■ "What I think is as important as what you think; I have the right to speak my voice."

■ "My requests are as important as your requests—or even *more* important."

■ "My well-being is as important as your well-being—or even *more* important."

QUESTION: But suppose I say I have the right to do what I want, even though other people feel bad. Won't I become cold and heartless?

ANSWER: We're not saying you should be uncaring; only that you need to take back the rights your Inner Critic is trying to take away from you. Once you do this, you will become free; once you have become free, you can then choose to be caring, but now it will not be a driven choice. And because it will be free, your caring will be much more effective.

-5-
Resisting Pressure From Others

In its attempt to protect you, your Inner Critic may tell you that you should do what other people want, so you don't make waves and

ELEVEN MORE CHALLENGING METHODS 155

upset them (what this really means is: so you don't incur their disapproval). This will result in pretzelizing yourself—twisting yourself into a pretzel. This form of giving in to pressure from others is another power giveaway. Here are some suggested challenges:

1. EVENT: Mom wants you to call her every day, and you don't want to.

2. CHALLENGES:
- "I'm not here to live up to your expectations."
- "I wasn't put on this earth to live up to other people's expectations of how I should perform."
- "I have the right not to do what other people want."

-6-
Reducing Your Concern About What Other People Might Think

Your Inner Critic is keenly aware of what other people might be thinking about you. In its zeal to "protect" you, it will do its best to make you conform so as not to trigger other people's criticism.[4] When you want to do something from your natural self, your Inner Critic may remind you that other people may not like it. It may demand that you pretzelize yourself.

When you pretzelize yourself to please other people, however, you give away your power to do what you want.

1. EVENT: You want to do something that others might criticize: e.g., wear your hair a new way, marry someone of a different race or religion, pursue a career that you really enjoy but that might not result in a large income. Or perhaps you want to say No to drugs or alcohol, you want to declare your love for someone, or you want to stick to your moral standards in the face of opposition.

You feel uncomfortable because your Inner Critic stands ready to pounce, should you not conform.

2. CHALLENGES:
- "I no longer choose to give away my power to other people"
- "I have the right to do what *I* want, not pretzelize myself to please other people."
- "I have the right to live by *my* moral values, not the hand-me-down values of other people."
- "I have the right to make a mistake, if that's what I'll be doing in making this decision."

-7-
Challenging Responsibility Commands

Your Inner Critic will tell you that you are responsible for other people's negative feelings (and sometimes their behavior and physical health). Furthermore, it will inflict emotional punishment (in the form of guilt) if you were to "make" other people feel bad. So your Inner Critic says you'd better sacrifice yourself and put others' feelings first. This is yet another form of power giveaway.

1. EVENTS: Someone says "You'll hurt my feelings (or make me angry, depressed, or unable to cope—or give me a heart attack) if you carry out your plans (e.g., to leave me, marry someone I don't approve of, not visit me, move away from this city, follow a career I don't approve of)."

2. CHALLENGES:

■ "I'm not responsible for other people's negative feelings; that's their stuff, for them to work on if they choose. (Because one of my values is to be caring, I may offer to help them work on their stuff, but I'm not responsible for that stuff)."

■ "I have the right to do what I want."

-8-
Challenging Guilt Feelings About The Present

Your Inner Critic will tell you that the reason you *feel* guilty is that you *are* guilty; it will tell you that you *are* guilty because you have committed a crime; and it will tell you that you should be punished for that crime, either by feeling the pain your Inner Critic inflicts or by some other punishment. Moreover, it will try its best to brainwash you into believing all the other propaganda about guilt feelings mentioned in Chapter 5.

CHALLENGES:

■ "Just because I *feel* guilty doesn't mean I *am* guilty."

■ "Feeling guilty will not make me a better person; it will just make me a miserable person. I can be a better person not through punishment but by listening to my Inner Guide."

■ "Just because I feel guilty doesn't mean I have to be programmed by that feeling; I'm free to do whatever I want, living from my natural self."[5]

-9-
Challenging Guilt Feelings About The Past

Not only does your Inner Critic like to punish you with guilt feelings about the present, it enjoys punishing you by reminding you of all the things you did "wrong" in the past.

The key to working with these Inner Critic messages is to realize that they are based on shoulds to have been more aware, more competent, and more advanced—all grandiose standards your Inner Critic tries to impose in its efforts to hold you to 100% perfection.

In addition to the challenges mentioned in the section above, here are some special ones for guilt feelings about events in the past:

■ "I have the right to have been in the state of mind I was in when I did certain things—to have been less aware than I am now, less competent, and less advanced. I could not have been something I wasn't."

■ "Just because I now know what was best to have done doesn't mean I knew then. I didn't know then."

■ "I did the best I could, based on my state of mind at the time."

■ "Just because I made mistakes in the past doesn't mean I was (or am) defective, evil, or bad."

■ "I have the right to have done things imperfectly."

-10-
Challenging Negative Predictions

In its self-appointed role as protector, your Inner Critic will make negative predictions about any new behavior you might try. For example, if you're thinking about going to a party, your Inner Critic will say: "Don't go; you won't have a good time." If you're thinking about trying to get a new job or applying for college, your Inner Critic will say, "Don't do it; you'll just get rejected."

Here's how to challenge negative predictions:

1. EVENT: You think about trying something new. Your Inner Critic says, "Don't try that; you'll fail."

2. CHALLENGE: "What do **you** know, Inner Critic. You're not an expert on this subject. I know you're just trying to protect me by

making me fearful and reluctant, but who needs protection like that? I'm going to figure out if this is what I really want to try, then assess the risks if I fail, and then do it or not based on the facts, not on the fear you're making me feel."

-11-
Overcoming Worry

Yes, worry is another result of Inner Critic functioning. You'll need to be especially watchful during times when you are apt to be more vulnerable to your Inner Critic.

For example, as you do this work, you'll find that your Inner Critic will tend to pounce when you're tired, when you wake up in the middle of the night, or when your feelings are running high.

Situations such as getting married, going through a separation or divorce, the death of someone close to you, trying something new, appearing before an audience, being evaluated, having a request refused, making a court appearance, the failure of some project, and losing your job are times of great opportunity for the Inner Critic. Vacations, holidays, birthdays, and other anniversaries are especially critical, as are times when you are travelling with others (especially on camping trips). Illnesses may make you more vulnerable, as may other biological events such as low blood sugar and pre-menstrual syndrome.

When you're in one of these vulnerable situations, you'll need to remind yourself that the negativity you're feeling is just Inner Critic stuff. Here's an example of dealing with a "Middle of the Night" (MOTN) thought, using a reframing process:

1. EVENT: You wake up in the middle of the night with worries that go around and around in your mind, and you can't get back to sleep.

2. CHALLENGE: "This is just my Inner Critic talking. It's the middle of the night and I'm having some MOTN negativity. Whatever feelings I'm having are not to be trusted. I'm just having an Inner Critic attack."

In the next chapter you'll see how the challenging methods are combined to address specific problems.

NOTES

1. The "basic you" is called the essential self or the Transcendental Self (T-self). The T-self is who you are at the core level of your being. It is basically an observer. Everything else about you is something "added on." Note that you do not *have* a T-self; you *are* a T-self. So if you search for it, as Hume (1978) did, you will never find it, simply because you are the searcher. This self is similar to Husserl's (1960) transcendental ego or Kant's (1900) transcendental unity of apperception. See Ryle (1949, pp. 195-198) for a discussion of the systematically elusive self. See Evans (1970) for an excellent book on the subject. *[From p. 151]*

2. Fusion of the present situation with a prototype from the past is the Anthetic explanation for what psychoanalysis refers to as transference. *[From p. 152]*

3. Many women have been trained in childhood to give away their power to men; both sexes have been trained to give away their power to anyone who seems confident, charismatic, and authoritative. *[From p. 153]*

4. To be criticized by someone, your Inner Critic tells you, is terrible; it means that you are defective. *[From p. 155]*

5. When you live from your natural self, this means living from the energies of your primary self, channelled by the structures of your secondary self. If you are to have a happy and fulfilling life, these structures must be informed by the Anthetic values of love, caring behavior, and responsible living, to be mentioned in Chapter 17. *[From p. 156]*

11

Putting It All Together: Some Examples

NOW THAT YOU'VE BECOME ACQUAINTED with the basic Inner Critic challenges, let's take a look at some examples to see how those challenges can be combined to address specific problems.[1] We will present examples from four areas: depression, writers' problems, fear of success, and aphilia (inability to love).

OVERCOMING DEPRESSION

Depression is like a dark cloud that seems to come out of nowhere. It can range anywhere from a mild glumness to a deep and pervasive hopelessness, together with the inability to concentrate, resistance to doing the most minor tasks, and the feeling that there's nothing whatever that makes life worth living. Anthetic Therapy holds that whether it's mild or severe, any given depression has a number of sustaining elements, most of which are created by the Inner Critic.[2]

Take the case of Paula, 47, divorced with no children. She told me (Jim) she had just been fired from her job as office manager of a small computer firm, and she was feeling worthless and depressed. Instead of aggressively looking for a new job, she stayed in her apartment almost every day watching soap operas on TV. When she did go out, it took her an hour to decide what clothes to wear. Her mother called several times a week, complaining that Paula was not visiting her. Paula felt guilty but couldn't bring herself to visit her mother.

Paula's life had few pleasures, and whenever she did engage in pleasurable activities, she felt guilty. "I can't enjoy anything," she said. "How can I enjoy anything? I keep thinking about all the people in the world who are worse off than I am. I've even been afraid to get back into therapy, because it seems so self-indulgent."

In addition, Paula felt basically flawed because, after years of therapy, she still needed more therapy. She compared herself to her former fellow-workers, who, she thought, were getting along much better. "Everybody else seems to have it together," she said. "But not me. I'm afraid I'm going to become a street person, a bag lady, and have to live on dog food."

Paula reported having few friends. She avoided other people because she thought they could see her defectiveness and were silently critical of it. If someone didn't smile at her, she thought she was being rejected.

I began by teaching her Anthetic challenging. The first challenge was a de-fusion: "Just because I got fired doesn't mean I'm worthless." This was difficult for Paula to accept; her believability score was 5%.

She scored higher on releasing statements; for example, "I have the right to fail" (40%) and "I have the right to be what you call self-indulgent" (60%). When she said "I have the right to enjoy life even if everyone else in the world is miserable," her face brightened. She believed it 95%. I directed her to say it a number of times, until her score hit 100%. "That's true!" she finally said. "I see it now."

I then directed Paula in responsibility disentangling. I asked her to say, "I'm not responsible for fixing other people or for making them happy, especially Mom." At first, she added a buffer: "I'm not responsible for making others happy, because I don't have enough time or money to help everyone." I pointed out the buffer to her, then suggested the following releasing statement: "I have the right not to make other people happy even if I have enough time and money to do so." Her eyes sparkled as she said this. Finally, she said, "I have the right to be selfish!" At this point, her face was transformed. Whereas before it had been sad and downcast, now she was smiling. I asked her to say "I have the right to be selfish" a number of times, and when she had finished, she began laughing.

"I don't feel depressed any more," she said. She was silent a moment. "But I'm sure it's going to come back."

"And now you can use the Anthetic challenges to pull yourself out of it again," I told her.

"Yes." She was silent again. "I never had tools like these before. I went to another therapist for a year, and he told me to dispute my negative beliefs, but I just couldn't do it. The beliefs kept winning out over me. It's much easier now that I know they're not *my* beliefs; they come from my Inner Critic." She switched to a new topic. "But why should I keep needing therapy? Other people are getting along okay without it."

I then directed Paula in some new challenging statements: "Just because I need therapy doesn't mean I'm a bad person," "I have the right to move at my own pace," and "I have the right to be depressed for the rest of my life."

"But I don't *want* to be depressed," she protested. I explained again the function of taking back rights: this was only with regard to her Inner Critic. The goal of releasing statements was simply to get free. Once she got free, whatever action she chose would be up to her.

When she left after this first session, she said she was feeling better than she had in years.

During the second session, I checked to see if she had been using the challenges. She reported some success in using them during the week, but then on Sunday a telephone call from her mother sent her into a downward spiral of depression that she couldn't pull herself out of.

Anthetic Dialogue with Mom in the empty chair revealed a parent who was subtly judgmental and manipulative. The result was the undermining of Paula's self-confidence.

What also emerged was a series of early childhood learnings imposed by (or modeled by) Mom: e.g., "Put other people first," "Be responsible for their feelings," and "Don't do pleasurable things, because they're trivial, silly, and unproductive." Using releasing statements, Paula challenged each of these dysfunctional beliefs, whereupon she felt much better.

The focus of the third session was on Paula's relationships. She thought that people didn't like her. Many cognitive-behavioral therapists would focus on this as a presumably mistaken inference, together with other such inferences as "When people don't smile at me, it's because they don't like me."

For the Anthetic Therapist, however, inference-testing usually comes after Inner Critic challenging. The primary goal is getting free from constrictions, and in this case the constriction was caused by her overvaluation of other people's opinions. I taught her to challenge this overvaluation, using the following statement: "I'm not here to live up to your expectations," together with the additional challenge, "You're here to live up to *my* expectations."

Immediately after this last challenge, Paula reported feeling prickly sensations all over her body. This occasionally occurs when people make a profound shift in psychic structure as a result of challenging the Inner Critic. She repeated the challenge a number of times, and each time she became more animated. She laughed with joy as she realized the truth of the challenge. The prickly sensations vanished as the structural transformation was completed (from Inner Critic bound energies to free energies), and the new configuration became more familiar and comfortable.

We experimented with more challenges: "I'm going to start pleasing myself, and if you don't like it, the hell with you." "I'm tired of twisting myself into a pretzel to please you." "I'm going to do what *I* like from now on, and if you don't like me, you're losing out on knowing a wonderful person." She addressed these messages to a number of people whom she imagined sitting in the empty chair: Mom, Dad, friends.[3]

Paula continued in therapy for six more sessions, during which time I taught her additional Anthetic Dialogue skills to supplement her challenging skills. Near the end of this time she had obtained a new job that was much better than her old one. She had a new boyfriend. She was beginning to make new friends who were less judgmental than the old ones. She was much happier and was thinking about going back to school for an advanced degree. The depression was still lurking at the edges of her awareness, but it had much less power now.

OVERCOMING WRITERS' PROBLEMS

Special problems often plague people whose work involves writing, whether it's writing letters, term papers, business reports, newspaper and magazine articles, fiction, or a thesis or dissertation. Among these problems are writer's block, fear of finishing, procrastination, coping with criticism, and handling rejections. Each of these problems is caused directly or indirectly by the Inner

Critic.

Ernie, age 23, suffered from all five of the above problems. He came for his first session with me (Jim) clearly distraught. Immediately after obtaining a degree in journalism, he had landed a job as a reporter for a weekly newspaper. He held the job for a year, and when he received a small inheritance, he decided to quit and use the money to support himself while he got established as a free-lance writer. His plan was to earn an income by writing newspaper and magazine articles while also working on a novel.

"I do some work for the newspaper I used to work for," he told me, "but when I get an assignment, I keep putting it off. If there are interviews involved, I can usually do them right away, but I wait till the day before the deadline to do the actual writing, and I have to stay up till 2 and 3 a.m. to finish it.

"And I haven't worked on my novel for weeks. When I sit down to write, my mind goes blank. Or I find a million other things that need doing.

"Another problem is that I've got about half a dozen articles that I've started but never finished. I'm good on ideas but bad on producing. I'm also good at writing query letters, but when an editor accepts my idea, I can't seem to write the article. I did finish one article and sent it out 'on spec,' but it got rejected. I was a basket case for days afterward.

"So I asked my girlfriend to critique a second article before I sent it to a publisher, and we got in a big argument. I thought she was being too picky, and she told me I couldn't take criticism, and I guess she was right.

"I know I can write, because I got good grades in my writing courses in school, and the newspaper editor I worked for liked my work, but I'm afraid something psychological is messing me up. I'm desperate; I'm afraid I'm going to run out of money pretty soon. I've got to make a success of writing somehow, because there's nothing else I really want to do."

From long experience in working with writers, I knew that the Inner Critic was probably the cause of Ernie's problems. In fact, one reason for the high rate of alcoholism among writers is that the alcohol anesthetizes the Inner Critic. Writers can write better after a few drinks, but, of course, the side effects can be devastating.

As I worked with Ernie, the following messages emerged from his Inner Critic:

1. "You should write perfect (or near-perfect) articles, right from

the start."

2. "You should finish your novel, or you're a failure, because fiction writing is 'better' than nonfiction writing. At the same time, you *shouldn't* finish your novel, because if you do, you'll have to send it out to publishers, and it might be accepted and published, and then people will criticize it when they see how awful it is. So you'd better play it safe by not finishing it."

3. "Basically, you're a failure at writing. You'd better give it up and get an eight-to-five job." When Ernie tried to dispute this message by saying, "But I had a job as a reporter, and they liked me," his Inner Critic said, "They just hired you because they felt sorry for you."

When I taught Ernie to use Anthetic Dialogue to work on his procrastination, he said (to "the publishers," imagined as sitting in an empty chair), "I'll be damned if I'll jump through your hoops. I'll hold back. I'll put things off, or maybe not do them at all." This, too, involved an Inner Critic message: "If someone tells you what to do, and you do it, you're a slave because, you're knuckling under, and you shouldn't be a slave. So in order to prove you're not a slave, you shouldn't do what they tell you."

As each Inner Critic message emerged, I helped Ernie challenge it. The most powerful message was number one above. Basically, this was a command, or should, to be perfect. In order to counter it, I suggested that Ernie declare, "I have the right to write garbage. I have the right to write by free association, just putting down whatever words come into my head, even if they don't make sense."

There was a practical reason for using this method, too: It's easier to edit something that has already been written than to write from scratch. Ernie immediately saw the usefulness of this approach.

The second most powerful Inner Critic message was number three above, about failure. Ernie's challenging statement was, "I have the right to fail. I have the right to fail at free-lance writing. And even ask for my old job back."

At this point, his Inner Critic pounced again: "What will people think when they see you come back with your hat in your hand, asking for your old job back?"

Ernie's challenge (as he spoke to "people"): "I'm not here to meet your expectations. I'm here for myself. And just because I ask for my old job back doesn't mean I'm defective in any way. I'm still a good person."

After three sessions, Ernie reported he was using the "garbage first" technique successfully. His novel was still on hold, but he was producing articles ahead of time and getting checks for them. He said he would be back later to work some more on his novel-writing blocks.

OVERCOMING FEAR OF SUCCESS

Hardly anyone walks into a therapist's office complaining of fear of success. Instead, if you have this problem, you may experience it as:

- getting excited at the beginning of a project, then losing interest somewhere in the middle—or near the end;
- functioning well only in a crisis; slacking off when things are going well; and
- feeling blocked by some mysterious force that seems to keep you from succeeding.

In each case, what's really happening may be fear of success. And in each case, the Inner Critic is involved.

Robert, age 19, came to see me (Jim) feeling depressed and confused. "It's like I've got some nemesis," he told me. "Some force out there that's against me."

After a year of a pre-law program, Robert had switched fields because he got bored. He began a major in business administration, with a focus on accounting. But then he lost interest in that, too, and dropped out of college altogether.

He got a job selling insurance, but sales were poor, largely because he couldn't bring himself to make the required number of sales calls. When he began getting dunning notices from creditors, he increased his sales efforts and began making money. But as soon as things were going well, he lost interest again, and sales fell, along with his commissions.

Anthetic Dialogue work revealed a failure script imposed by his Inner Critic based on a "should" not to surpass his father. The father had completed high school and could only get menial jobs. Robert feared success because, as he put it, "My success would be a slap in the face to the old man."

Robert's challenges to his Inner Critic were: "I have the right to surpass my father" and "I have the right to insult my father, to give him a slap in the face, by my success."

At first, Robert felt appalled at his audacity in making these challenges, but after saying them a few times, he realized they made sense. He believed them 100%.

Finally, he added a "Just Because" challenge: "Just because I might succeed doesn't mean I'm injuring my father. But if he is offended, that's just his stuff. Any decent father would *want* his son to surpass him."

"This work is awesome," Robert told me. "I didn't know all those things were inside me." He subsequently got vocational testing, left his insurance job, and returned to school to study business administration again. He was now armed with the following knowledge: "If I lose interest in my career, it may be a clue to my fear of surpassing Dad. All I have to do then is challenge my Inner Critic."

Three years later, he reported by telephone that he was graduating and planned to go on to get an M.B.A. "The challenges are working," he said. "Dad does feel a bit jealous of my education, and he does put me down once in a while about all the 'impractical book-learning' I'm getting, but he likes the fact that I'm doing so well, too."

OVERCOMING APHILIA:
The Inability To Be Loving

Some people take pride in being tough and strong. They see tenderness and love as weakness. They see psychotherapy as a cop-out for sissies. And they see love not as the expression of warm feelings but as the giving of material things.

We call them "Tough" people to distinguish them from "Tender" people, another category that is used in Anthetic Therapy. (Two additional categories are "Dependent" and "Self-sufficient.")[4]

People in the Tough category are usually men. Extreme examples of Tough people are responsible for most of the evil in the world—exploitation, crime, wars, and other forms of inhumanity. These extreme examples include spouse-batterers, child-abusers, dictators, con men, gang members, international terrorists, Nazi party members, and criminals in general. Less extreme examples include hard-hearted and hard-driving business executives, government officials, military leaders—along with counselors and psychotherapists who are judgmental and confrontational.

Tough people hate to perceive themselves as wimps and weaklings. They get debuffered when they lose a contest, when they feel

168 DISARMING YOUR INNER CRITIC

taken advantage of, or when they feel insulted. The debuffering is experienced as humiliation, and they are often driven to seek revenge, which, when they achieve it, gives them a buffer that balances the scales.

Tough people are judgmental toward any "weakness" they perceive in themselves and others. They may be chronically angry, and they lack the ability to empathize with others.

Their glorification of toughness leads them to become, in popular language, hard-hearted. They are often described by others as callous, cold-blooded, insensitive, and ungiving. Their relationships are stormy and short-lived.

While some Tough people (strangely enough) are also Dependent, most are Self-sufficient. The Inner Critic of the Self-sufficient type imposes shoulds to be independent, never to need or ask for help. The result is a "TSS" type: Tough and Self-sufficient. Usually lone wolves.

Above all, TSS people have great difficulty in expressing what we have come to call Anthetic love: love that is expressed as a warm feeling, not as the giving of material things. To put this another way, TSS people are unable to soften their heart toward others.

TSS people appear to be so cold and calculating that they have been described as lacking a superego or conscience—or, as we would say, an Inner Critic. Clinical experience shows, however, that they do have an Inner Critic. It's just that the shoulds it imposes are different from those of Tender people. Tough people's shoulds are to fight, to win, never to be taken advantage of, never to be insulted or humiliated, never to appear weak or soft, never to be needy.

Since TSS people don't believe they have any personal problems, we rarely see them as clients unless they appear in our consulting room in couple counseling, brought there by a partner. They come for therapy reluctantly. Which is sad, because TSS people's relationships are terrible.

Take the case of Eric, 51, the president of a small manufacturing company, who came to see me (Jim) with his wife, Jane, for couple counseling. She had threatened to leave him if he didn't join her in seeking help.

A former army officer, Eric was handsome, charming, well-dressed, distinguished-looking, and self-assured. His handshake was firm, and he looked me in the eye when he gave it. He also gave me a wink, as though to say, "You and I, we're both men of the world. We know that women get emotional and irrational; I'm just here to help her get straightened out."

Jane had several complaints, all typical of the Tender wives of TSS men. Her chief complaint was the lack of romance in the relationship. "He was very romantic when we were courting," she said. "He brought me flowers and candy and sent me little love notes and told me he loved me. Now? Zilch! Nothing."

Eric looked up at the ceiling, rolled his eyes, tilted his head slightly, and tightened his mouth—all signs of judgmentalism.

"She's too damned demanding," he said. "I need my space, and she'd like to suffocate me. That lovey-dovey stuff is all right for kids but not for us old married folks. Tell her she's expecting too much, Doc."

"I can't do that," I said. "Part of my job is to help each of you make requests so you can get what you want in this marriage."

"Well," he said, "I've got a request. I request that she get off my back about all these ideas she's got. She asks me if I love her, and I have to keep telling her a million times a day. When we got married, I told her I loved her. She knows I love her. I work hard every day so she can have a good life."

"It's not material things I'm asking for," she said. "I want to *feel* that you love me. I don't feel loved. And you may think this is a little thing, but it's a big thing." She stopped talking and bit her lower lip. "I don't know that I want to go on being married to you if you can't be affectionate toward me."

The room was silent.

Finally, he said to me, "Okay, maybe I need to learn something about loving. I don't want to lose her. I didn't know she felt this bad." His eyes misted over: A Tough Self-sufficient man beginning to get in touch with his neediness.

I directed him in Inner Critic work using the Anthetic Dialogue method. His shoulds were: to be strong, not to be a wimp, not to give in, and to dominate. I explained again how his Inner Critic had taken away his power.

"What power?" he asked. He was very attentive when it came to the possibility that he had lost some personal power.

"The power to be tender, soft, and submissive," I said. "To be the whole person that you are."

"But I don't want to be submissive."

"Then you'll be driven to dominate," I told him. "And you'll never have the pleasure of letting your love flow freely, or of surrendering in a sexual situation, because you'll have to be in control at all times. And that's just one example. And here's another: If you have to dominate, you won't be able to really listen to your wife, and if you can't listen to her, you won't have a very satisfying relationship."

He saw the logic of it. He said he knew he had problems with both sex and listening, in addition to expressing love. "She tells me I keep trying to fix her problems instead of just listen," he said. So he decided to take back his right to be tender, soft, and submissive. Even wimpy. During this process he became more and more uncomfortable, shifting uneasily in his chair.

And as he continued to make releasing statements, he had a stronger and stronger reaction.

"This feels weird!" he said. "It feels like my skin is tingling all over."

"That means that a big shift is happening to you," I told him. "Anything else you're feeling?"

"A lot lighter," he reported. "This is wonderful!"

The next few sessions were taken up with coaching Eric in making the releasing statements correctly. I explained to the couple that once Eric got free, he would be able to express love (if he chose) but now from his heart, not from the shoulds imposed by his Inner Critic.

As Eric got more and more free, Jane reported noticing a change: he became more loving and considerate. But he still had a few blocks. For example, he couldn't say "I love you" to her.

Anthetic Dialogue revealed that Eric thought lovey-dovey stuff was mushy and sissyish—not very manly. He then took back his right to be mushy, sissyish, and non-manly. This was even harder than the other releasing statements, and again he felt the tingling.

It took several sessions for Eric to overcome his blocks to lovey-dovey stuff, but he did. I explained the concept of Anthetic love (described in Chapter 17), and they both liked it. Eric was finally able to write love poems to his wife, which thrilled her immensely. Before, she had asked him over and over to bring her flowers, which he had finally done, telling her "Okay! Here's your damn flowers!" Now he brought flowers lovingly.

After three months of Anthetic therapy, Eric was able to soften his hardened heart so love could begin flowing through him. He learned to listen to Jane without trying to problem-solve. He also

PUTTING IT ALL TOGETHER   171

began to do more delegating at the office so he would have more time for his family. He still had a strong need to control, which came up every once in a while and had to be dealt with. The couple's sex life improved, as did their relationship in general.

The process was not without problems for Jane. She found herself feeling anxious about the changes in her husband. Inner Critic work helped with this issue, as well as with the judgmentalism she had been expressing toward Eric.

The first three items mentioned above—depression, writing blocks, and fear of success—are common problems described in many professional books and journal articles. However, inability to love is rarely mentioned as a psychological problem; in fact, after an extensive review of the literature, we could not find a single reference to this issue.[5] It is not listed in DSM-IV, the standard catalog of mental disorders.

So we decided to name a new syndrome—aphilia—caused directly by the Inner Critic and found in most couple problems and many individual problems. Just as aphasia is loss of the ability to comprehend or use words, so aphilia is loss of the ability to feel and express love. It is pandemic, so much so that it goes unremarked in our society. People have just stopped expecting to experience love, especially intense love.

More on this topic will be presented in Chapter 17; until then, we'll continue our discussion of Anthetic challenging, beginning with some information that will deepen your understanding of the process, to be presented in the next chapter.

NOTES

1. The examples presented in this chapter are condensed; each session, of course, took longer, with many obstacles which had to be overcome. *[From p. 160]*

2. Some depressions, of course, have biological causes. Here we are referring only to the psychological factors in depression. In addition, we are speaking primarily about dysphoria and dysthymia, not major depression. *[From p. 160]*

3. It might appear that challenges such as "I'm going to please myself" would result in making Paula uncaring and self-centered. Such was not the case, since she found that caring about other people became pleasing to herself, once it was no longer driven by a should. This is a common discovery among Anthetic

172 DISARMING YOUR INNER CRITIC

Therapy clients: once their reactivity is reduced, love and caring can flow freely and naturally. *[From p. 163]*

4. Just as Tough people take pride in being tough, so Tender people take pride in being sensitive, loving and caring, and Self-sufficient people take pride in being independent. Each type creates surface "acts" that are driven by shoulds. To create each act, the Inner Critic commands the submergence of the polar opposite of the act. As mentioned previously, our Anthetic categories were inspired by the work of Karen Horney. Horney's work, of course, did not connect the categories to the Inner Critic's commands. *[From p. 167]*

5. Freud, of course, declared that mental health consists of the ability to love and work, although this idea appears nowhere in his writings. We are indebted to Erik Erikson for the comment; Erikson said Freud told it to him at a convention. In Volume II of the *Collected Papers,* Freud did write (1912, p. 332) that the physician "must be content to win back a part of the [patient's] capacity for work and enjoyment...." *[From p. 171]*

12

Suggestions for Making Your Challenging More Effective

For some people, learning the basic steps of Anthetic challenging is easy. After a one-hour session, they quickly learn to make releasing statements, the most frequently used challenge. The effects are immediate and dramatic. As people get released, they become playful, they smile and laugh a lot, and they feel more relaxed and easygoing.

For others, however, challenging is difficult. So enmeshed are they with the Inner Critic that it may take two or three training sessions to learn the skills. And some people may take longer.

But even those people who learn quickly may find that the Inner Critic begins to fight back, using more subtle weapons than before. Such people may find it tough going for a while until they have learned the finer points of challenging.

This chapter will discuss these finer points to help you increase the effectiveness of your work.

How to Think About Your Inner Critic

A good way to think about your Inner Critic is to see it as a sort of crazy uncle who lives with you, up in the third story of your house, in a locked room with barred windows. From time to time your crazy uncle leans out the window and hurls insults at passersby. He may say the most outrageous things, just as might an inmate a mental institution where you happen to be visiting, but as long as you realize that this person is not speaking rationally, you will know that what he says is not to be trusted. So if you are the target of one of your crazy uncle's insults, all you have to do is realize that he's crazy. Furthermore, it's important not to argue with him, since arguing with a crazy person does no good. Here's a challenge you can use to disengage from (not shut up) your Inner Critic:

■ CHALLENGE: "You can scream all you want, Inner Critic, but I'm not going to believe you."

Believing what your Inner Critic says leads to inner slavery; buying out of what your Inner Critic says leads to inner liberation. Disbelieving your Inner Critic is based on your understanding that its voice comes from desperation, anxiety, and judgmentalism and is therefore absurd.

The point of this method is that you don't have to debate with your Inner Critic; all you have to do is realize that it bombards you with negativity, which is simply its emotional reactions—not a series of facts—and therefore not to be trusted as something realistic or objective.

How to Think About The Disarming Process

It's useful to think of disarming your Inner Critic as the process of draining it of energy. Your strategy in doing this must be based on the following principles:

■ The Inner Critic has no energy of its own. It has energy for one reason and one reason only: because you have given it energy.

■ There is only one way you can give energy to the Inner Critic: you give it energy because you *buy into* the commands it gives you. This is the only power it has.

■ Disarming your Inner Critic, then, consists of one single strategy: refusing to buy into its messages.

■ You can refuse to buy into most Inner Critic messages for the following reason: the message is either a judgmental putdown, a command, or a constriction—and not a supposedly factual statement at all. Since the message does not take the form of a factual statement, there is no need whatever to debate the message with your Inner Critic.

Dehypnotizing The Devalued Self

As we mentioned briefly in Chapter 6, all the negative feelings you have about yourself come from a kind of trance; that is, from the fact that your Inner Critic has hypnotized your natural self into thinking and feeling that it's defective, worthless, shameful, and inferior.[1] It's as though your natural self is under a magic spell cast by your Inner Critic. The magic spell is what creates machinery. To put this another way, if you are in a trance, it's because your machinery has taken over.

What is needed, then, is a dehypnotizing process, one that awakens your natural self to its wonderfulness and preciousness. In other words, challenging not only drains your Inner Critic of energy, it also helps your natural self throw off the trance under which it has been living.

Here's how this happens: As you challenge your Inner Critic, not only do you disengage from it and buy out of its messages, there's another process that occurs. When your devalued natural self overhears your challenges, it takes heart and is encouraged to cast off the overlay of devaluation—the hypnotic trance under which it has been operating. This process occurs automatically.

As the elements of your natural self begin to feel accepted, they become more willing to emerge into consciousness. The devaluational overlay is gradually removed, revealing your natural self in all its glory.

The Process Of Challenging

At first your challenging may be painful, because you will be poking away at the electric fence, whereas before, you were content to stay in the center of the pasture, under that nice tree. However, although you may feel some pain at first, you'll now have tools to deal with it. You'll know that every instance of psychological pain will be a clue to your Inner Critic, and you will be armed with methods for getting released. Every time you challenge your Inner Critic, any discomfort you feel will be reduced. As you become more and more proficient in the challenging skills, the pain will get less and less, and you'll begin to feel exhilarated each time you challenge your Inner Critic.

176 DISARMING YOUR INNER CRITIC

As your challenging continues, your Inner Critic will begin to shrink and have less power. After awhile, it will appear ridiculous. As it tries in vain to control you, you may feel sorry for it, which is a good sign that you're making progress. You'll begin to have some compassion for it, too, and you may address it by saying, "I know you're driven by fear, Inner Critic, but no matter what drives you, I don't want you to run my life any more."[2]

Your Inner Critic will now be a pale shadow of its former self. However, it's important not to relax your vigilance, because from time to time it might pounce with as much ferocity as before.

But more often, you'll be surprised when you discover that your Inner Critic's voice has become less forceful. You might say, as did one of our clients, "I've noticed that my Inner Critic doesn't jump on me as much as it used to. I'll do something or think something and say, 'Gee, wasn't my Inner Critic supposed to jump on me just then?' Now, if I feel anything at all, it's just the slightest little twinge."

When Working On A Personal Problem, Challenging Must Come First

It's important that Anthetic challenging is the first step you take in working on any problem. Achieving inner freedom will clear the decks so you can see the problem clearly, uncontaminated by any Inner Critic stuff. Otherwise, you might find yourself diligently pursuing goals that you don't really want.

Consider the case of Scotty, who was going to law school, and whose grades were gradually falling. "Dad wants me to join his law firm when I graduate," he told me (Jim), "but the way I'm going now, I may flunk out of school. I've got to find out what's wrong with me." To keep himself "on track," Scotty had tried positive thinking, Integrity Therapy, and Solution-Focused Training, but nothing had worked in making him buckle down and study.

Anthetic Dialogue revealed a strong Inner Critic whose messages were: "You should do what Dad wants" and "You shouldn't let Dad down."

His challenges were: "I have the right to do what *I* want" and "I have the right to let Dad down." These challenges were hard to make, but as he repeated them, he began smiling broadly.

"You know what?" he said. "I hate law school. I always wanted to be a gourmet chef. I love cooking. Dad said I could always do that as a hobby, but dammit, I want to do it full time. Isn't that ridiculous?"

"Not at all," I said. "But your Inner Critic thinks it's ridiculous."

Our next session was devoted to how to tell Dad of Scotty's decision to leave law school and enroll in a cooking school. Dad was upset and angry, but Scotty was determined. Scotty was an only child, and from the time he was born, his father had dreams of the two of them working together. Scotty's dad finally accepted his son's decision, although it was a disappointment to him. In a session with the two of them, the father was able to say, "Well, if it makes him happy, I guess I'll have to say okay."

Had Scotty not gotten released from his Inner Critic, he might have successfully used willpower to achieve what he saw as his goal: to get through law school and begin a career as an attorney. "I had a narrow escape," he said. "I'm glad I found out about the Inner Critic!"

Another reason to do Anthetic challenging first is that it gives you an opportunity to do the deeper work of getting free. If you simply dispute your inferences, you might not have this opportunity.

Consider the case of Sally and her husband Ed. In the course of couple counseling, Sally said to me (Kathy), "I want to buy some new dining room furniture, but if I ask him, I think Ed will be angry at me. It scares me silly. Right now he's not saying anything, and I'm sure that means he's angry." Ed opened his mouth and was about to respond, when I gestured to him to be silent.

"Would you like to work with the scared feeling?" I asked Sally. She said Yes. "Do you know what challenge to use?" I asked. It seemed to me that Sally's fear was a clue to a should.

"Yes, I guess so," she replied. "Ed, even though you might get angry at me I still have the right to request that we buy furniture."

"Right!" I said. "Now you can check out with Ed whether he's angry at you." She did so, and Ed said he wasn't; he was thinking about new furniture himself.

Sally's belief that Ed was angry was an assumption on her part—an inference to be tested, not an established fact. At this point she could have tested her inference simply by checking with Ed as to whether he was indeed angry. But had she done that first, she would have missed the opportunity to do the deeper work necessary for achieving inner freedom.

In other words, Sally's Inner Critic was telling her two things: One, that Ed's silence meant he was angry (the inference), and two, that Ed's anger meant she was bad (the Inner Critic's pejorative message).

Sally was directed to challenge the second message first, because the second message was the one that took away her right. So the rule about sequences is this:

First, take back any rights.

Second, check out any inferences you've made.

Prerequisites For Successful Challenging

At the end of some of the previous chapters are lists of prerequisites for successful challenging. Here are some more:

■ **You'll need to learn the skills of critical thinking.** Challenging your Inner Critic requires the ability to think critically. This means being able to question and evaluate every belief you hold, even (or especially) your most cherished beliefs. The reason for doing this radical questioning is that the beliefs you are strongly attached to may be the very ones that are sabotaging your life.

■ **You must have a clear idea of where your Inner Critic came from.** Although part of your Inner Critic came from society (and, of course, some of its messages you thought up yourself), most of your Inner Critic came from your parents, teachers, religious authorities, and other people (the prototypes) who programmed you while you were growing up. This programming was installed in your Inner Critic, and now, your Inner Critic makes you feel bad the same way those people made you feel bad.[3]

We want to tell you in no uncertain terms that your Inner Critic was not implanted by God. It is not "natural"; it is unnatural. It was imposed on you without your knowledge.

■ **You'll need to know how your Inner Critic functions.** You must understand how it generates shoulds, makes you feel twinges or jolts of pain when you disobey the shoulds, then drives you to create reactive self-structure to cope with the pain.

■ **You'll need to be in touch with your feelings so you can recognize when your Inner Critic pounces.** Your feelings are clues to Inner Critic functioning. The clues include feelings of be-

MAKING YOUR CHALLENGING MORE EFFECTIVE 179

ing pressured and burdened, along with twinges of guilt, shame, defectiveness, and inferiority.

■ **You'll need to know how destructive your Inner Critic is.** Throughout this book we have tried to show how powerful your Inner Critic is and what a negative influence it has on your thoughts, feelings, and behavior. You need to have a thorough understanding of how it influences every aspect of your life.

As a prerequisite for learning the challenging skills, you must be able to say with great conviction: "I am thoroughly convinced that my Inner Critic is a destructive force that has been causing psychological pain and mental suffering. I do not see any value whatever in using it as a guide to living."

To be able to say this, you must have a thorough awareness of the negative consequences of obeying your Inner Critic. Chapter 7 describes most of these consequences. Our hope is that once you see a full listing of them, you will realize the heavy price you pay for submitting to the dictates of your Inner Critic, and you will decide to choose inner freedom as your primary value.

■ **You'll need to see the Inner Critic as the source of your negative feelings.** Although other people can trigger your negative feelings, you must be convinced that your Inner Critic, along with the machinery it produces, is the primary cause of those negative feelings. The Inner Critic is responsible not only for feelings of defectiveness, shame, guilt, inferiority, and magnified fear, it is also responsible for hurt feelings, anger, and judgmentalism.

To overcome the impact of these negative feelings, all you need to do is work on your Inner Critic, dismantling whatever mechanisms that got triggered.

Remember the land mine metaphor? It's as though you are sown with land mines, and when someone pokes one, it explodes. As each land mine explodes, you must dismantle it, using your Anthetic challenging skills. When you have dismantled all the land mines, people can poke all they want, and there will be no land mines to explode.

Here's another metaphor: You might see yourself as a jukebox, loaded with a certain number of negative records. When someone pushes the right button, a negative record plays. What you need to do is use Anthetic challenging to disconnect the wiring between the button and the negative record.

■ **You'll need to know why your Inner Critic should be challenged**. Anthetic challenging must be based on your understanding of the following reason for not trusting your Inner Critic: Your Inner Critic, while appearing to help you, is actually the source of most of the pain and suffering you experience—feelings of guilt, defectiveness, shame, and inferiority. In addition, it creates depression and intensifies whatever fear you feel. The messages of your Inner Critic are to be challenged simply because you have chosen not to invite any form of mental suffering into your life.

Values Necessary For Successful Challenging

If you want to be successful in your challenging, it is absolutely essential that you choose three important values. Here's what you must be willing to say:

■ **"I choose inner freedom above all other values."** Inner freedom means freedom from the oppression of your Inner Critic. It must be a primary value for you; that is, you most hold it above all other values. Here's why: Once you have inner freedom, any other values can be chosen freely; if you do not have it, any other value may be contaminated by reactivity.

■ **"Because I am dedicated to inner freedom, I am willing to use any negative feeling I have as a possible clue to Inner Critic functioning."** No negative feeling—e.g., anger or hurt—must be considered as a terminal feeling; that is, as valid, appropriate, legitimate, normal, natural, and therefore not material to work with. All negative feelings—including anger and hurt—must be seen as possible clues to your Inner Critic's oppression.[4]

■ **"I choose pleasure and happiness as a value; I realize that psychological pain and suffering are not useful in my life in any way whatever."** This includes the realization that there is no such thing as "healthy" guilt or "healthy" shame, no matter what the experts say. Both guilt and shame are forms of pain and suffering. To argue in favor of needing "just a little guilt" or "just a little shame" is arguing in favor of "just a little torture," and any torture will diminish your pleasure and happiness.

Values You Will Have To Give Up

The above values must come before all other values, including the following:

■ **Balance.** Some people value balance. They say, "I need a certain amount of Inner Critic to balance the other parts of me. Why not have a happy medium?" Of course, they may have a medium, but it won't be happy. Any time you welcome the Inner Critic, you'll be welcoming emotional pain.

■ **Avoidance of pain.** People may say, "I don't want to deal with any commands my Inner Critic delivers; I just want to obey them and avoid pain; I want to keep my defenses; I want to be safe, even at the price of living a life that is not as fulfilling as it could be." Such people think they're avoiding emotional pain, but they're not: they'll feel the emotional pain of lack of fulfillment.

■ **Living a life of reactive duty, obligation, and propriety.** Quite a few people choose not to be liberated from inner constrictedness and mental anguish. They say, "I'd rather be constricted; I don't want to be free." They are willing to put up with the emotional suffering that happens as a result of living a reactively righteous life.

■ **Spontaneity.** Some people say, "To me it's more important to be spontaneous than to stop and analyze my feelings so I can be free from my Inner Critic." To do Anthetic challenging, you must interrupt spontaneity temporarily and examine what you're doing. If, however, you choose spontaneity over Inner Critic work, you'll simply have reactive spontaneity. Resulting, of course, in spontaneous pain and suffering.

■ **Popularity.** The position here is "I might not have any friends left if I got free from my Inner Critic; I'd rather have friends." Such people may have what appear to be friends, but the price will be high: self-constrictedness.

You Must Be Willing To Create New Values

Finally, you must be willing to create your own values, not rely on hand-me-down values imposed by other people. You must be willing to stop idolizing "normal standards"—that is, statistical normality (i.e., "what most people do") as "the single criterion for the desirable or even allowable" (Wright, 1983, p. 122).

Being In A Group Will Help

If you are a member of a training group working on Anthetic skills, you'll find it extraordinarily helpful as you watch other people take back their rights and get released. You'll be able to say, "If they can do it, I can too. If they have rights, so do I." And then you can move on to: "I can do it even if they can't; I can take back my rights even if they choose not to."

Anthetic Practice In Everyday Life

If you value inner freedom, you will want to engage in Anthetic practice. That is, once you learn the skills of Anthetic challenging, you may choose to deliberately put yourself in positions where your Inner Critic will pounce, so you can have more practice in challenging. This represents another 180-degree turn—a move from "This is scary, I should avoid it" to "This is scary, I can use it in my practice."

To engage in Anthetic practice, you must put yourself in "pounceworthy" positions. Here are some experiments that are practically guaranteed to provide this result:

- Take dancing lessons in a class, not privately. Get out on the dance floor, even though you don't know how to do the step perfectly. Make sure everyone is watching as you try to perform. Improvise your own dance when you don't know what to do.

- Invest in the stock market. If your stock goes up, notice how buffered you feel. (But also notice that your Inner Critic may pounce by telling you that you should have bought twice as many shares.) If your stock goes down or stays steady, while other stocks are rising, notice what your Inner Critic tells you. When you sell, notice how buffered you feel if the stock then goes down; if it goes up, notice how your Inner Critic pounces.

- Ask for tips on the stock market from your broker or from friends. Don't buy anything, but keep track of the prices of the stocks. If one of them starts going up, observe your Inner Critic telling you what you should have done.

- Go to a Chinese restaurant with friends. If others eat with

MAKING YOUR CHALLENGING MORE EFFECTIVE 183

chopsticks, ask for a fork. While everyone else orders a combination of Chinese dishes for the group to share, order one Chinese dish for yourself alone. (Don't tell anyone you're doing an experiment.)

■ Go to a restaurant with friends; if they want to split the check, ask the waitperson for a separate check.

■ Go to a restaurant by yourself and have dinner alone so everyone can see you have no partner.

■ Go to a restaurant, with or without friends—especially an expensive restaurant. Tie your napkin around your neck. Drink your soup out of the bowl. Put your elbows on the table. Sing a little song between bites. Whistle the parts where you don't know the words (put in some fancy effects if you wish). Slouch in your chair between courses. If the service was not good, do not leave a tip.

■ When you go to a restaurant, take along an attache case full of "meal supplements": your vitamin bottles, salt substitute, special sauces, spices, grated cheese, bacon bits, a can of whipped cream in an insulated bag (for your dessert), and a bottle of Pepto-Bismol or antacids (just in case). Line these items up on the table and rearrange them from time to time in different aesthetically pleasing configurations. Look around to see if anyone is admiring your boldness and creativity.

■ On the bus, read a book on sex (e.g., "Frigidity" or "Impotence"), and hold it so everyone can see the title.

■ If you want to buy contraceptives at a drug store, wait till there's another customer standing nearby who can overhear you asking where they are—in a loud voice.

■ Go to an automobile dealer to buy a car. Bargain as hard as you can about the price. Start by offering a ridiculously low price. Resist any attempts on the part of the salesperson to sell you any extras you don't want.

■ Give a public performance of some kind: sing before an audience (do a little dance while you sing); join Toastmasters and learn public speaking; tell a funny story to a group of friends.

■ Go to a lecture that might be sparsely attended. Sit somewhere near the back. When the speaker asks everybody to move up front, remain in your seat.

■ Go to another lecture and sit in the first row of seats. If, after a while, you decide the lecture is not very good, get up and leave.

■ Make the following request to your spouse, lover, or friend:

"I'd like you to give me a compliment so I can practice responding to them. But make sure it's sincere." When you get the compliment, make the following releasing statement: "I have the right to accept this compliment." Then say "Thank you." Don't add anything; especially don't make a self-discount such as "I was just lucky."

■ Ask for more compliments, as in the experiment above. This time, when you get each compliment, agree enthusiastically with the person who gave it; e.g., "Yes, you're right! I did a great job! I'm glad you saw it! And I thought I was especially good at such-and-such."

■ If the person you asked can't come up with any compliments, be aware of being debuffered, and explore your feelings. If the person not only can't come up with a compliment but also zings you judgmentally for even asking, note your twinges of pain. Say "Ouch!" if you wish. Make the necessary releasing statements. (You might also want to reassess your relationship with that person.)

■ Now pick someone who, you think, might not like you—and ask that person for compliments, but don't tell her or him you're doing an experiment.

■ Think about people you love; that is, people that you have warm feelings toward. Tell each person about your love for him or her. Just say: "You know, (person's name), I have a lot of warm and loving feelings toward you."

■ Ask someone (a friend or spouse) for feedback about your judgmentalism. For example: "I want to keep track of each time I'm being judgmental. Would you tell me whenever you see it?" (Each time you get the feedback, make a releasing statement: "I have the right to be judgmental.")

■ Give yourself an "A" for doing each of the above experiments; give yourself ten A's for doing the one in the preceding paragraph. (Realize that each "A" is probably a buffer, but give yourself the "A" anyway.)

■ If your Inner Critic is attacking you for not doing one or more of the above experiments, do some Anthetic challenging.

If you're finding it difficult to learn the challenging skills, take heart. The next chapters will present solutions to some of the many problems people have in learning this unusual new way to achieve inner liberation.

NOTES

1. Negative feelings such as anger, judgmentalism, and hurt also have their source in reactivity (i.e., machinery, stuff, or a trance). *[From p. 175]*

2. It's important not to express premature compassion for your Inner Critic. If you behave compassionately toward it before you have disarmed it, it will take your compassion as encouragement, and this will give it strength. *[From p. 176]*

3. Of course, it was your *interpretation* of the prototype situations that made you feel bad. To put this another way, it was what you learned (emotionally and cognitively), not what actually happened. *[From p. 178]*

4. The term "negative feeling" does not imply that some feelings are not OK; it's simply a convenient way of referring to anger, guilt, hurt, shame, etc.—feelings that are painful. *[From p. 180]*

13

Strategies That Don't Always Work

THE INNER CRITIC IS AN IDEA whose time has come, and more and more psychology writers are including this concept in their books. Unfortunately, we have found that some of their methods for overcoming the Inner Critic's influence do not work very well—and may, in fact, simply add more reactivity to your life. Here are some of our findings:

Simple exhortation won't work. In other words, challenging cannot be done by trying to "stop putting yourself down," "dropping self-blame," or "banishing self-condemnation," as many authorities recommend. Precisely-targeted challenging is needed, not vague exhortations.

"Letting go of shoulds," "releasing guilt and shame," or saying "Cancel" are techniques that don't work, either. They often lead to struggles with your Inner Critic. Never struggle with it. Just quietly disengage from it by challenging it.

It's not enough just to be aware of your Inner Critic.[1] You need to challenge what it says.

Don't try to ignore your Inner Critic, "tune it out," "set it aside," or "put it to one side."[2] You've got to listen to what it says so you can target your challenges accurately. In any case, no matter where it has been "put," it will continue to exercise its power.

Challenging cannot be done by doing conventional positive thinking; that is, making such affirmations as "I have no Inner Critic," "I am perfectly free," "My Inner Critic has no power over me," or "My life is happy and free from conflict." Such affirmations are simply attempts at "frosting the garbage"—covering up your machinery with a fancy facade of pseudo mental health. If you try to do this, you'll find that your negativity will sneak out sideways in a form that's more difficult for you to recognize and deal with.[3]

It's okay to *tell* your Inner Critic to shut up, but don't make it your goal to shut it up. Saying "Shut up!" is just a way of expressing anger. Don't try to silence your Inner Critic, eliminate it, erase its tapes, banish it, or let go of it (if that means eliminating it).

Shutting up your Inner Critic prevents you from doing the targeted challenging that's needed, because if you have turned off its voice, you won't know what it's saying. You need to know exactly what it's saying so you can formulate the correct releasing statement.

Silencing your Inner Critic will also drive it underground, where it will continue to function, but now unbeknownst to you.[4] Remember: it can't hurt you unless you buy into its commands. If you take back your rights, there's no way in the world it can affect you, so you can afford to let it complain all it wants. Keep it around so you can monitor it.

By the same token, let your negative feelings exist. Don't try to banish them, let go of them, transcend them, rise above them, transform them, or eliminate them. Don't say "I release all my past negative feelings," if this means eliminating them. They too may be driven underground and may come out in sneaky ways. Work on your Inner Critic instead. You'll find that the more Inner Critic work you do, the more your negative feelings will automatically diminish.

Don't try to eliminate such words as "should," "must," and "ought" from your vocabulary. This is very important. Such elimination has three disadvantages: One, it prevents you from using recipe shoulds. Two, it prevents you from knowing when your Inner Critic is pouncing. Three, it lends itself so easily to adding one more should to your burden: "You shouldn't use the words should, must, or ought."[5]

Don't debate with your Inner Critic. Don't argue with it, verbally dispute what it says, or try to get it to change its mind. For instance, if your Inner Critic says you should do something, don't ask, "Why should I?" Asking questions just gets you into a debate, and your purpose is not to debate with your Inner Critic but to get disengaged from it by buying out of what it says. Your Inner Critic is not open to being reasoned with. It doesn't understand that kind of language.

For challenging most Inner Critic messages, you don't need any evidence whatever.[6] As soon as you see that the message contains a should or is judgmental, you can dismiss it immediately without any need to search for factual refutation. Here's why: No amount of factual evidence will ever "refute" a should, because a should is not a factual statement; it's simply a command. Likewise, no amount of factual evidence will ever "refute" the punishment delivered by your Inner Critic if you disobey the should, because such punishment is simply your Inner Critic expressing itself emotionally, and you can't refute an emotion (you can only refute a would-be fact). Your Inner Critic's emotional expression may be camouflaged as a factual statement, but it isn't; it's a pseudo-fact, a factoid.

If your Inner Critic makes a supposedly factual statement, don't attempt to critique it until you have worked with the imperative should by making a releasing statement. Take the case of John. "You're always late for business meetings," John's Inner Critic told him. "You should be on time; otherwise, you're an incompetent manager." John began with a releasing statement: "I have the right to be late as many times as I want." It was important for John not to defend himself against the Inner Critic's charge by asking, "What do you mean, always? I'm not always late. Sometimes I'm on time." Such a defense would support John's buffer (being on time) and would reinforce the power of the Inner Critic to oppress him. That is, John would be *agreeing* with the Inner Critic's should, not buying out of it.

Don't negotiate with your Inner Critic. Don't say, for example, "I'll let you out for a few minutes a day if you'll give me some peace the rest of the time."

Don't see your Inner Critic as a polarity that must be integrated as a helpful guide in living your life.[7] Remember: it's trying to sabotage you. Don't create any place in your life for the mental suffering that comes from such sabotage. Unless, of course, you don't mind suffering.

Don't use the two-chair Gestalt technique, moving back and forth several times between the chairs. The purpose of this technique is to create harmony between the inner figures. What you want is disengagement from your Inner Critic, not harmony.

STRATEGIES THAT DON'T ALWAYS WORK   189

If you do empty chair work, use the Anthetic Dialogue method, with anywhere from four to eight chairs for the inner figures that will emerge. It's best to have one inner figure per chair. If you don't have those extra chairs, you won't be able to maintain the integrity of each inner figure. What you'll find is that a new inner figure may *replace* an old one, leading you to think that one inner figure (e.g., the Inner Critic) is changing, when what's really happening is a simple replacement.

Don't try to change your Inner Critic.[8] Don't try to soften it, transform it into something kind and caring, or convert it into a caretaker inner figure. All you have to do is get unhooked from your Inner Critic; that is, disengage from your enmeshment with it. The releasing happens on your side; it happens no matter what your Inner Critic says or does. If you seem to succeed in transforming it, what's happening is just a replacement (see above); it's probably your Inner Guide coming on the scene, while your Inner Critic goes underground, and you will not have done any targeted challenging.

Don't try to "heal the split" between your Inner Critic and your self, whatever that might mean. What you need to do is deepen the split—get disengaged from your Inner Critic so you will be in a position to challenge its negative messages.

Don't use the technique of atonement to silence your Inner Critic.[9] You may indeed wish to atone for (that is, make amends for or reparations for) an injury you have done to someone, and it may be an appropriate behavior, but if you value inner freedom, you'll want to make amends from a free position, not one driven by the shoulds of your Inner Critic.

Don't try to befriend your Inner Critic. It may tell you it's willing to be friends, but if you accept this offer, you'll find the same old imperative shoulds dressed up in "friendly" and more subtle forms.

By the same token, don't look for a grain of truth in what the Inner Critic is saying.[10] It's too easy to accept the judgmental way the grain of truth is expressed. Instead, look to your Inner Guide for truth.

Don't express compassion for your Inner Critic until you've disarmed it. Premature compassion will weaken your challenging efforts.[11]

Don't thank your Inner Critic for what it does in the present. Some therapists suggest saying, "Thank you, Inner Critic, but I'm going to do what I want." Thanking your Inner Critic will give it a

190   DISARMING YOUR INNER CRITIC

certain amount of encouragement. You have nothing to thank it for and no reason to encourage it. (However, once you've done some challenging, you can thank your Inner Critic for protecting you when you were a child. Just be sure to tell it you don't need that kind of protection any more.)

Don't call on some part of you to challenge your Inner Critic.[12] If you do this, you'll just add an unnecessary task to your challenging, and you may not be able to elicit such a voice in yourself. You yourself must be the one who does the challenging. You can and should, of course, use your Inner Guide to support your efforts, as you listen to its advice, encouragement, and reassurance.

Don't use challenging to acquire buffers. For example, if you are feeling depressed because of a recent failure, don't say "I have the right to succeed," hoping this will enable you to actually succeed and thereby get a buffer. You'll need to say, "I have the right to fail as many times as necessary—and I'm still a good person." In other words, no matter what your imperative should demands, your releasing statement must give you the right to do the opposite.

Don't challenge by saying, "I have the right to do what I want without feeling guilty." After challenging, you may still feel guilty, but if challenging has been successful, you will no longer be driven by the guilty feeling. You will be able to choose your behavior from a free position. (And you'll find that the more challenging you do, the more your guilt feelings will gradually diminish.)

Don't challenge by using the word "because." For example, don't say, "I have the right to say No to my friend because she always says No to me." Whatever follows the "because" will be a buffer, and buffers are unreliable. You need to take back your right no matter what your friend does.

Don't challenge by saying "I have the right to X, but I don't want to." That kind of statement, we've found, is an indication of an incomplete release. We're not sure why this is the case, but our hypothesis is that saying "but I don't want to" permits the Inner Critic to smuggle itself back into the releasing statement, this time disguised as a "want."

Your challenging statement must be strong and unequivocal. A powerful way to challenge is to say "I have the right to X, and I *just might do it.*" This challenge, of course, does not commit you to any particular course of action once you get free.

What Might Or Might Not Work

Here are some methods that may or may not work. Some of them don't work because they lack precision; others just don't have enough bite.[13]

■ **Forgiving yourself.** Let's take a look at the basic concept of forgiving. To forgive someone seems to have three possible meanings: (1) to stop feeling resentment toward a person who has injured you; (2) to give up any expectation that the offender must pay a penalty; and/or (3) to no longer blame the offender for the injury.

Let's assume that self-forgiveness means applying these meanings to yourself. The implication is that there has been an offender and an injury. The question is who this offender is—and whether an injury has actually been inflicted. The only candidate for wrongdoing seems to be the natural self—the part that is often called your Inner Child. Self-forgiveness may mean something like, "You committed some sort of crime, Inner Child, but I absolve you of any penalty, and I no longer blame you." If that's the case, then the sneaky Inner Critic has been smuggled into the process again, since it is only in *its* eyes that the Inner Child has done wrong. What needs to be done is not to forgive your Inner Child, since no crime has been committed. What is needed is simply your realization of that fact, through making a releasing statement.

However, there could be another meaning of self-forgiveness. If it simply means "Just because I did such-and-such doesn't mean that I was a bad person," then it is simply another name for a defusing statement. Most people, however, do not ascribe this meaning to self-forgiveness.

■ **Converting the should into a could or preference.** Some writers recommend such a substitution: Instead of saying "I *should* make more money," they recommend saying "I *could* make more money" or "I *prefer* to make more money."[14] If this releases you from the grip of the Inner Critic, fine—but there are three dangers with this method: (1) The chances are good that it would be a simple verbal shift of terminology, without an underlying release; (2) You might not prefer to make more money at all, so the switch would be false; and (3) It might obscure the functioning of the Inner Critic by not exposing it clearly, and it would now be

192 DISARMING YOUR INNER CRITIC

sneakier than ever.[15]

■ **Saying "I can choose."** If you use this as a challenging statement, and it works, fine. But there are two disadvantages to the "I can choose" statement: One, most people find that it doesn't have as much bite as taking back rights. Two, it has to do only with behavior ("I can choose not to send Christmas cards") and doesn't address the Inner Critic directly.

It has seemed to our clients that the "I can choose" statement should come *after* the "I have the right" statement. In other words, first take back your rights, then make a choice.

The reason for this recommended sequence is the fact that any choice can still be driven by your Inner Critic.

■ **Saying "It's OK for me to be, do, or feel something."** This challenge works best *after* you've become proficient in using releasing statements to take back your rights. Most of our clients and group members found that if used *instead* of releasing statements, it doesn't have enough bite.

■ **Saying "I deserve X."**[16] This works well if you have gotten released first. Unfortunately, the Inner Critic might sneak in here because to deserve something usually requires a reason, and the reason is probably that you must be worthy of what you deserve, as in "I deserve to get paid because I worked hard." If you say "I deserve X," your Inner Critic might say, "The hell you do, you phony!" The result could be a debate over factual evidence, which your Inner Critic will win, even if it loses (because it has snookered you into debating on its territory). However, if "I deserve X" means "I deserve X for no reason whatever," it will work fine. But it's best to first make a releasing statement.

■ **Giving yourself permission.**[17] This technique calls for saying "I give myself permission to do such-and-such" instead of "I have the right to do such-and-such." It may lead to release, but there's a danger here. For most people, permission implies a permitter and conjures up scenes where some authority figure from childhood has relented and said it's okay to do something. Better to take back your rights (which were yours all along) than give yourself permission. To most people, taking back rights seems to make a stronger statement than giving oneself permission.

■ **Being given a right (or permission) by someone else.** If you're talking with someone (e.g., a friend or therapist), that person might feel like helping you by saying, "You have the right to do such-and-such" or "It's OK for you to do such-and-such." This

STRATEGIES THAT DON'T ALWAYS WORK   193

statement might get you released—but the source of the release is someone else; you will not have learned the skill yourself. In addition, it may put you in a child-like petitionary position instead of a fully empowered position. It's better if you make the releasing statement yourself, in order to strengthen your skills—and because the releasing statement will have more bite because it is self-generated.

■ **Repeating the affirmation, "I now drain you of energy, Inner Critic."** This will work only if you have in fact been draining your Inner Critic of energy by doing Anthetic challenging.

■ **Simply contradicting your Inner Critic.**[18] For example, if your Inner Critic says, "You are selfish," this technique calls for you to say the opposite: "I am unselfish." If you use this method, you will probably open the door to a big argument from your Inner Critic. In addition, this method just defends your buffers. If you want to contradict your Inner Critic at all, it's best to do it only after you have gotten released.

■ **Meditating by focusing on something.** This will work temporarily by distracting you from the Inner Critic's messages, but when you're through meditating, your Inner Critic will still be there. No bite at all with this method.

■ **Focusing on the here and now.** This is a valuable skill to have, but it can also be simply a temporary distraction. Our clinical experience shows that in itself it does not result in getting released from the Inner Critic. Again, no bite.[19]

■ **Meditating by simply noting every time you hear the voice of your Inner Critic.** If you meditate, it's useful to note every time your Inner Critic appears, but you won't get free from it unless you add the step of challenging it.

■ **Being absorbed in something (e.g., dancing, rock climbing, yoga, work).** Like focused meditation, these things will distract you, and you'll feel good while you're doing them, but when you're finished, you'll find that your Inner Critic is still there.

■ **Giving back negative feelings to other people.** A common technique is to "give back" shame, guilt, confusion, anger, and other negative feelings to the person from your past who first "gave" them to you. Time and again we have heard people say, "It was not my shame; it was my mother's; so I gave it back to her." Unfortunately, our clinical experience has been that after doing this kind of work, people still seem to have a lot of shame.

Joan said, "My cousin sexually abused me when I was younger; he gave me his shame, and so he became shameless. Now I have to give it back to him. But it isn't working." I (Kathy) asked Joan to address her Inner Critic and get released by saying, "Just because I was sexually abused doesn't mean I did anything shameful." She did so, and it worked beautifully. The shame about sexual abuse came not from her cousin but from her mother, who shamed her for having sexual feelings and who installed that shame in Joan's Inner Critic. The shame then got triggered by the sexual abuse.

If someone shamed you or made you feel guilty, it's not a good idea to "give it back," because what you got was not that person's shame but his or her judgmentalism, which you incorporated in your Inner Critic and which *then* created the shame. It's difficult or impossible to give that kind of judgmentalism back, whatever that might mean.

But there are two exceptions to what we've been saying:

First, if you have *imitated* someone's shame, guilt, judgmentlism, confusion, anger, etc., then you can indeed give that back. You can say, "I've been using you as a model, taking on your way of thinking, feeling, and behaving, and I'm going to give all those things back to you." Such giving back makes your boundaries stronger.

Second, if you learned a dysfunctional way of thinking or behaving from your parents, you can give that back. For example, you can say, "I learned from you, Mom, that I am responsible for other people's negative feelings. I give that learning back to you. I'm not responsible for anyone's feelings."

■ **Using the "so what" technique.** This involves stating a worry (i.e., an Inner Critic belief), then asking yourself, "So what?"[20] For example:

"I feel like I'll get hurt again." "So what?"

"People will discover I'm not perfect." "So what?"

This method will work if "so what" means something like "the consequences of this are not really catastrophic." Our clients found, however, that it's not as effective as Anthetic challenging.

■ **Experiential disconfirmation.**[21] This is a process that occurs when you have something shameful to say, and you expect the listener to be shocked and judgmental when they hear it, but when you finally do say it, he or she is accepting of what you say, thereby disconfirming your expectations.[22] If you have a good non-judgmental therapist, this process can happen, and it can lead you on your own to adopt the belief that you had the right to say what you said. It may, however, make you dependent on external validation.

It's certainly a good thing to experience this kind of disconfirmation, but it's better if you yourself can challenge the shamefulness. Then you'll be able to speak your voice even if the listener (therapist or not) is indeed shocked and judgmental. You'll be able to say, "That's just the other person's stuff."

■ **Turn it over to God or your Higher Self.** This works well with such things as fear and the need to control situations or people, but it doesn't work well with the emotional punishments of defectiveness, shame, inferiority, or guilt. You'll need to challenge your Inner Critic to overcome these feelings.

■ **Thought stopping.** This technique consists of saying (mentally or out loud) "Stop!" whenever you have an Inner Critic attack. When it does seem to work, it does so by driving the Inner Critic underground, where it continues to function, although now without giving you any clues you can easily recognize. It's best not to silence your Inner Critic's voice but instead keep monitoring it.

■ **Realizing your uniqueness.** If you're feeling bad about yourself, according to some authors, you should realize you're like a snowflake, completely different from all the other snowflakes. It's not clear how uniqueness can make you feel better, since you can be unique and still have a strong Inner Critic who says your uniqueness is defective, shameful, and inferior.

■ **Understanding that the Inner Critic is motivated by anxiety.**[23] It certainly is true that the Inner Critic is motivated by anxiety, and this realization will certainly help you understand the dynamics of your Inner Critic, but it won't help you address and challenge the specific dysfunctional beliefs that your Inner Critic tries to impose.

■ **Replacing negative thoughts with positive affirmations.** Saying, for example, "I am a worthwhile person" may lead to replacing negative self-evaluations with positive ones (especially if you repeat it many times), but because it does not target specific shoulds, it will not necessarily lead to your taking back the rights your Inner Critic has tried to take away from you. These rights must be targeted one by one, using releasing statements. That is, if your Inner Critic says you are a klutz, you must say, "I have the right to be what you call a klutz."

■ **Simply engaging in the forbidden behavior.** This may work if your Inner Critic is not very strong. Otherwise, it will be painful unless you have disarmed your Inner Critic first. This pain may occur right away, or it may hit you a few hours or days after the behavior, a process we call Inner Critic backlash. In some people, this has been severe enough to cause a major depression.

That is exactly what happened to Fred, a heterosexual 34-year-old carpenter, who went to an encounter group, where the leader asked each person to reveal some deep, dark secret.

Fred's secret was that in childhood he had had a homosexual experience, but he was reluctant to reveal it to the group. After considerable persuasion by the group members as well as the leader, he decided to disobey his Inner Critic, which had been imposing a should not to tell anyone. When he had told his secret, the group was accepting, to his surprise, and he felt elated.

That night in bed, however, his Inner Critic pounced. Whereas before he had merely felt defective, now he felt an immense attack of shame and inferiority. He went into a depression, which required institutionalization.

If You See a Demonstration, It May Look Deceptively Simple

This concludes our presentation of what works and what doesn't. We'd like to add one more comment: We presented a workshop on Anthetic Therapy at a recent conference of the American Association of Sex Educators, Counselors and Therapists. We began by telling our audience that Anthetic Inner Critic work is complex and requires extensive training. Then we did a demonstration with a volunteer from the audience, and, as usual, it worked beautifully. In about five minutes, she easily got released from a number of shoulds.

After the workshop, a colleague, impressed with the speed and elegance of our work, asked,"What do you mean, extensive training is needed. What you did looks very simple to me."

"It isn't," I (Jim) told him. "There are many ways it can go wrong.[24] Anthetic challenging is a complex process, and there are many traps and obstacles."

Some of these traps and obstacles will be described in the chapters to come. We want to give you as much help as possible in achieving success in your challenging.

But if you're a therapist, please don't do this work without being trained, since you might unwittingly add additional constricting shoulds to your client's burden. Of course, you wouldn't know this; all you'd know is "This method doesn't seem to be working."

If you're still having problems with Anthetic challenging, take heart. The reason may be that you have come to believe the Inner Critic's propaganda about itself. The next chapter will take a look at how the Inner Critic tries to indoctrinate you with its disinformation and what you can do about it.

NOTES

1. Writers who recommend simple awareness include Carson (1983), Stone & Winkelman (1989), and Cornell (1993). *[From p. 186]*

2. McGavin (1994, p. 4) writes about the method of "putting the Inner Critic aside." She reports, however, that it doesn't work, since the Inner Critic's thoughts "just creep back and emerge later." *[From p. 186]*

3. Once you've done enough challenging, you can indeed make some of these positive affirmations—and believe them, because they'll be true. *[From p. 187]*

4. If your Inner Critic has been driven underground, all you may know are the following clues to that submergence: (a) You seem to have high standards that are difficult to meet; (b) Other people seem to make demands on you that are hard for you to deal with; and (c) You suffer from one or more of the problems described in Chapter 7. *[From p. 187]*

5. Albert Ellis (Ellis & Yeager 1989, p. 97) recommends replacing "must" (and probably "should," too) with "had better." He seems to have made exactly this change in his own writings, whenever he wants to make a suggestion to the reader. Our clients, however, thought "had better" sounded more Inner Criticky than "should." They said it reminded them of Mom and Dad saying, "You had better get in here, do your homework, brush your teeth, and get ready for bed, or you'll get a spanking!"

If you have a should not to say "should," you can take back your rights by saying, "I have the right to say 'should' any time I want." When our clients make this releasing statement, they usually laugh with pleasure, and their whole bodies relax—good indications they have just gotten free. *[From p. 187]*

6. Rational-Emotive Behavior Therapy's "irrational beliefs" are the end result of Inner Critic messages. For REBT, the chief method of overcoming such beliefs is to verbally dispute them, using what is called a "logico-empirical method of scientific questioning, challenging, and debating" (Ellis et al. 1988, p. 53). "For every belief expressed by a client, the appropriate RET question is, 'Where is the evidence that what you believe is true?'" (Walen, DiGiuseppe, & Wessler 1980,

p. 6). REBT has so far not used the concept of the Inner Critic. *[From p. 6]*

7. It seems useful to integrate the Inner Critic only in the sense of acknowledging its existence, accepting it as one of your inner figures, and letting it be what it is. The notion of integrating, however, is often taken to mean that the Inner Critic's guidance should be considered useful. In Gestalt Therapy the Inner Critic is called the top dog, and the gestaltist principle of integration is usually construed as integrating the top dog as a useful part of the personality. For examples, see Baumgardner (1975, p. 67); Fantz (1975, p. 88); Latner (1973, p. 156); Perls (1969, p. 19); Erving & Miriam Polster (1973, pp. 62 & 248); Resnick (1975, p. 227); and Simkin (1976, p. 10). *[From p. 188]*

8. Don't try to change or transform any inner figure. It is possible to *disengage* from an inner figure so it no longer programs you. It also is possible to drain energy from an inner figure so it is no longer driven to affect your life. It's also possible to orchestrate an inner figure so it plays a less important role in your life. And it's possible to see more deeply into the structure of an inner figure in order to understand what drives it (e.g., to see the fear—sometimes panic—that drives the Inner Critic).

However, Western thinking seems to want to control, shape, change, and transform everything it comes across, and when this is applied to the mind and its contents, repression usually occurs, with the result that the item *seems* to be transformed but has really been simply driven underground and/or exchanged for another inner figure. In dealing with inner figures, and especially with the Inner Critic, we recommend the Taoist principle of *wu-wei*, or non-interference—letting the figure be what it is without any heavy-handed shaping or transforming. At the same time, we recommend disengaging so as to become liberated from being driven by the inner figure. *[From p. 189]*

9. Atonement is one method recommended by McKay & Fanning to silence your Inner Critic. "Sensible shoulds," they write, "may be 'healthy,' whereupon the only way to stop your critic is to initiate the process of atonement" (1987, p. 120). *[From p. 189]*

10. Cornell (1993, p. 79) recommends looking for the grain of truth in the Inner Critic's messages. *[From p. 189]*

11. Cornell (1993) declares that in working with the Inner Critic, "nothing is stronger than compassion" (p. 78). *[From p. 189]*

12. Calling on a "healthy voice" inside you to serve as the challenger is advocated by McKay and Fanning (1987, p. 7). *[From p. 190]*

13. "Bite" refers to the force of a philosophical argument, the explanatory power of a concept or theory, or the effectiveness of a psychological method. Arguments, concepts, theories, and methods are said to vary in their bitefulness. *[From p. 191]*

STRATEGIES THAT DON'T ALWAYS WORK   199

14. Keyes (1979, p. xvi; 1987, p. 41) recommends "upgrading" or "upleveling" addictions and demands (i.e., shoulds) to preferences. Farmer (1989, p. 162) also recommends replacing shoulds with preferences. Ellis (1979, p. 18), sees shoulds as resulting from the escalation of preferences and recommends changing them back into preferences (Ellis 1990, p. 143). AT holds that some shoulds never were preferences to begin with (e.g., "You should clean up your plate, even though you're not hungry"). See J. Elliott (1995) for a discussion of this issue. *[From p. 191]*

15. For more information on the method of converting shoulds to preferences, see J. E. Elliott (1995). *[From p. 192]*

16. Sondra Ray recommends "I deserve" (1976). *[From p. 192]*

17. In Transactional Analysis, "permissions" appear to be like rights but are offered by the therapist to the client (Woollams & Brown 1979, pp. 180 & 215). Anthetic Therapy teaches the skills of challenging so clients can do this for themselves. It's much more powerful that way—and the client is armed with skills that can be used the rest of her or his life. *[From p. 192]*

18. Contradicting the Inner Critic is the method recommended by John Bradshaw. Instead of saying "I am selfish," he suggests, say "I am unselfish" (1988, p. 191). *[From p. 193]*

19. Butler reports a comment of Transactional Analysts Bob and Mary Goulding: "Most of the difficulty people have is not staying in the here-and-now, by anticipating the future or rehashing the past. There is usually no way of feeling bad if I stay in the present, in this place, unless this is a bad place, and then I will get the hell out of it" (Butler 1981, pp. 58f). *[From p. 193]*

20. The "so what" technique is recommended by Jane and Robert Handly (1990). *[From p. 194]*

21. The term "experiential disconfirmation" came from Safran & Segal (1990). *[From p. 194]*

22. Experiential disconfirmation is the chief method used by Weiss & Sampson (1986), originators of Control Mastery Theory. According to this form of psychoanalysis, patients who experience guilt will test their therapists, unconsciously seeking disconfirmation of their "grim unconscious beliefs." If the therapist simply accepts what the patient says, disconfirmation occurs, and the guilt feelings are alleviated.

We suspect that there are two non-specific factors leading to the effectiveness of most forms of psychotherapy: (1) the process of experiential disconfirmation, which then (2) permits the client to explore and express her or his feelings freely. As the client does this exploration and expression, she or he may almost accidentally do some sort of unsystematic Inner Critic challenging. *[From p. 194]*

23. Becoming more understanding of what drives your Inner Critic is recommended by Hal and Sidra Stone (1992). *[From p. 195]*

200 DISARMING YOUR INNER CRITIC

24. Trainees in our Professional Training Program are required not only to learn the challenging methods presented in this book, they are also required to do intensive individual work on themselves using Anthetic methods so they can learn the skills for overcoming their own reactivity. If these skills are not learned, that reactivity will contaminate the therapeutic process with clients. We call this contamination the Semmelweis effect.   *[From p. 196]*

14

How to Challenge Your Inner Critic's Propaganda Messages

SINCE YOUR INNER CRITIC WANTS TO SURVIVE, it will do its utmost to persuade you to value it. Its goal is to prevent you from even thinking about reducing its power. To achieve this goal, it will bombard you with a variety of propaganda messages.[1] If you explore your Inner Critic's propaganda, you'll see that most of it is designed to do three things:

First, to prevent you from realizing its power and pervasiveness;

Second, to persuade you not to work on weakening that power; and

Third, to prevent you from exploring the machinery (i.e., reactivity) that was created in response to Inner Critic oppression.

Here are some of the propaganda messages your Inner Critic may try to make you believe, together with some suggested challenges:[2]

■ PROPAGANDA MESSAGE #1:"You don't have an Inner Critic." Occasionally, people will say "I don't have any guilt feelings. I have no shame, no feelings of inferiority, no feelings of defectiveness. I accept myself 100%. I just don't have any personal problems. In fact, I don't have an Inner Critic." These were the words of Matt, an experienced clinical psychologist who was a member of one of our professional training workshops.

202 DISARMING YOUR INNER CRITIC

When confronted by others in the group, Matt showed clear indications of defensiveness—a compulsive need to explain and justify—which was a good clue that his Inner Critic was operating. Anthetic Dialogue revealed strong shoulds to be mentally healthy, a common condition among therapists and counselors.

Most people don't realize how ridiculously easy it is to submerge your Inner Critic's voice; you simply won't know it's there.[3]

Les, one of our group members, explained why some people might be in denial about the Inner Critic. "Once you do Inner Critic work," he said, "you begin to see that all your life you have been manipulated, when you thought all along you were free. That's painful to realize. So people might deny the existence of the Inner Critic to protect themselves from the possibility of feeling that pain."

The key issue here is whether you value inner freedom. If you do, you'll be enthusiastically suspicious of any propaganda message from your Inner Critic that it doesn't really exist.

■ SUGGESTED CHALLENGE: "Just because I'm not aware of my Inner Critic doesn't mean I don't have one. Because I value inner freedom, I'm going to keep an open mind about Inner Critic functioning in myself. That way, I can spot it when it occurs."

QUESTION: But what if the Inner Critic is not the source of mental suffering? What if it is also the source of positive guidance?

ANSWER: The way we have defined the Inner Critic here is that it is the source of emotional punishments. That is, any internal agency or inner figure that imposes suffering is what we call "the Inner Critic." On the other hand, any internal agency or inner figure that loves you unconditionally, that never punishes you with mental suffering, and that is the source of positive guidance is what we call the Inner Guide.

QUESTION: But mightn't it be the case that some entity other than the Inner Critic is the source of shoulds and mental suffering?

ANSWER: If that were true, we'd just call it the Inner Critic and continue to teach our challenging methods.

QUESTION: Your definitions seem so arbitrary. How can you play so fast and loose with these concepts?

CHALLENGING PROPAGANDA MESSAGES   203

ANSWER: Elements in the inner world are unlike those in the external world. External elements remain pretty much what they are, no matter how we think about them. Inner elements are more malleable. We can group them together in whatever ways we wish and give that grouping a single name.

QUESTION: But how do you know that mental suffering is connected with shoulds?

ANSWER: Try it yourself. Disobey an imperative should (or just think about disobeying it). Then if you are in touch with your feelings, you'll feel the twinge of discomfort or punishment we've been talking about. (If, after reading the foregoing, you feel indignant, that's caused by your Inner Critic, too.)

QUESTION: But I don't *want* to disobey a should. Why would I do that?

ANSWER: For the sake of this experiment. So you can see where the electric fence is.

QUESTION: Why do you keep blaming the Inner Critic?

ANSWER: Because it's the culprit. It's the one that sabotages your happiness and effectiveness. The Inner Critic, of course, would be happy if you tried to defend it.

QUESTION: When you talk about the Inner Critic, aren't you just saying "The devil made me do it"?

ANSWER: The Inner Critic doesn't make you do anything—unless you value it as a source of guidance and decide to obey its commands. You are responsible for that decision, and you are responsible for your behavior as a result of that decision. In any case, we want you to buy out of what the "devil" tells you, not shift responsibility to it.

* * *

■ PROPAGANDA MESSAGE #2: "Your Inner Critic is useful, not destructive; you need it as a motivator or evaluator, at least some of the time." This is the most common propaganda message, and it's often a powerful one. Your Inner Critic will try to brainwash you into thinking that it is a positive influence in your life, or can become one provided it is properly transformed. It will tell you that you need it, that if you don't obey it, all kinds of dire things will happen.

The truth is, however, that you don't need an Inner Critic. You can use natural-self motivation rather than Inner Critic motivation. Natural-self motivation will work even better, because what you do will be grounded in your deepest wants and needs instead of coming from rules that are imposed on you, backed by the threat of punishment if you don't obey.

True, obeying your Inner Critic may produce good results temporarily. For example, your Inner Critic may make you study hard for an exam or apply for a well-paying job. But in the long run it will cause you unhappiness through the mental suffering it imposes whenever you disobey it.

■ SUGGESTED CHALLENGE: "Because I value inner freedom, happiness, and peace of mind, and because I choose not to invite mental suffering into my life, I totally reject you, Inner Critic, as a useful guide to my thinking, feeling, and behaving. I am determined to challenge every single message you give me."

QUESTION: "But can't I use the Inner Critic as a kind of reinforcement to help me satisfy a natural-self desire?"

ANSWER: You can if you don't mind constrictedness and suffering, which is what your Inner Critic specializes in. In addition, reliance on the Inner Critic will tend to cover up your natural-self desires, so you won't be quite sure what those desires are. Finally, if you rely on the Inner Critic for any of your motivation, some part of you will tend to rebel by procrastinating, making mistakes, and forgetting important things.

■ PROPAGANDA MESSAGE #3: "Even though it may be destructive, your Inner Critic can't possibly be as influential in your life as this book says it is."

The Inner Critic likes to make people think it's simply a minor irritant. For example, Francine said, "I can't believe the Inner Critic has such a powerful effect on my life. I'm getting along okay, and I'm working on the few problems I have, but I just don't see that my Inner Critic is responsible for everything."

Like Francine, many people acknowledge the existence of the Inner Critic but are in denial about the widespread negativity it introduces into their lives. What we've tried to do in this book is

CHALLENGING PROPAGANDA MESSAGES   205

present the many forms of this destructiveness. We hope we've been successful.

■ SUGGESTED CHALLENGE: "Because I value happiness, effectiveness, and peace of mind, I am open to the possibility that my Inner Critic is a much more powerful factor in my life than I have previously thought. I'm going to try a few challenges to see what results I get. If my Inner Critic is more powerful than I thought, I want to know about it."

■ PROPAGANDA MESSAGE #4: "You need your Inner Critic to tell you what to do. Without it, you wouldn't have anything to guide your behavior." This is one of the most common fears that prevent people from doing Anthetic challenging. The Inner Critic wants you to believe that it's the sole source of guidance.

However, when people neutralize the power of the Inner Critic, what they discover is that a new inner figure emerges—the Inner Guide (see Chapter 5). The Inner Guide offers positive guidance, loving encouragement, and emotional support in place of the Inner Critic's threats of harsh punishments.

■ SUGGESTED CHALLENGE: "Just because I don't obey my Inner Critic doesn't mean I am left without a source of guidance; I have my Inner Guide."

■ PROPAGANDA MESSAGE #5: "All you need to do is avoid negativity, not work on your Inner Critic." Some people believe the way to achieve happiness is simply to avoid thoughts of negativity. Here are some of the statements they make:

• "Well, maybe I do have an Inner Critic, but I can deal with it by putting it out of my mind, just not focusing on it, and it will go away."

• "I don't like to think about negative things. Since you become what you think, you become negative when you dwell on negative feelings."

Your Inner Critic would love it if you would put its negativity out of your mind. It wants to survive, and it hopes you will not become conscious of it, because if you did, you might decide to start neutralizing its power. So it thrives on secrecy. Our clinical experience has shown that putting your Inner Critic out of your mind just drives it underground. The result is that you will almost certainly continue to have problems, but now they'll be puzzling, because their source will be submerged.

206 DISARMING YOUR INNER CRITIC

■ SUGGESTED CHALLENGE: "Because I value inner freedom as the pathway to happiness, effectiveness, and peace of mind, I choose not to believe any propaganda that tells me to avoid confronting negativity. I see that what blocks me from achieving inner freedom is negativity. I know that the first step in overcoming that negativity is exploring it in great detail."

■ PROPAGANDA MESSAGE #6: "All you really need is something to take your mind off your problems." Your Inner Critic always wants you to avoid confronting it, so it loves to encourage you to use distractions to divert your attention from its impact on your life. Here are some of its propaganda messages: "You'd be better off just taking up a new hobby. You know you feel better when you dance or do yoga; why not just do that? Or maybe you just need to get a better job. Why not take a walk in the woods and get back to nature? Or take a trip somewhere interesting. Maybe move to a new place (the geographical cure). Find someone to love you. At all costs—forget about working on your Inner Critic."

■ SUGGESTED CHALLENGE: "Since I value inner freedom, I choose to face and challenge my Inner Critic, not avoid it through distractions, even though facing it may be uncomfortable at first. Just because distractions make me feel good temporarily doesn't mean they're good for me in the long run."

■ PROPAGANDA MESSAGE #7:"You don't need Inner Critic work; you'd be better off following a spiritual path instead." Here your Inner Critic may suggest that you use spirituality to transcend your negativity and rise above it. True, a spiritual path is certainly important, but there's no need to use it as a *substitute* for challenging your Inner Critic. Why not pursue both?

Moreover, it's important to look carefully at the concept of transcendence. If it simply means disengaging, that's a useful move. If, on the other hand, transcending your negativity means eliminating it, you'll never know whether it has simply been driven underground.

In any case, if you don't do Inner Critic work first, your Inner Critic may become woven into your spirituality. For example, you may use your spiritual path as a buffer. If that's the case, you may feel judgmental toward people who are not as "spiritually advanced" as you are.[4] Another danger is that your Inner Critic may, for its own antihedonic purposes, command that you pursue a stoical or ascetic path.

■ SUGGESTED CHALLENGE: "I see what you're up to, Inner Critic. You want to prevent me from focusing on you. But I *am* going to focus on you, because I don't want you running my life any more. I can do Inner Critic work *and* have a spiritual life."

■ PROPAGANDA MESSAGE #8: "You can't change the way you are." As you'll recall, this is the Popeye Syndrome (See terminalism, Chapter 7). When you accept this Inner Critic message, the argument states: "I am the way I am; that's *me*. It's just my nature to think, feel, and behave the way I do. If I changed, I wouldn't be me any more. You're asking me to change, which means you're asking me not to be me." The Inner Critic wants you to think you're like a material object with fixed qualities. That way, it can control you better.[5]

■ SUGGESTED CHALLENGE: "You're wrong, Inner Critic. I *have* my thoughts, I *have* my feelings, I *have* my personality traits, and I *have* my behavior—but I am not my thoughts, feelings, personality traits, or behavior.[6] Who I am is a Transcendendtal Self (an essential self), not these accidental things that are subject to change."

■ PROPAGANDA MESSAGE #9: "You just have some bad habits or character flaws." For example, Henry told me (Jim): "I don't think my Inner Critic is responsible for any of my problems. It's just that I have some bad habits, and I'm trying to overcome them through willpower. For one thing, I'm lazy."

I explained "terminalism" to Henry—the mistaken idea that concepts such as habits and personality traits provide terminal explanations for behavior; that is, explanations that are not connected to any deeper dynamics.

"The reason you're having trouble overcoming what you call laziness," I told Henry "is that you haven't explored the deeper sources that are driving this habit. When you do, you'll find that the Inner Critic is the ultimate cause. Once you deal with that culprit, your problems will be easier to solve, with little or no willpower at all, but with a combination of wantpower and skillpower."

■ SUGGESTED CHALLENGE: "I know you don't want me to explore myself more deeply, Inner Critic, but I have the right to do that. I'm not going to assume that my problems are simply caused by terminal habits and traits that require willpower to overcome. I have the right to look deeper to see what's driving them."

■ PROPAGANDA MESSAGE #10: "You must have a defective gene that's causing your problems." "I've tried everything," Jenny told me (Kathy). "Psychoanalysis, Gestalt Therapy, est—and nothing works. I'm about ready to give up on psychotherapy. I guess my problems are really due to a defective gene; there's nothing I can do about them."

People often believe this propaganda message because they've had so much difficulty working on themselves, and the Inner Critic wants them to give up so it can function without any obstacles.[7]

■ SUGGESTED CHALLENGE: "Just because work on myself in the past has been difficult doesn't mean that psychotherapy doesn't work. I'm going to give Anthetic challenging a try."

■ PROPAGANDA MESSAGE #11:"Why not just eat—or take a drink or a drug—and feel better." This is a self-medication propaganda message from your Inner Critic, who says, "How about some comforting food, alcohol, or drugs? Why not just anesthetize your painful feelings?"

True, these things will give you a temporary fix and dull the pain. Like getting an injection of novocaine instead of having your tooth filled. But there's a price to pay for medicating your Inner Critic. First, you'll find yourself needing more and more of the medication. Second, you'll discover after a while that the medication no longer makes you feel good, it just provides a form of oblivion. Third, you'll wake up one day to discover that you have become physiologically addicted.

■ SUGGESTED CHALLENGE: "Just because you want me to dull the pain so you can continue controlling my life doesn't mean I have to keep doing that. I'm not going to give in to your temptations, because I want a *happy* life, not an unconscious life."

■ PROPAGANDA MESSAGE #12: "Your problem is not your Inner Critic; it's just that you're too self-conscious." "Stop analyzing yourself," says your Inner Critic. "Just be spontaneous, go with the flow, don't think so much, don't be so introspective, just be yourself. Give up this incessant self-preoccupation. Why not just accept yourself instead of questioning everything you do? It just makes you self-conscious."

It's true that self-analysis can be interminable and futile—if all you do is go over and over something in your mind and remind yourself of how awful it is. If, on the other hand, you use your thinking ability to analyze and challenge your Inner Critic, you'll get free from this awfulness, and you will indeed be able to accept yourself. Then your natural self will be liberated; you can be spontaneous and go with the flow, but you (instead of your machinery) will now decide when to be spontaneous.

As you practice the Anthetic challenging skills, you'll find that self-consciousness is no longer painful; it will be a pleasure. In other words, self-consciousness is painful only to the extent that you have a strong Inner Critic that kicks in when you start exploring yourself.

■ SUGGESTED CHALLENGE: "I know you want me to stop exploring myself, Inner Critic, because I might discover how you've been oppressing me. But I'm not going to stop."

■ PROPAGANDA MESSAGE #13: "If you were to get released from your Inner Critic, you would just be making excuses for your behavior." Your Inner Critic wants to hold you to a strict code of behavior; it doesn't want you to make "excuses" for deviating. It will punish whatever it sees as excuses.

In other words, to your Inner Critic, making excuses is being irresponsible, and being irresponsible means not obeying your shoulds. For example, Martin's Inner Critic told him, "You really screwed up; that was a terrible thing you did." He challenged this by saying, "I have the right to do what you call screw up," whereupon his Inner Critic responded, "That's a copout; you're just making excuses. You're irresponsible." Martin was able to challenge this second-order Inner Critic attack by saying, "I recognize your voice, Inner Critic, because you're using Inner Critic language, talking to me about excuses and being irresponsible. I have the right to do what you call cop out and make excuses and be irresponsible any time I want."[8]

QUESTION: But aren't some people irresponsible? And isn't it a good idea to be a responsible person?

ANSWER: Yes to both questions. Being responsible (see Chapter 17) is an important value to hold. But the issue is not whether to be responsible; it's whether you're going to be a responsible person because of the threat of punishment by your

Inner Critic or whether you choose freely to be responsible because you care about people. If your "responsibleness" comes from your Inner Critic, it will inevitably be contaminated by Inner Critic messages—and will wind up having destructive effects.[9]

■ SUGGESTED CHALLENGES: (1) "I have the right to make excuses." (2) "I have the right to be what you call irresponsible." (3) "I have the right to do what you call cop out."

■ PROPAGANDA MESSAGE #14:"Your Inner Critic is protecting you; what would you do without it?" Your Inner Critic will tell you that when it imposes constrictedness in your life, its purpose is to protect you against pain. However, this protection doesn't work. You'll feel pain anyway whenever you disobey your Inner Critic's shoulds.

■ SUGGESTED CHALLENGE: "Inner Critic, I know you say you're protecting me, but who needs protection like this? Certainly not me. I'm not going to believe what you say any more."

■ PROPAGANDA MESSAGE #15: "If you give up your Inner Critic, you'll just do anything you want, and you might make a fool of yourself." Your Inner Critic sets you up for its game by proposing the following: "Doing what you want means making a fool of yourself. So let me 'protect' you from the crime I've just charged you with."

Once you give up living according to Inner Critic commands, you might do a lot of new things, and you might not do them perfectly, and at that point your Inner Critic could well pounce with some backlash: "Look what you've done now that you no longer have my guidance and protection!"

Note, too, that "making a fool of yourself" means "What will people think?" Your Inner Critic loves to make you conform by telling you to live by other people's values. It's safe.

■ SUGGESTED CHALLENGE: "I have the right to do anything I want—even what you call 'making a fool of myself.'

QUESTION: But, to take this to extremes, do I have the right to kill someone? That doesn't seem right.

ANSWER: We're not saying that you have a legal or moral right to kill someone. But if someone were attacking you, you might be constrained by shoulds not to injure, or kill, someone, and you might be killed or injured yourself. So you've got to have the right. Once you take back that right, you can decide what to do, and that decision is a separate issue.

■ PROPAGANDA MESSAGE #16: "You should keep your hangups because they make you unique and colorful; it's just that you're a bit eccentric." While it's true that hangups tend to make people unique, colorful, and eccentric, the price is heavy (see Chapter 7 for a discussion of that price). And as you get free from your Inner Critic, you'll discover that you can be unique, colorful, and eccentric (if you wish) but without all the pain and suffering that accompany reactivity.

■ SUGGESTED CHALLENGE: "Just because I challenge my Inner Critic and overcome my reactivity doesn't mean I won't be unique, colorful, and eccentric. In fact, I'll be free to be even more unique, colorful, and eccentric."

We hope these descriptions of your Inner Critic's propaganda messages will help you spot some of the problems you may be experiencing with challenging. Now, in the next chapter, let's turn our attention to some additional problems.

NOTES

1. So strong is the propaganda power of the Inner Critic that it has led some writers to believe that this internal tyrant can have a beneficial role. Freud, for example, thought the ego ideal (a part of the superego, or Inner Critic) represents humanity's "higher nature" (1923/1949, p. 37). Fenichel states that the superego can serve as the source of protection and as a provider of reassuring love (1945, p. 105). Schafer declares that the superego can provide love (1960, p. 186). Susan Campbell maintains that the Inner Critic is a valuable and useful part (1984, pp. 136f). Stone and Winkelman, originators of the Voice Dialogue method, contend that the Inner Critic provides "some valuable services...." It "points out, in no uncertain terms, that there is something wrong and we had better correct it." Moreover, "the critic forces us to look at the distasteful sides of ourselves...." (1989, p. 121). Such writers usually fail to make the distinction between Inner Critic and Inner Guide.

Some writers recommend obeying the Inner Critic; for example, Richard Bandler, a founder of Neuro-Linguistic Programming, writes that the Inner Critic "could be right. Maybe you ought to listen to what it says...." (1985, p. 70).

212 DISARMING YOUR INNER CRITIC

One strand of thought in Transactional Analysis regards the Inner Critic (i.e., "Critical Parent") as at times a positive force in the personality. For example, Jack Dusay declares, "Displaying a healthy amount of Critical Parent protects a person and prevents him/her from being a slave to other people's whims." A person with a low Critical Parent, he contends, "neither stands up for his/her rights nor defends his/her opinions" (1977, pp. 27f). In a lecture I once attended (Jim), Dusay said that all the ego states should be of roughly equal strength.

Norman Vincent Peale, a popularizer of positive thinking, calls the Inner Critic the censor and urges people to trust it and heed its counsel, otherwise it will create "self-disgust" or "gnawing regret." The censor, Peale contends, is "something God put in each of us in order to hear His voice" (1992, p. 15). *[From p. 201]*

2. Unlike releasing statements, challenges of the Inner Critic's propaganda messages do involve verbal disputing. However, don't make the mistake of thinking your goal is to change your Inner Critic's mind. All you need do is realize that your Inner Critic is wrong; the challenges help solidify your position. *[From p. 201]*

3. How will you know you have an Inner Critic if you can't hear its voice? You'll know it by its effects: the symptoms described in Chapter 7. *[From p. 202]*

4. Two comments about spirituality: First, the Inner Critic's influence can also be seen in religious intolerance, especially that which serves as the basis for holy wars between competing religions. Second, an examination of the stories and parables presented by some Christian and Eastern mystics reveals a pervasive judgmentalism—the antithesis of the love and compassion they advocate. *[From p. 207]*

5. As mentioned previously, French philosopher Jean-Paul Sartre (1956a&b) describes our tendency to think we are like material objects. He distinguishes between an object (*en-soi*, "in itself") and a person (*pour-soi*, "for itself"). A person is what he makes of himself. To act otherwise is to imitate an object; i.e., to act in bad faith. To put this another way, there is no such thing as unchangeable "human nature." A material object, on the other hand, has a fixed nature, or essence. *[From p. 207]*

6. "I am not my thoughts, feelings, personality traits or behavior" is the famous Psychosynthesis disidentification technique (Assagioli 1965). *[From p. 207]*

7. Some psychological problems do indeed have a neurological aspect or are caused by something organic; a medical checkup will determine whether this is the case. *[From p. 208]*

8. What we are writing about here is reactive responsibility: your Inner Critic's attempt to make you obey by using shoulds. Anthetic responsibility is discussed in Chapter 17. *[From p. 209]*

9. The term "being responsible" may simply mean "fulfilling one's commitments and being caring toward others." When contaminated by the Inner Critic, however, "being responsible" may be driven by shoulds, in which case it can lead to perfectionism, judgmentalism, and attempts to control others. *[From p. 210]*

15

Overcoming The Problems and Pitfalls Of Challenging

Your Inner Critic has been with you for years. It knows you through and through, and it has developed subtle ways of controlling you. As you continue the work of Anthetic challenging, your Inner Critic will become even more subtle and sneaky. It will find quite new ways of harassing you. This chapter will present some methods for dealing with the problems that arise when the Inner Critic becomes sneaky.

New Shoulds

Since everything is grist for your Inner Critic's mill, you may discover you have acquired some new shoulds you never had before. Here are some possibilities:

■ As you look back on the reactive decisions you've made in your life, your Inner Critic may pounce about them, perhaps telling you that you've made too many serious mistakes. You can get free by taking back your right to make mistakes.

■ Your Inner Critic may contaminate the process of your challenging. You might, for example, believe, "I should challenge my Inner Critic" (a constricting should). You'll need to get released from this by saying "I have the right not to challenge my Inner Critic any time I want."

This is an example of paradoxical challenging: taking back a right that seems at first glance to go against the whole process of challenging. But Anthetic challenging must be done from a free position, not a driven one, which means that you must get free from all shoulds—even what might be called Anthetic shoulds.

■ Your Inner Critic might impose a should to choose inner freedom. You might believe (because of your Inner Critic message), "If I don't choose inner freedom, I'm stupid." If this happens, you'll need to challenge your should by saying "I have the right not to choose inner freedom"—another paradoxical challenge.

■ Your Inner Critic may pounce about its own pouncing. Let's say you think you're doing well at challenging, and you're beginning to experience the joyous exuberance that is the sign of inner freedom. At this point you might think you've finally got your Inner Critic totally defeated.

Rest assured, however, that your Inner Critic will not give up; it will just switch the material it uses. For example, if you experience your Inner Critic pouncing, you may say, disparagingly, "There I go again, putting myself down" or "There I go again, falling into that trap! I shouldn't do that. Can't I ever learn to stay out of my Inner Critic trance?"

You can get released from this new should, again by making a paradoxical challenge: "I have the right to put myself down as often as I want and fall into as many trances and traps as necessary."

This is important: The goal of Anthetic challenging is not to make sure you never again fall into an Inner Critic trance. That's an impossible ideal. The truth is that from time to time your machinery will inevitably get triggered. So the goal is simply to have the skills necessary to get released whenever you do fall into a trance.

QUESTION: But doesn't that kind of challenging defeat the whole purpose of challenging?
ANSWER: Not at all. Inner freedom must come first. It must be your primary value and your top priority. And even if you have a should to get free, you must challenge that should, too. Once you get released from that particular should, you will be free to choose inner freedom, if you wish. But this time your choice will come from a want, not a should.

■ Your Inner Critic might zing you for slowness in learning the challenging skills. It might negatively compare you with others, complaining about your lack of progress. You can get released by saying, "I have the right to move at my own pace, not someone else's pace."

■ As you continue your work of challenging, your Inner Critic might change its voice from that of a harsh, authoritarian taskmaster to one of sweet reasonableness, solid logic, pseudo-maturity, and positive mental health. It may sound rational, polished, and so slick that you will be convinced that you have at last transformed it into a benevolent force.

But no matter how logical and reasonable your Inner Critic sounds, you must remember the infallible criterion for identifying it: If you don't follow its commands, you'll feel twinges (or jolts) of emotional punishment.

■ Your Inner Critic might adopt a confrontational pseudo-constructive tone. It may say things like "Snap out of it; get on track; get some focus; do something productive; quit wasting time; have a sense of direction." This may sound reasonable to you, as it did to Ben.

Ben was a 42-year-old stock broker, whose problem was procrastination. When I (Jim) directed him to enact the role of advice-giver, he delivered the messages in the paragraph above.

Ben named the advice-giver "Buddy" and thought he was "right on target." As Ben did Anthetic Dialogue, Buddy talked to "The Kid"—Ben's "immature" and resistant self. The Kid responded with, "Yeah, Buddy, I know. I been outta sorts lately, on a treadmill, not getting anywhere, losing spirit, just drifting. Keep at me, will you? I need a kick in the pants to get going."

As we discussed this interaction, Ben was astounded to discover that this apparently constructive voice was really that of his Inner Critic. Once he could label it correctly, he was able to get free from it.

As he got free, he functioned more and more from his natural self, and his procrastination vanished.

■ As you continue the process of Anthetic challenging, you'll recognize that many things you once thought were ego-syntonic are simply stuff—that is, ego-dystonic problems.

As this stuff is revealed to you, your Inner Critic may impose on you a new should: not to have stuff. Therefore, before you can work on your stuff, you may have to get released from your shoulds not to have stuff. Then you can work on the stuff. Another paradox.

For example, Maria, a 30-year-old second grade teacher, was telling me (Jim) about her new boyfriend. "I feel uncomfortable around him," she said, "because of the clothes he wears. I'm worried about what other people might think. But that's ridiculous. I feel ashamed to worry this way. It means that I'm not doing this work right. To be free, I shouldn't be so concerned about what other people might think."

"Is your Inner Critic telling you not to have stuff?" I asked.

"Not at all," she said. "It's just that I don't want to give away my power to other people. Isn't that one of the things you mentioned in your lecture?"

"Yes," I replied. But then I directed Maria in Anthetic Dialogue, and it turned out that her Inner Critic was indeed imposing a should not to be concerned about what other people might think.

I explained to Maria that she needed to challenge on two levels. The first level addressed the should about having stuff ("I shouldn't be concerned about what other people think"). The challenges were: "I have the right to worry about what other people might think" and "Just because I worry about what other people might think doesn't mean I'm a bad person."

Work on the second level can then address the other should ("I should be concerned about what other people might think"). The challenges were: "I have the right to be with someone toward whom other people might feel critical," "Just because they feel judgmental toward him doesn't mean anything about me, even though they might think it does," and "I'm not here to live up to their expectations."

Her challenges were all successful and, when she had delivered them in the above sequence, she was able to sort out the "should tangle" that had occurred. She was then able to become more easygoing toward her boyfriend, as well as toward "other people."

Remember that the Inner Critic can convert anything written here into grist for its nefarious mill: new material for oppressing you. For example, as you read this, you might be thinking there's something wrong with you for having all these shoulds. But there's nothing "wrong" about having shoulds. Everyone has them: Zen masters, saints, swamis, psychotherapists, founders of schools of psychotherapy, the authors of this book.

To be human is to have shoulds. To be human is to have machinery, reactivity, stuff, negative feelings, and so on.

QUESTION: But isn't the Inner Critic right some of the time?
ANSWER: Hardly ever. For one thing, most of its messages consist of commands, judgmental statements, and the infliction of emotional punishments. None of these are possible facts at all. A command is simply an order; either you obey it or you don't, but it's not a fact. Judgmentalism is simply an emotional attack, clothed in pseudo-factual language (e.g., "You're stupid!"). Emotional punishments are just twinges and jolts of pain. They're not facts, either.

However, the Inner Critic can take a grain of truth expressed in a recipe should ("You should study if you want to pass this exam") and transform it into an Inner Critic imperative should ("You're a bad person if you don't study").

It can also take a kernel of truth ("You failed an exam") and wrap it in a judgmental attack ("You're a failure; you'll flunk out of school"). When it does this, it creates a pseudo-fact that we call a factoid. It can do this with anything, so you've got to be able to distinguish recipe shoulds from imperative shoulds, and you've got to be able to analyze factoids into their two parts: kernel of truth plus what the Inner Critic adds.

When the Inner Critic predicts disaster and inflicts magnified fear, it comes the closest to presenting something that might look like a fact. But it's just a prediction, not a fact, and the Inner Critic is notoriously inaccurate in its predictions, because it thinks so impulsively.

Inner Critic Backlash

As we mentioned previously, you might think that once you have successfully challenged your Inner Critic, gotten free, and engaged in new behavior—that now you're finished. Not true. At this point, you'll need to watch out for Inner Critic backlash—the pouncing of your Inner Critic after you've performed some action that defies it.

Carole, for example, was one of our group members who was working on getting in touch with and expressing her feelings. Her blocks were the following shoulds: "I shouldn't tell Ron (another group member) that I think he's self-centered, and I want him to change. I should be nice. I shouldn't be rude. I shouldn't hurt anyone's feelings. I shouldn't try to change other people."

First, Carole made a releasing statement: "I have the right to say what I see and ask for what I want." She then made her request to Ron to work on his self-centeredness. We checked with Ron, who said he felt okay, and that he wasn't sure he was self-centered. Carole felt the usual feelings of joy and exhilaration after getting released, but on the way home after the group, she experienced an acute Inner Critic attack.

"How dare you say a thing like that!" her Inner Critic scolded. "You should have been nice. You shouldn't hurt people's feelings. What have you done!"

She bought into these messages and experienced a sleepless night. In the next group session she mentioned this to me (Kathy), saying, "I don't think this challenging stuff works, Dr. Elliott. I felt so bad after I said that thing to Ron. I don't think I'll do that any more."

I explained backlash to her and asked her to make one more releasing statement: "Just because I felt bad doesn't mean I did something wrong." This releasing statement worked. At a later session, other people gave Ron feedback about his self-centeredness, and he decided maybe they were right and that he had some stuff to work on. "Maybe that's why my relationships have been so lousy," he said with a wry smile. Having learned to speak her voice in the group, and armed with releasing statements, Carole was now able to tell her boyfriend some things about his patriarchal personality that she wanted him to change. It turned out that he didn't want to change, and she broke up with him. "It was painful," she said, "but better to break up now than after we were married."

To summarize: Inner Critic backlash does not mean your challenging isn't working. It just means that you have some additional challenging to do.

Troubleshooting:
Why Isn't Your Challenging Working?

If your challenging does not work—if you still feel heavy, and you achieve only a small (or even a zero) Believability Score on your challenging statements—here are some possible reasons:

■ **Value problems.** This is by far the most common reason for difficulties in learning the challenging skills. You may not hold inner freedom as a primary value. You may put other values above inner freedom. For example, you may decide that:
- My relationship (e.g., "my marriage") is more important than inner freedom.
- It's more important to be a "nice" person than to achieve inner freedom.
- It's more important to get love and approval from others than to achieve inner freedom.
- It's more important to maintain my pride and dignity than to achieve inner freedom.

If you give any value priority over inner freedom, it will be difficult for you to get released.

■ **Underestimating your Inner Critic's power.** You may find it difficult to believe that your Inner Critic's messages really are so destructive or pervasive; that they have such a powerful impact on your life; that doing Inner Critic work is so important. So you may not be highly motivated to do the challenging. If this is the case, please re-read Chapter 7, which presents descriptions of a wide range of psychological problems and shows their connections to the Inner Critic.

■ **Disengagement problems.** You may be finding it difficult to take some distance from your Inner Critic. Its voice may seem so much like your own that you can't step back from it and see it as something that is not-you. If this is the case, you may need individual work with a Certified Anthetic Therapist or help from an Anthetic Training Group.

■ **Falling for your Inner Critic's trick of proposing a debate.** When you say "I have the right to such-and-such," your Inner Critic may try to engage you in an intellectual debate, asking, "Where's your evidence for that?" Your answer must be: "I don't need any evidence. I'm just taking back the right you tried to take away."

Do not under any circumstances debate with your Inner Critic.

Let's take a look at the case of Dennis, a 42-year-old advertising copywriter who had just been fired and was experiencing depression. "I'm a failure," he told me (Jim). "I went to a therapist, who asked me, 'Where is it written that you're a failure?' "It's not written anywhere,' I told him. 'I just know I'm a failure.'

"The therapist said, 'Well, a failure means a failure 100% of the time. Do you fail 100% of the time?' I told him I didn't. He asked me to say 'I don't always fail; I succeed at some things.' But it didn't help. A voice inside me said, 'Even if you succeed at some things, you're still a failure.' And I still felt depressed."

I explained to Dennis that arguing with the Inner Critic will not lead to inner freedom. And even if you win such an argument, I added, it will simply put a buffer in place. This may buy off the Inner Critic's attacks temporarily, but after a while, your Inner Critic will demand more buffers.

For example, if you complete a project successfully, you can tell your Inner Critic, "See? You're wrong! I really am successful!" Your Inner Critic will probably agree, but sooner or later it will say, "Okay, now what? You've got to do even better, or I'll continue to call you a failure."

That's the Inner Critic's game; it might be called "the more and more game." Playing such a game leads people to drive themselves to achieve, in order to prove to the Inner Critic that they're really OK. This single-minded striving for success not only leads to workaholism, stress and burnout, it also destroys relationships.

The solution to this problem is simply to buy out of the Inner Critic's game right from the start. You do that by using your Anthetic challenging skills.

Now, back to Dennis. During Anthetic Dialogue, I taught him the following releasing statements: "I have the right to fail" and "I have the right to be what you call a failure." As he said these words, he grinned widely. "That's right!" he said. "I don't have to play the Inner Critic's game at all."

We then worked on other Inner Critic disempowerments. Dennis's depression lifted somewhat in that first session. In later sessions Dennis learned more challenges, until finally his depression vanished.

■ **Difficulties in recognizing shoulds.** One of the most difficult problems in challenging your Inner Critic is identifying your shoulds. This is a problem because shoulds almost always masquerade as needs, wants, preferences, and "normal desires." Shouldn'ts have been known to appear in the guise of ordinary dislikes and aversions.

How can you tell the difference? If you don't obey the should or shouldn't, you feel a twinge or jolt of pain. If you don't get a want, you just feel disappointed.

■ **Incorrect releasing statements.** You may not be formulating your releasing statements correctly. If so, you'll need help from a therapist trained in Anthetic Inner Critic work.

Take the case of Jeremy, who came to one of our workshops on Disarming Your Inner Critic and seemed to learn the challenging methods quickly. On the second day of the workshop he said, "This stuff isn't working. My Inner Critic has been predicting failure for my business project. I challenged it by saying 'I have the right to succeed.' I must have said this a thousand times, but it didn't work. My Inner Critic has just as much power as it ever had."

"Do you have a should not to succeed?" I (Kathy) asked him.

"No."

"Challenging won't work if you take back your right to do something that you have no shoulds about. In your case your Inner Critic is predicting failure, so a releasing statement won't address this issue. What you need to say is 'What do you know, Inner Critic? You're no expert on whether I'll succeed or not. You're just mindlessly trying to protect me by persuading me not to take any risks.'"

He made this challenging statement, and it worked. I could tell by the broad smile on his face.

■ **"Action shoulds" that block you from achieving inner freedom.** An action should is a should to take action once you get free. Take the case of Ann, 45, who worked in a travel agency. "I'm lonely and depressed," she told me (Jim). "I moved to California five years ago, and I haven't made any friends. I want to invite people over for dinner, but I can't. I'm sure they wouldn't approve of the hovel I live in."

I asked her, "What is your Inner Critic saying?"

"I'm blocking," she replied. "My mind is a blank." She thought for a few minutes. "I was blocking because if I tell you what my Inner Critic says, I'll have to challenge it. Then I'll get free. And then I'll have to invite people over. And I don't really want to do that."

So Ann had to work on a second-order should: "If I get free from my Inner Critic, I should invite people over."

Ann's releasing statement was: "Just because I get free from my Inner Critic doesn't mean I have to invite people over." The releasing statement worked: an action should had been blocking her—a should to take action once she got free.

There's no reason in the world to take action once you get free. That is, getting released (as we mentioned previously, in Chapter 9) is like buying a fishing license; once you get it, you don't necessarily have to go fishing.

■ **Unrealistic expectations.** You may be expecting that once you get released, you'll stay released. So you may be surprised when your Inner Critic pounces again about the same issue. "I can get released, all right," Janet said, "but there's a price to pay. It backfires on me." What she meant was that after she got released and began engaging in some new behavior, Inner Critic backlash struck. Her Inner Critic again hit her with a jolt of punishment. She hadn't expected it.

"That's just your Inner Critic pouncing again," I (Jim) told her. "All you have to do is challenge it again." She was surprised to learn that challenging was an ongoing process. She was able to continue challenging, and she discovered, as do most people, that the more she challenged it, the less energy her Inner Critic had.

The case of Irma illustrates another kind of unrealistic expectation. "Even if I wiped out my Inner Critic," she said, "the feeling that I'm bad would still be there."

I (Kathy) told her two things: "First of all, your goal should not be to wipe out your Inner Critic—just to get disengaged from it. Second, the bad feeling may still be there; it's just that you no longer believe it as though it were a factual statement about yourself. And as you continue challenging, the bad feeling will gradually diminish."

Frank presented a similar complaint: "I keep challenging, but I still have negative feelings." I (Kathy) explained that challenging may not immediately eliminate negative feelings.

Anthetic challenging has only one immediate goal: to help you buy out of believing that you should obey your Inner Critic's commands. The more you do this challenging, the weaker your negative feelings will become.

■ **Problems with the Inner Critic Police.** As you get free from your Inner Critic and begin to live from your natural self, you might expect that other people will like the new you. We're sorry to say that's not always true.

Remember that your friends and relatives are used to the old you: a reactive person—one who has been willing to pretzelize herself or himself in order to please them—someone who is willing to be controlled and manipulated—someone who doesn't like conflict, who avoids making waves, who dislikes saying No. So as you recover from your reactivity, people may not approve.

As you grow in inner liberation, you may find that others will try to police you back into your reactive life style. They may call you cold, self-centered, insensitive, inconsiderate, and selfish, simply because you will no longer be putting them first. So you may need one more challenge: "I have the right to be what you call cold, self-centered, and selfish—that is, to put myself first."

As they see you becoming liberated, these people may get angry at you, partly because they themselves are not free. The message of the anger will be: "How dare you get away with being free when I'm not able to!"

You will be called inconsistent, unreasonable, and irresponsible—all Inner Critic terms: labels used by people who would like to control you. The Inner Critic police may try to shame you when you compete (especially if you were to win the competition), or make you feel guilty when you display your expertise or when you make a lot of money. Unfortunately, the world is full of people who will do their best to get you to behave in ways that are convenient for and useful to them. You have the right to decide how you will live your life. This life is too precious to let others live it for you.

■ **Replays: stuff from the past.** Replays are based on early decisions made in childhood that have the power to lock your Inner Critic in place. Each replay has a negative payoff that looks like an accident of fate, but it's not. It's something planned and driven by unconscious machinery. Your Anthetic Therapist can suggest ways of identifying the replay and dismantling it. Prototype work will be needed to discover the original source of your Inner Critic messages (K. J. Elliott 1995).

■ **Attachment to a non-Anthetic school of therapy or system of personal growth.** If you've been in therapy a long time, or if you've had a lot of training and experience as a therapist, you may have great difficulty doing Anthetic challenging. It may seem senseless to you. One reason may be that your theoretical attachments will prevent you from creating the philosophical foundation necessary to generate successful challenging statements.

To put this another way, you may see Anthetic concepts, not as they are presented here, but through the lens of another theoretical framework. For example, you may see the Inner Critic simply as the Freudian superego. Or you may have difficulty fitting Anthetic ideas into an object relations framework. Or you may think Anthetic Therapy is irreligious, because you think the Inner Critic's voice is the voice of God. In addition, you may think the concept of sin is useful in guiding your behavior, instead of seeing it as another indication of Inner Critic functioning.

If you have become attached to a non-Anthetic philosophy, you may need to ask your Anthetic Therapist to teach you the skills of disengaging from any ideological commitments that are blocking you from becoming free.

■ **Learning challenging methods from a therapist not trained in Anthetic Therapy.** If you are learning challenging from a therapist who is not certified as an Anthetic Therapist, there is a danger that has been reported by some of our clients. Untrained therapists, through subtle judgmentalism and other forms of reactivity, may unwittingly burden you with new shoulds, and you'll continue to feel heavy, oppressed, and constricted.[1]

■ **Not adopting a defiant and rebellious attitude toward your Inner Critic.** When you confront your Inner Critic, the more defiant and rebellious you are, the more powerful your challenging will be. Getting angry at your Inner Critic helps, too. In the beginning you can't afford to be gentle with this inner saboteur. Later, once your Inner Critic is pretty much deflated, you can afford to be understanding and sympathetic, if you wish.

■ **Not making "absolute" releasing statements.** Your releasing statements must not be qualified in any way. Our clinical experience shows that you must aim at absolute freedom—no matter what. For example, saying "I have the right to quit my job, but I don't want to" will not be very effective. Anthetic Dialogue has revealed that these last five words refer to obeying the Inner Critic but now in the guise of a want. Absoluteness, on the other hand, makes your releasing statement a live option (even if you ultimately choose not to do it) instead of a theoretically interesting but never-to-be-chosen possibility.

Likewise, you may attempt to challenge your Inner Critic by saying "I have the right to make mistakes because other people make mistakes, too." This, too, lacks bite.

For maximum effectiveness, you must say "I have the right to make mistakes even if everybody else is perfect." Absoluteness in a releasing statement makes it firm and solid: your right no matter what happens.

Remember: the option need not be actually carried out. Releasing statements have one purpose only: to get free from your Inner Critic.

The Need For Feedback

Your Inner Critic is so subtle and sneaky (especially after you've begun to challenge it) that it's sometimes difficult to tell when it's pouncing. As one of our group members said, "I've had it for 40 years, and it seems comfortable, familiar, and natural. It has taken me many months to catch on to all the things it's been doing."

Ideally, you need someone who will give you feedback whenever she or he sees your Inner Critic functioning. If the person has been certified as an Anthetic Therapist you'll get useful feedback. Even better is being in an Anthetic Training Group, so you can get feedback from more than one person.

Catch-22 In Inner Critic Work

There is one problem in helping people learn Anthetic challenging that is so difficult we have not yet found an effective way to overcome it. Some people are so resistant to doing this work that they never can begin, and there seems to be no entry point to help them. Here are three examples:

■ **People who have difficulty listening to feedback because they hear it as criticism.** While many people are acutely aware of the Inner Critic's punitive voice, some are not. Inner Critic functioning feels so normal to them that they cannot recognize it as destructive.

Now, in order to teach people to do Anthetic challenging, we must give them feedback about clues to the Inner Critic shoulds that are to be challenged. That is, from time to time we say, "That's your Inner Critic." If, because of their reactivity, people hear this feedback as an accusation, they won't be able to benefit from it. They'll simply defend themselves by saying, "No, it isn't."

Consciously, they'll feel reluctant to consider feedback about their Inner Critic. They may also feel angry at anyone who offers such feedback. They may also believe there is no such thing as an Inner Critic, or that there is an Inner Critic, but it really is (or can become) helpful. What's happening unconsciously, however, is that their Inner Critic is blocking the person from realizing its existence and destructiveness.

Now, if they could learn to do Anthetic challenging, they would be able to listen non-defensively to the feedback. However, in order to learn challenging, they must first be able to listen to feedback about the Inner Critic.

And that's the Catch-22 vicious circle.

■ **People who have difficulty learning because to learn something radically new means giving up a previous system of thought that served as a buffer.** This, of course, comes from a message from the Inner Critic that says "Stay attached to your previous way of thinking. It's a good buffer for you, since you can identify yourself as a "such-and-such" (e.g., psychoanalyst, Buddhist, existentialist). Such people will have difficulty learning anything radically new, like Anthetic challenging, since they will have too much invested in the buffer of "knowing it all already." Their pride will prevent them from moving out of their old paradigm.

And they probably won't be able to work on their pride until they can learn the challenging skills. Another Catch-22 vicious circle.

■ **People who are so committed and attached to a system of thought that they cannot step outside it temporarily to examine Anthetic Therapy from a neutral position.** Some schools of psychotherapy are ideologies; that is, they demand strict obedience and discourage any of their followers from thinking critically about the system's concepts, principles, and theories. These demands then become internalized in the Inner Critic.

Even when an ideology doesn't serve as a buffer, you may be so attached to it that you can't disengage from it in order to see Anthetic Therapy on its own terms. Any attachment to a school of thought may prevent you from having the necessary theoretical foundation for learning the challenging skills.

As we have mentioned, people who fall into the above three categories are in a Catch-22 position. They can't be open to learning the challenging skills because of their Inner Critic, and they can't challenge their Inner Critic because they can't learn the challenging skills.

228 DISARMING YOUR INNER CRITIC

There are some additional obstacles to learning Anthetic challenging, as reflected in the following statements made by clients:

■ "Whoever gives me feedback about my stuff is one up on me. Therefore, if I consider your feedback, I'm one down, so I refuse to listen to it. I do not welcome it." This comes from an Inner Critic message designed to "protect" the person from changing.

To get free from this message requires the following de-fusing challenge: "Just because you give me feedback doesn't mean you're one up; just because I listen to it doesn't mean I'm one down."

■ "I won't listen to your feedback unless you listen to mine." Here the person values justice over her or his own inner freedom. (We call this a justice script.)

To give up this justice script, there must be a value shift from justice to inner freedom. The person wholly dedicated to inner freedom would say "Give me lots of feedback about what you see as my stuff. You don't have to receive any from me. If I'm the only one who gets feedback, it just means I'll be further ahead in getting free from my Inner Critic; it's your loss, not mine. I'm not lowered by it (unless I believe my Inner Critic when it says I am, in which case, I have stuff to work on)."

■ "Whoever gives me feedback about my stuff may be just avoiding her or his own problems, so I won't listen to it." This, too, is a justice script: "I won't think about my stuff until you stop denying yours."

■ "You shouldn't take other people's inventory." This is one of the principles of Alcoholics Anonymous. It was originally designed to keep the recovering alcoholic focused on her or his own work. Although it admirably serves this function, the rule deprives people of the benefits of listening to and benefiting from feedback.

■ "I won't even consider your feedback, because it doesn't fit in with my own reality." Marie made this statement in our orientation group for people who wanted to qualify for our regular training group. She had said, "I did a really stupid thing today" and then went on to describe the event. "That sounds like your Inner Critic," I (Jim) told her. "No, it isn't!" she said. "It *was* a stupid thing."

I then explained that one of the skills needed for membership in the training group was that of processing feedback. This skill, I explained, is very simple: it consists of neither immediately accepting nor summarily rejecting feedback—but simply saying "Let me think about that." I asked if she would like to learn that skill.

"Look," she said angrily. "I've done a lot of work on myself over the last ten years, and I feel like I'm in a really good place now. When I was growing up, my parents told me a lot of things that I believed and then later found out weren't true. And when I began my recovery, it was easy for me to believe someone else's truth. But now I'm not going to do that here. What you said just doesn't fit in with my own truth. That was not my Inner Critic."

I explained again that the skill of processing feedback was not about accepting feedback; it was simply about considering it seriously. I added that since the Inner Critic might be unconscious, you could never tell that you *didn't* have one, since if you checked inside and didn't find the Inner Critic's voice, it might be that it was unconscious, and no one can know what is below the level of consciousness.[2]

Marie's anger continued. She wanted to be in our training group, but she did not want to learn the skill of processing feedback. I said we couldn't accept her if she didn't want to learn the skills that the other people were committed to learning.

Unfortunately, Marie could not even begin to challenge her Inner Critic, since she was not willing to process feedback.

■ "How could you possibly know what's going on inside me? I'm the only one who knows that." This way of rejecting feedback is based on the mistaken idea that you are the best authority on your inner world. It's not always true. To understand this, all you have to do is recall the commonly-cited example of the man in the encounter group who, when told he looked angry, shouted, "I'm not angry, dammit!" while pounding on the arms of his chair.

Pseudochallenging

Some people are able to say the challenging words but do not seem to get released. Even though their Believability Scores are high, their challenging seems mechanical, and they do not report any of the benefits of challenging. It took us a while to realize the interrelated reasons for the difference between these less effective challengers and those who were more skillful.

The most important reason is that the less effective challengers are not really challenging; they're engaging in pseudochallenging, just going through the motions. Why do they want to challenge at all? Usually, because of shoulds to challenge.

Second, they are not committed to inner freedom as their top priority. Third, they believe the Inner Critic can be a useful guide. Finally, they are not defiant and rebellious enough.

Not everyone can learn the challenging skills. Some are not ready.[3]

Problems Doing Critical Thinking

Critical thinking is not the same as being critical. It means being able to question and evaluate your beliefs: to convert each belief, no matter how much it seems to be true, into a hypothesis (or assumption) to be tested. It means asking whether there are adequate reasons that support the belief. It also means asking what it would take to falsify the belief and looking carefully and impartially at all the evidence that might make it false. Finally, it means carefully considering every alternative belief or explanation.

This must be done in a thoroughgoing way. You must be prepared to challenge every belief you have. If you do not have this attitude of critical thinking, it will be difficult for you to challenge your Inner Critic.

Theoretical Positions That Interfere With Learning to Challenge

In addition to the above problems that get in the way of successful Anthetic challenging, you may also have some theoretical positions that interfere with your challenging efforts. These positions may be reflected in one or more of the following objections:

■ **"Working on my Inner Critic and other inner figures makes me too fragmented."** Frances was a 34-year-old humanistic psychologist who had come to couple therapy with her husband, a nurse. He complained of depression and low self-esteem. Frances said to me (Jim): "Thinking about the self-parts y'all describe just prevents me from having a holistic concept of myself. You can't separate people into parts like that."

The truth is, I told her, each person has these parts already, but they're usually all fused together. The more fused they are, the more reactive the person will be. What Anthetic Therapy accomplishes is separating the parts, so they can be dealt with. The more "air" there is between the parts, the more free the person will be from their mechanical influence. Once the parts are separated, a new kind of merging can take place—one that is now a matter of choice, not a compulsion. So you wind up being whole in a new way: "back together," so to speak, but now with inner freedom.[4]

Frances struggled with this concept through the first four couple sessions. When she saw her husband do Inner Critic challenging easily and productively, and reduce his Elliott Depression Test score from 10 to 2, she decided to try it herself.[5]

She was surprised at how effective it was. "I guess I had one of those ideological commitments you talk about," she said. "I had been taught in graduate school not to be fragmented."

"I have the right to be fragmented" was one of her releasing statements. "Yes," I told her, "and you are the one in charge of what seem to be the fragments. This will give you the holistic unity that's important."

As Frances learned to challenge her Inner Critic, she also built a foundation to learn to reduce her anger and judgmentalism.

■ **"Struggling against something, as you recommend, simply gives it more power."** Followers of Eastern philosophies sometimes offer this argument. However, Anthetic practice doesn't involve struggle against an adversary. It means simply buying out of your belief that you have no rights. If this process seems to be a struggle in which you must dominate or change your Inner Critic, it won't work.

■ **"Negative feelings are just illusions."** "I read a book," said Irene, "that said since God is love and God is all, then love is all—and there's no room for anything else, such as negative feelings. You just have to realize the truth of this, and your negative feelings will vanish. What do you think of this idea?"

I (Jim) told her that all she had to do to convince herself of the reality of such negative feelings as anger, anxiety, or shame was to feel it in herself or see it in someone else. I've heard of cases of desperate people, feeling intense anxiety, calling a transpersonal hotline and being told that their feelings are just illusions. This, to say the least, has not proven helpful. If you believe that any feelings are illusions, you will probably just submerge them.

■ **"Anthetic challenging presents itself as offering a quickie cure for problems which are really deep-seated and which require a lengthy process to solve."** It's true: in some cases Anthetic Therapy changes people as though by magic and in only a few sessions, especially cases of depression, low self-esteem, and anxiety. In many cases, such as reducing anger and judgmentalism, change takes somewhat longer—five to fifteen sessions, or more. Couple therapy, which is more complex, may take even longer.

So we are not suggesting that this approach always produces fast results. But it does so often enough. We have begun a research program, which will provide statistical evidence for the relatively rapid success of this method in treating introjective depression.

■ **"This whole thing is just too simplistic."** Aren't there any other reasons for having psychological problems? It can't just be a matter of the Inner Critic. Things are much more complex than that." True, the Inner Critic isn't the sole factor in problems. But it's the one log that's blocking all the others in the logjam. Once it is dealt with, there will certainly be other problems—but now they'll be easier to deal with.

To use a different metaphor, bypassing the Inner Critic in your work on yourself is like having surgery without anesthesia. It's painful.

■ **"This challenging work is too intellectual. It takes me away from my feelings."** True, part of Anthetic challenging is intellectual. It will take you away from your feelings. But only temporarily. They'll be back. The intellectual work needs to be done so you can process your negative feelings. If you don't process them—if you stay in them all the time—they'll run your life, and you'll wonder why you have so many difficult personal problems.

■ **"It's just natural to have negative feelings."** Melanie made this statement in one of our sessions. "Sure it is," I (Jim) answered. "Which is to say it's 'natural' to be reactive—given the upbringing we all had. And so we all have negative feelings. The question is whether we just accept them or learn the skills for processing them, thereby reducing their power, once we locate their source in the Inner Critic."

■ **"The concept of the Inner Critic seems ontologically flawed. You talk as though it's a kind of homunculus inside us. You are anthropomorphizing."** The Inner Critic, as presented here, is certainly a semi-autonomous figure, with power, feelings, and purposes. If your ontology is restricted to physicalist or mechanist categories (Pepper 1950), you will not be able to sense its presence. On the other hand, if your ontology is broad enough to include mentalist items, you will be able to sense the presence of the Inner Critic in the same way that you sense your thoughts, feelings, images, and impulses. Our clinical experience provides plenty of support for these assertions. Some people, however, report an inability to "perceive" the Inner Critic, just as some people are unable to form images in the mind or see certain colors.

■ **"I want to keep my Inner Critic and use it as a signal that something needs attending to."** You can certainly use your Inner Critic's messages as a signal that something needs attending to. The question is whether you attend to it by obeying your Inner Critic's commands or by getting released from them.

■ **"What's wrong with criticism? Don't we benefit from literary criticism?"** The Inner Critic doesn't evaluate you the way a good literary critic evaluates a piece of fiction. It imposes shoulds, demands that you obey them, then zings you with emotional punishment if you disobey. The analogy fails.

■ **"I'm a writer, and my Inner Critic is the one who critiques my writing and improves it. I don't want to give that up."** This objection was made by a writer of short stories. I (Jim) told him: "You'll find that your Inner Critic likes to attach itself to other inner figures in an effort at camouflage. In this case, it may be masquerading as that part of you that does the editing once you've finished writing.

"The price of valuing your Inner Critic as an editor, however, is high: your Inner Critic inflicts emotional punishment if your writing doesn't meet its standards. This will tend to inhibit the creative part of you that does the writing, because you need a free flow of thoughts and ideas for good writing. You may also find that you need alcohol to anesthetize your Inner Critic so you can liberate that free flow.

"Once you disarm your Inner Critic, you'll find that some other part of you can critique your writing—without punishing you."

■ **"I don't believe it's my Inner Critic that generates negative feelings; it's some other inner figure—my Little Boy, for example."** The Inner Critic has the ability to fuse itself with other inner figures, so it may appear to you as an Inner Child figure. If your Little Boy appears to be the source of negative feelings, it's only because he has believed what the Inner Critic told him.

In any case, in order to challenge your Inner Critic effectively, you must separate it from any inner figures with which it has become fused. Otherwise, your challenging efforts will lack focus.

More Statements That Indicate Problems in Challenging

■ **"I'd be crazy to accept myself."** Cynthia came to see me (Jim) because she was many pounds overweight. I explained Inner Critic work to her and how it leads to self-acceptance. "But it would be crazy to accept myself at this weight," she told me. "It would mean encouraging something that would destroy me, like cancer."

I explained to her that acceptance of something about oneself doesn't mean encouraging it; all it means is neutralizing the Inner Critic's judgmental statements toward it. She gradually came to see self-acceptance simply as non-disparagement and began to learn the challenging skills.

■ **"When you say that my Inner Critic is responsible for my problems, you're just blaming the victim."** Fixing responsibility, we believe, is not blaming. When my automobile mechanic says "The trouble is in your carburetor, not your fuel line," she's not blaming anybody for anything. She's just telling me what problem needs to be corrected.

Blame means judgmentalism, and a neutral diagnosis is not judgmental.

■ **"Challenging sounds so angry and adversarial."** This is another instance of buying into Inner Critic propaganda, the purpose of which is to prevent you from doing any challenging. In this case the Inner Critic is pejoratizing simple, ordinary, assertive disengagement. You may first have to challenge this message of pejoratism by saying "I have the right to be what you call angry and adversarial. I value inner freedom more than I value what you call niceness and politeness."

■ **"You seem to want me to make a devil or an enemy out of my Inner Critic. I don't want to do that, because that approach interferes with my ability to work with it by listening to it in a friendly way."** It's important to realize that your Inner Critic is already your enemy. It wants to constrict your life by punishing you if you transgress. Sure, it often thinks it's trying to help you by protecting you and keeping you safe, but what it protects you from is living a full life.

On the subject of being friendly with your Inner Critic, we can say from our clinical work with thousands of clients: It isn't effective. Your Inner Critic is an adversary. It wants to torture you. If you try to befriend it, it says "At last! Now I've got a free hand in constricting this person!"

■ **"My Inner Critic has needs, too. Shouldn't those needs be honored? For example, it's motivated by anxiety. Why not just reassure it?"** Reassuring your Inner Critic, we've found, just doesn't have enough bite. It's not very powerful in helping you get released. Your Inner Critic may appreciate any reassurance you give it, but that reassurance seems merely to lead it to use more subtle constrictions.[6]

■ **"Getting released seems like disowning my Inner Critic. I created it, and I want to take responsibility for it, not disown it."** We are not recommending disowning it. It's *your* Inner Critic; it got installed through your childhood decisions to believe what the outer critics said, and you are indeed responsible for its existence. And you're also responsible for your constrictedness and emotional suffering if you continue to welcome its efforts to keep you in line by threatening to punish you if you stray.

■ **"But I don't *feel* any emotional suffering."** You won't, as long as you obey your Inner Critic's commands. However, those commands will constrict your life and lead to unhappiness.

■ **"But it doesn't feel like my life is constricted."** You may have lived with constrictedness so long that it feels quite normal to you.

■ **"I battled with my Inner Critic, but I lost."** Said George: "I fought my Inner Critic all night, but it didn't do any good." What George meant, it turned out, was that he had been trying to silence his Inner Critic. "This strategy doesn't work very well," I told him. "It's okay to let your Inner Critic keep talking. All you have to do is buy out of what it's telling you."

■ **"I believe my challenges intellectually but not emotionally."** At first glance, this might be seen as an inability to challenge properly, but that may not be the case. It's best to think of this problem as "Part of me believes the challenge, but a stronger part doesn't." What you need to do is encourage the less strong part so it can gain strength.

In other words, believing a challenging statement "intellectually" is okay. You may not need to believe it emotionally at all. All you need to do is believe it.[7]

■ **"I find it hard to believe my challenges."** Sometimes people will say "I can say the challenging words, but I don't believe them." It's true, of course, that just saying the words mechanically won't work. You must believe what you are saying. But if you can just say the words mechanically at first, you may find that this voicing will trigger the beginnings of your belief.

It's best to say the words out loud in the presence of another person. See what reasons there are for believing the challenge; e.g., "I have the right not to call my mother. That's true because my Inner Critic is trying to take away my rights, and I am now taking them back." (Remember: valuing inner freedom is the *only* reason for believing the challenges.) Then ask yourself what your Believability Score is (Chapter 12). Most people find that as they repeat the challenges again and again, this percentage rises.

■ **"I don't really have those rights you say I'm supposed to have, because if I don't do what people want, they'll feel bad."** Meg spoke about calling her mother: "I have to call my mother every day, and if I don't, she raises holy hell. How can I say I have the right not to call her? If I don't, she'll make my life miserable."

Taking back a right is separate from what you actually do. You take back your rights from the Inner Critic, which has taken them away. Once you do that, you may decide to continue what you've been doing, especially if the external consequences will not be pleasant if you don't. But now you do it freely, whereas before you were programmed.

But suppose you decide not to continue. And suppose some other person will then try to make your life miserable. You may need to make an additional challenge: "If someone makes my life miserable because I don't do exactly what they want, I have the right to disconnect from that person, partially or completely."

It's unfortunately true that if you choose to act from your natural self instead of your Inner Critic, some people will not like your new behavior. They will not support your inner freedom. They may do their best to police you back in shape by trying to make you feel guilty for not living up to their expectations.

And now you'll discover who your real friends are.

■ **"I don't like to do this work."** Said Sharon: "I feel very reluctant to do this work. Do I have to challenge my Inner Critic 24 hours a day?"

Reluctance to challenge can occur for at least two reasons:

- It's sometimes a signal that you have a strong stake in

maintaining your Inner Critic as the dominant force in your life. You certainly have the right to obey your Inner Critic, but it's important to realize the price you'll pay, either in a constricted life (that you may not even be aware of) and/or mental suffering, crippled relationships, low self-esteem, depression, and lack of happiness (all of which you will be aware of).

If you understand the price and are willing to accept impoverishment and/or suffering—and you realize that it's totally unnecessary to have it—then there's probably no way we can persuade you to choose otherwise.

• A more common reason for reluctance to challenge is that suggestions to challenge have become converted into new shoulds by the tricky Inner Critic. When that happens, you think the only way you can maintain some semblance of freedom is to resist the process of challenging. The way out of this tangle is to use a paradoxical challenge: "I have the right not to challenge my Inner Critic."

Once people catch on to the process of challenging, it becomes second nature—a happy and satisfying experience each time they do it. They would never think of asking whether they have to challenge 24 hours a day, just as they would never think of asking "Do I have to be happy and free 24 hours a day?"

■ **"I may have the right to do something, but I couldn't accept myself if I were to do it."** This statement may mean "I've said the words, but I don't really believe I have the right." It may also mean that the challenges are not precisely targeted.

But the most probable meaning is that the Inner Critic is so powerful and so firmly entrenched that it may be impossible to disarm it, simply because the person has not chosen to value inner freedom above everything else. Unless this value is chosen, successful challenging will be impossible.

■ **"Challenging the Inner Critic doesn't work for me."** This statement may mean you just need some training in the challenging skills, either in an Anthetic training group or with an Anthetic Therapist. It might also indicate a strong attachment to a reactive, Inner Critic-based value system. Some people find it very difficult to shift to values that support their challenging.

Because your Inner Critic protected you against childhood pain and perhaps shaped you into a person other people find attractive, it has great subjective value. Even though it produces constriction and suffering, it still gives you a feeling of control and "rightness."

238 DISARMING YOUR INNER CRITIC

Therefore, only if you fully realize the disadvantages of living from your Inner Critic will it be possible to make the necessary shift in values.

■ **"I've been making releasing statements all week, but they haven't worked."** Lorene, my client, told me (Jim) this at the beginning of our second session.

"What has your Inner Critic been saying?" I asked.

"It's been jumping on me for making mistakes in the business reports I write."

"What have you been saying to challenge it?"

"I've been saying things like 'I can't be right all the time,' 'I can't please everyone,' and 'Nobody's perfect.'"

"Statements like those won't work very well," I told her. "They're not releasing statements. The first two are just statements of your inability to do things. The last one probably means you don't have to be perfect as long as other people don't have to be perfect, either. What you need to say are releasing statements that take back your rights.

"Each releasing statement," I added, "*must* begin with the words 'I have the right.' And each releasing statement must add the reverse of the shouldn't. For example, if your Inner Critic says 'You shouldn't make mistakes,' you need to say 'I have the right to make mistakes. In other words, you must take what your Inner Critic says you *shouldn't* do and give yourself the absolute right to do it. These principles are essential for effective challenging.

"Don't say 'I can't please everyone.' Say 'I have the right *never* to please anyone.' If you make an 'I can't' statement, you're on the wrong track. Finally, don't say 'Nobody's perfect.' Instead, say 'I have the right to be imperfect even if everybody else is perfect.'"

Even after you've learned the correct way of making releasing statements, we've found, the Inner Critic will try to move in and make you change your statements slightly so they're less effective. If you stick to the exact forms prescribed in this book, you'll find that your releasing statements will have the best chance of working.

It's important to check with your Anthetic Therapist to make sure you're saying the releasing statements correctly.

■ **"You emphasize negativity too much."** Said Janice: "I don't want to do this work, because I feel uncomfortable about all the emphasis on negativity. Why don't you focus on the positive instead?"

"Your Inner Critic would love it if you avoided negativity," I (Jim) told her, "because it uses negativity to control you, and if you avoid looking at that negativity, your Inner Critic can oppress you to its heart's content. The truth is, the negativity of the reactive self must be addressed first. Only then can positive feelings emerge, based on the natural self."

■ **"I'm still not sure the Inner Critic actually exists. How do you know it does?"** Of course, the Inner Critic doesn't exist the way material objects exist. It's an inner figure, and it exists in the mind. It's a constellation of thoughts, feelings, and impulses, and it has the power to impose shoulds and inflict emotional punishments if the shoulds are disobeyed. I (Jim) discovered this through Anthetic Dialogue. Essentially, I asked a client to move to a chair opposite, then look back and speak to "himself" or "herself." Without any suggestions on my part, what emerged was a series of shoulds and shouldn'ts, followed by such messages as "If you don't obey these shoulds, you're defective, shameful, guilty, and inferior." I gave the name "Inner Critic" to the source of these messages.

To put this another way: The existence of the Inner Critic is inferred from its voice in the same way that the existence of a magnetic field is inferred from the behavior of iron filings on a piece of paper with a magnet beneath it.

In any case, you may view the Inner Critic as a construct (Vaihinger 1935).

■ **"I think my Inner Critic can be useful."** If you believe this, you believe that constrictedness and emotional suffering can be useful. If you believe *that*, you can certainly expect to have some emotional suffering in your life. We ourselves wouldn't consciousciously choose to suffer, but if someone does choose suffering as a value, we can't argue with that choice except to say that in addition to causing many psychological problems, suffering isn't really necessary, nor is it much fun.

■ **"My Inner Critic is very perceptive. I don't want to do without its perceptiveness."** True, your Inner Critic is keenly perceptive. It can spot your tiniest flaw. As you work to disarm it, however, you'll find yourself still able to be perceptive—but without the emotional punishments that your Inner Critic inflicts.

■ **"I don't want to do this work, because it feels so strange and unnatural."** If challenging feels strange and unnatural, it means you're doing it right. What has happened is that your reactive self has come to feel familiar and normal, simply because it has been around a long time. A prisoner who wears shackles may come to believe that shackles are normal. Getting unshackled may feel unfamiliar at first, even scary.

If you have challenged your Inner Critic's propaganda, sidestepped all the ineffective methods for challenging, overcome any new shoulds that might be imposed, there still might be some fears that are holding you back from doing effective challenging. Those fears will be discussed in the next chapter.

NOTES

1. When we present workshops at professional conferences, what we do looks deceptively simple. Therapists who go back home and try it with their clients report difficulty in making it work. In some cases, this is because the therapists are not skilled in the finer points of challenging. In most cases, it's because the therapists are committed to a model whose goal is shaping the client's personality instead of liberating the natural self. If the therapist has not done intensive work on her or his own Inner Critic, reactivity will get woven into the work done with the client. This is why we require that our trainees work extensively on themselves before becoming certified as Anthetic Therapists. *[From p. 225]*

2. If you do not believe that the concept of the subconscious mind (or unconscious) is useful, you will not, of course, be able to consider that the Inner Critic might be unconscious. You may, however, have trouble explaining the source of ideas that pop into your head. If this source is not the subconscious mind, what is it? You may also have trouble explaining the process whereby one says "When someone gave me feedback that I was angry, I rejected it. But then the next day, I realized that I really had been angry and, in fact, had been angry for years without knowing it." The subconscious mind is inferred in order to explain what might otherwise appear to be terminal elements, disconnected from any deeper dynamic forces. *[From p. 229]*

3. Anthetic Therapy does not use the medical model, which is based on the assumption that if the client undergoes a procedure, that's all that's needed to result in a "cure." Instead, it's based on a learning model. Only those who are ready to learn and have a certain amount of motivation can benefit. *[From p. 229]*

4. An important concept in Anthetic Therapy is the Anthetic De-fusion Growth Process:

Stage One is fusion. You are fused not only with your Inner Critic but also with other things: your negative beliefs, your parents, other people, ideas, possessions. Another term for fusion is enmeshment.

PROBLEMS & PITFALLS 241

Stage Two is disengagement. After experiencing Anthetic Dialogue, you become disengaged from the items with which you were formerly fused, or enmeshed.

Stage Three is individuation. When you are in this stage, you are now free to merge (a term that replaces "fuse") with anything you wish, and you can also be disengaged, should you choose to be. Another term for Stage Three is psychic mobility.

Those familiar with the work of Martin Heidegger (1962) might find it illuminating to compare Stage 1 with *Zuhandenheit* (the "ready-to-hand") and Stage 2 with *Vorhandenheit* (the "present-at-hand"). It is our contention that Stage 3 opens up the possibility of what we call "communion," which might be compared with Heidegger's concept of opening to *das Anwesen*. *[From p. 230]*

5. The Elliott Depression Test is simple. We ask the client to rate his or her depression on a scale of zero to 10. *[From p. 231]*

6. Stone and Stone (1993) recommend becoming a nurturing parent to the Inner Critic (p. 190). *[From p. 235]*

7. It may be worth repeating that "believing a releasing statement" does not mean gathering enough evidence to refute the Inner Critic's message. What it means is realizing that the message coming from the Inner Critic consists of a command plus the threat of an emotional punishment if the command is disobeyed. Neither of these is susceptible to refutation, because neither is a would-be fact. If someone commands that you do something, you need not dispute the situation with that person; you just say "I have the right to do what I want, not what you want." "Believing the releasing statement" simply means believing that you do indeed have that right, based only on your commitment to inner freedom as a value that you hold above all other values. *[From p. 235]*

16

Overcoming Fears That May Block You from Effective Challenging

IN THE BEGINNING STAGES of learning the challenging skills, you may experience fears that impede your progress. These fears may seem quite realistic and objective to you, but we want to assure you that they are simply evidence that your Inner Critic is putting up a big fight to retain its grip on your life. In each case you need to challenge the fear. Here's a list of possible fears, along with some suggested challenges:

■ **Fear of becoming an uncaring person.** "Dr. Elliott, I'm afraid all this challenging is going to turn me into an awful person," said Teresa, a 28-year-old teacher of gifted children. Teresa had consulted me (Jim) because she had problems being assertive. "If I get free from my Inner Critic, I'm afraid I'll become uncaring, mean, selfish, and self-centered," she continued. "People are going to say, 'You used to be such a sweet person; you're not any more.' I don't want to be the kind of person who says I'm only going to do things for myself. But if I give up being guided by my Inner Critic, the only standard I'll have is 'Do I want to do this or not?'

"Also, you say that if I give up my Inner Critic, caring and love will fill in where the Inner Critic was. But I don't always feel caring and loving. So I can't rely on them all the time.

"Without caring and love," she added, "I wouldn't be living a worthwhile life, I wouldn't be able to help create the kind of world I want. I'm afraid I don't have enough love in me to do it. It won't be sufficient. But if you have a good sense of what your duty is, you can see yourself through times when love is not there.

"For example, what if parents don't feel loving toward their child? Won't they be able to be caring anyway out of a sense of duty? If my husband goes to the hospital, and I don't want to visit him, isn't it better to visit him out of a sense of duty and stand by your husband when he needs you, instead of not visiting him at all? If you just live for yourself, you'll feel isolated."

It was clear that Teresa was fused with her Inner Critic, which was using its usual propaganda to keep her in line. She thought the Inner Critic's thoughts were her own. Instead of responding to Teresa directly, I decided to use Anthetic Dialogue to help her disengage from that figure. Here's what she said to it: "You sound pretty pessimistic and cynical. And you have a lot of power. Your voice carries a lot of weight—it has a certain amount of seductiveness. For one thing, you're saying Dr. Elliott wants me to change my whole life, the implication being there's something wrong with me. I don't have to believe that. Just because I change my life doesn't mean there's been something wrong with me. And I can see now that you're just my Inner Critic.

"Now about love and caring. I know one thing for sure: I do much better when I come from a loving place. But when I'm influenced by you, Inner Critic, I can't be loving, because you tell me that caring for people is a should, not a free choice. It's a duty that comes from *you*, not a want that comes from my heart. Also, you speak as though what you say is the truth, and when I believe you, I think that's the way it is, and I can't see any other way. But there is another way to see this. I think I would be capable of love and caring as long as I didn't listen to you very much."

Once she had done this work, this particular fear disappeared, and Teresa was able to continue learning the Anthetic challenging skills. She learned to be more assertive, and not only did she retain her ability to be loving and caring, she found that her ability increased as she gradually neutralized the power of her Inner Critic.

Fear of becoming unloving and uncaring is a common obstacle to learning Anthetic challenging. What's difficult for most people to realize is that the ability to be loving and caring is the very thing that is blocked by the Inner Critic. For example, the Inner Critic may command you (through its shoulds) not to express love, because, it will say, you'll just get hurt again. It may tell you to harden your heart. It may tell you to seek revenge instead of love. It may make you cynical. It may tell you that loving feelings are too transitory to be of any value. It may make you tough and unfeeling. And it may command that you be self-sufficient.

The result of obeying these shoulds is that that people fall back on duty and obligation to motivate their caring behavior. That kind of caring is driven by the Inner Critic; it is reactive caring.

Because it will not be done freely from the natural self, it will almost certainly be contaminated by two elements. First, reciprocation will be demanded. When it is not given, anger and resentment will be the result.

In the most egregious cases, anger and judgmentalism will actually be seen as instances of love and caring; e.g., "I'm angry at you because I love you and care about you."

Second, reactive caring will try to pressure others to change "for their own good." The reactively caring person will be controlling.

In any case, because caring will be reactive, it can destroy relationships.

The natural self, on the other hand, is naturally loving. Once it is liberated from the grip of the Inner Critic, its love can flow naturally toward other people, and any caring behavior that is chosen will be backed by love instead of Inner Critic shoulds.

■ **Fear of freedom.** Some people find that inner freedom is fearful because it feels precarious. Take the case of Rita, a 34-year-old accountant. Rita consulted me (Kathy) for general feelings of living an unfulfilled life. I led her through the steps of Anthetic Dialogue and taught her the basic challenging skills. "I don't know," she said. "If I got free from my Inner Critic, I'm afraid that something nameless and disastrous would happen to me. If I gave up my old way of doing things, I'd be rudderless and adrift. I'd be in unfamiliar territory. In fact, after doing a little challenging and getting free, it feels like the ice is melting under me; like I don't have anything solid to stand on."

Rita took a week to think over whether she was willing to put inner freedom first in her life and finally decided that she did. It was a momentous value shift. "I think my Inner Critic is just trying to hang on," she told me. "It's making me scared. But I'm tired of being unhappy. I'm going to keep on challenging it. I see that it's my Inner Critic that's blocking me, and I do want to get free." Rita learned the releasing skills, and she reported that her new freedom was uncomfortable at first, but the increase in her joy more than made up for any discomfort. And the discomfort did vanish in a week.

Bob, a physician in general practice, had similar fears. He had come to see me (Jim) at the request of his wife. "She says I need to be more open," he told me. After learning the basic Anthetic challenging skills, Bob said he felt lighter and happier, but reported experiencing some resistance. "My reactive self, my old self," he said, "is familiar, even comfortable, in a sense. I've spent years living with it, and I know how to live with it, even though it feels depressing and painful at times. It got me through medical school, and it gives my life structure. This new openness and liberation I get from challenging is unfamiliar. It's like learning to type using the touch system after years of using the hunt-and-peck method."

All Bob needed to dispel his fears was to talk about them, whereupon he continued to learn more challenging skills. We finally identified his fear of speaking openly as a fear that his wife would be judgmental if he were to talk about his feelings. I taught him some Anthetic responses for listening to judgmentalism, and in the next session he reported that his wife was pleased with his new openness and wanted even more of it. However, her judgmentalism remained a problem, and he was able to persuade her to join him in couple counseling, where she learned the skills for Anthetic processing of judgmentalism. This took several sessions. The more she learned to process her judgmentalism and reduce it, the more open Bob became.

When Joy consulted me (Kathy), she described her life as a disaster. "My job is driving me nuts," she said. "And my boyfriend won't commit, but I can't seem to end the relationship, and my parents are angry at me for hanging on to him. I'm going to night school, and my grades are terrible." Joy, a 23-year-old dental assistant, described her efforts at personal change: "I tried giving up alcohol, I tried exercising regularly, I meditated, I did all the things that are supposed to make you feel better, but nothing worked."

Joy's shoulds were about being conscientious. I taught her the basic challenging skills, and, even though she believed her challenges only 60%, reported feeling somewhat better. "I'm not so hard on myself," she said. "But my way of seeing things is strange now. It's unmapped territory. I might lose what control I have over myself. I'd be adrift. I've never been free in my life, and if I got totally free, I wouldn't know what to do. I don't have any structure any more. It's like I'm standing on the border of new territory, and I feel reluctant to venture into this new freedom without a map."

It took Joy about two weeks to explore her new inner freedom and feel comfortable with it. As she did this, her Believability Score (Chapter 12) increased to 99%. She went to a vocational counselor, took a battery of tests and, based on the results, decided to apply for medical school. She took back her rights to "hurt" her boyfriend, and she gave him an ultimatum, which he rejected. They broke up.

She then learned to challenge her Inner Critic's predictions that she would never find anyone else. Her happiness level increased, and she reported at her last session that the beginnings of a map were appearing, to her great satisfaction. It was a map based no longer on her Inner Critic but on her natural self.

Here are some more statements made by people who have experienced unsettling feelings while beginning their recovery from reactivity:

■ "It's like I'm standing on a log that's rolling under me; I'll lose my footing. I'll lose control."

■ "As I get free, it feels like the ground is shifting under me."

■ "It feels like I'm an airplane on the ground, and the guy wires holding me down are being cut, one by one. It's scary, because I don't know how to fly yet."

■ "It's like I'm on a little island, just big enough to stand on, and I'm quite safe there as long as I stay, but you're asking me to leave, to jump into the water, and I don't know whether I'll be able to float."

Why all this uneasiness about shifting out of a reactive value system? We told each of the above clients roughly the same thing: "For years your Inner Critic has been protecting you from the anxiety that your natural self would experience if it ever got free. Your reactive self has provided control for your life—rigid, brittle control, costing you a heavy price in loss of effectiveness, creativity, and pleasure, but it's still the kind of control that offers protection from anxiety. It's no wonder you're afraid to give up this control."

We typically ask our clients to explore the drawbacks to living the old way of life and compare them to the advantages of the new way. "If you decide there are too many drawbacks to reactivity," we say, "you'll make a choice against it and in favor of inner freedom. And if you continue to practice your challenging skills, you'll find that new values will gradually replace the reactive values you are giving up. Once these new values are in place, you'll have the feeling of a more solid foundation under your feet, but this time, the foundation will be flexible instead of rigid, and it will be connected with what you want instead of what your Inner Critic thinks you should feel, think, and do."[1]

■ **Fear of being overwhelmed by emerging feelings.** This is a fear of "unwanted" thoughts, feelings, and behavior—all those things that have been submerged because they were condemned by the Inner Critic.[2] When they are in their submerged state, they seem to have great power; if they ever were to emerge, we think, they would overwhelm us with their bizarreness, shamefulness, and painfulness. So we are afraid of their emergence, and we feel our fear as "I think I'm going crazy." Of course, that's incorrect.

It often is uncomfortable at first to contact and welcome these disowned parts. But once we have taken back our rights to have them, they lose their scary power rapidly and then become new resources for us to draw on. When the submerged elements finally emerge and are accepted, they have hardly any negative power. As one client said, "Each part is like a frog who, when kissed by a princess, turns into a prince."

■ **Fear of self-image disconfirmation.** Not only does the emergence of submerged elements become scary because of the apparent power of those elements, it also would be scary if the emerging elements were to disconfirm your compensatory self-image. Let's examine this process in greater detail by looking at the case of Henry.

Henry was a civil engineer, 39, who worked for a successful San Francisco company and was about to become a partner in the firm. Henry wore a conservative three-piece suit. His hair was neatly trimmed. He sat very quietly and spoke with great precision. Whenever he was about to explain an important point, he tightened his mouth just before he spoke.

Henry consulted me (Jim) because he had been experiencing attacks of anxiety, which seemed to come out of the blue at odd moments throughout the day, but mostly while driving across the Golden Gate Bridge.

Anthetic Dialogue revealed that Henry's Inner Critic imposed shoulds to be logical, practical, precise, rational, and mature. He believed that every argument with his wife could be resolved through logical analysis. Whenever they had an argument, he would forcefully command her to "Think!" (This, however, didn't help much.)

Henry was so successful in obeying his shoulds that he felt no emotional punishment. Until the anxiety, that is.

His anxiety seemed ego-dystonic; it was like an alien intruder that he wanted to get rid of. That is, it created a disconfirmation of the should-backed elements in his idealized self-image. It didn't fit in with the picture he had of himself, which was that of a rational, well-balanced, mentally healthy person. So it worried him greatly. He thought it was a sign of impending insanity.

Because Henry valued his shoulds so much, he had some resistance to learning Anthetic challenging. His machinery made him *want* to be what his Inner Critic demanded.

After several sessions, I asked him to dialogue, not with his Inner Critic, but with his anxiety. My purpose was to help him discover its meaning by imagining "anxiety" in the empty chair, speaking to it, then switching chairs and responding while enacting "the anxiety."

When he enacted the anxiety he responded as follows: "I'm afraid you're getting too big for your britches. You're flying too high. You came from poverty, and that's all you are—poor folks. I'm here to keep you down, to protect you."

Henry's anxiety had been generated by his Inner Critic. He was now able to objectify his anxiety and dialogue with it whenever it appeared, which was one of the factors that led to its rapid reduction.

The way was then open for me to teach Henry some Anthetic challenging skills. The first skill was a "Just Because" challenge: "Just because I feel anxiety doesn't mean I'm going to go crazy." The second skill addressed the following Inner Critic should: "You shouldn't have so much anxiety." The skill was: "I have the right to have anxiety; and I have the right to have 'so much' anxiety; I even have the right to feel anxious all the time."

Having learned these skills, Henry's anxiety shifted from being ego-dystonic (something to be feared) to something he could accept and even, in a sense, be comfortable with. He no longer attempted to submerge it. He saw the anxiety simply as a signal from his Inner Critic that he was about to step over a boundary if he were to become a partner in the company.

Henry was then in a good position to learn an additional releasing statement: "I have the right to get too big for my britches; I have the right to fly too high; and I have the right to surpass my poor-folks childhood." As Henry continued practicing these challenging skills, his anxiety was further reduced.

As Henry continued working, he discovered a number of feelings and impulses that the Inner Critic would have pejoratized had they emerged: for example, raw sexuality, passionate love, and a kind of wild playfulness. At first he saw these as irrational, crazy, and irresponsible.

If those feelings and impulses had emerged, his buffers would have collapsed, and his self-image of pure rationality would have been disconfirmed, whereupon his Inner Critic would have pounced.

To understand this disconfirmation process, let's take a look at the structure of the self-image. The self-image contains "slots" for certain thoughts, feelings, images, and behaviors, but there may be places where there are no slots. For example, if you have a should to never have angry feelings, there may be no welcoming place in your self-image for any anger that may bubble up. If anger does emerge, not only will it not find a slot, it will also disconfirm your self-image as a rational, mature, sweet, loving, non-angry person—which means again that your Inner Critic would pounce.

We want to assure you that the more you challenge your Inner Critic, the more you will be able to handle the submerged elements that bubble up. To put this another way, there will be a welcoming slot in your self-image for each emerging element.

Henry was able to accept not only his anxiety but also his playfulness, sexuality, and ability to feel and express love. He wondered briefly whether to continue in his career as an engineer, then decided he would. He wore jeans to work one day and in other ways became more easygoing and relaxed. His fellow workers and clients were impressed by the personality transformation they saw, and his creativity began to blossom. He decided to stop using the name Henry and switched to his middle name, "Rick" (short for "Richard"), to reflect his new style. As partner in the firm, he introduced some innovative management procedures that led to more happiness and greater effectiveness for everyone.

■ **Fear of discomfort at confronting your Inner Critic.** For years you may have been avoiding emotional punishment by doing exactly what your Inner Critic commands. Even though such obedience has been producing a considerable amount of constrictedness, you may have been willing to accept it because of your fear of the Inner Critic's punishments. This fear is what anchors your attachment to a reactive way of life.

Because what you have is something like an addiction, it's reasonable to expect a few withdrawal symptoms when you begin recovering from that addiction. Since you'll be defying your Inner Critic instead of obeying it, you'll be up against what you've been avoiding all along: punishments generated by your Inner Critic. And you will no longer be getting your fix in the form of buffers.

Now, however, you'll be armed with skills for buying out of your Inner Critic's oppression—skills you can use immediately to neutralize your Inner Critic. For an instant, though, you might feel the pain of the electric fence.

If you simply disobey the Inner Critic and engage in oppositional behavior without using the Anthetic challenging skills, you may indeed feel the pain of the emotional punishments. If that happens, you may give up and say "This method doesn't work."

If, on the other hand, you use the skills *before* actually disobeying your Inner Critic, you will be able to defy it easily and painlessly.

■ **Fear of loss of a self-part.** Some people say, "I need my Inner Critic as a friend and guide; it's part of me; what would be left if I gave it up?"

The Inner Critic is indeed a constant presence, and it may feel much like a comfortable companion. But really, of course, it's merely a familiar enemy. Who needs "friends" like that?

■ **Fear of sadness.** From time to time, people who successfully challenge their Inner Critic will feel some sadness; perhaps even deep grief. This may seem scary until its source is located. The sadness is usually about missed opportunities in the past, resulting from constrictedness at the hands of your Inner Critic.

If you feel such sadness, you may need to grieve—perhaps, to cry—about your pre-Anthetic life.

■ **Fear of happiness.** "It's too scary to be happy. I'd feel guilty. Some unnamed entity would get me for it." This fear is common. It's a fear of being punished for having pleasure and may originate in early parental programming or in Oedipal/Electra mechanisms (If I love my opposite-sex parent and want that parent exclusively, my same-sex parent will punish me. If I actually win my opposite sex parent [e.g., through my same-sex parent's death], my punishment will be even more severe.) Anthetic challenging will release you from these blocks.

■ **Fear of loss of identity.** "Without my Inner Critic and reactive self, I wouldn't be the same person I am. I'd be somebody different. I don't want to lose my identity." These comments were expressed by Carolyn, an attorney who consulted me (Jim) for depression. I told her that sometimes the Inner Critic has become so much a part of a person's identity (along with all the reactive self structure) that she or he would feel quite strange without it.

It's true that when the Inner Critic is disarmed, there might be a vacuum at first, but it gets filled by the Inner Guide. At the same time, the reactive self structure gradually gets replaced by the growing natural self.

Indeed there is a loss of identity, I added: one's identity as a person who is reactive and plagued by puzzling problems. But there is also the gain of a new identity: the identity of oneself as a free, creative, and happy person.

■ **Fear of making mistakes if you become yourself.** "It's so frightening to be myself," said Rob, an elementary school teacher. "I might make some serious mistakes in my life. With my Inner Critic, I at least know I'll be safe." Rob found the following challenge helpful: "I have the right to make as many mistakes as I want."

■ **Fear of what other people will think.** Making mistakes was an issue for Susan, too. "If I can just keep a low profile," she said, "I'll never make any mistakes, and no one can criticize me."

If you give up your low profile and become your true self, of course, some people *will* criticize you, because you'll be standing out from the crowd.[3] The question is whether you want to continue to pay the price that the low profile is costing you.

Remember: If you have difficulty listening to criticism, you can overcome that problem by making challenging statements; for example, "Just because someone criticizes me doesn't mean I'm a bad person" and "I'm not here to live up to other people's expectations."

■ **Fear of God's retaliation.** Rona, a 29-year-old secretary, told me (Kathy) she wanted to break her engagement to her fiance. "We're both very religious," she said, "in fact, we met in church. I always wanted a husband who took religion seriously, and Bob fit that description. But in a few weeks I wasn't sure about him. He seemed to want to control every aspect of my life. When he proposed, he said God had told him we should get married, so how could I say No? But then he became so critical. I can't take it any more, and I've got to get out of this relationship, but Bob said I should keep my agreements, especially since God had commanded that we get married."

When Rona began the Anthetic Dialogue process, her Inner Critic said, "You made an agreement, and you should keep it. Something bad will happen to you if you break up with Bob, after what God told him. You should be humble and do God's will."

Rona's releasing statements were: "I have the right to go back on my agreements"; "Just because I say No to Bob doesn't mean something bad will happen to me"; "I have the right not to be humble"; and "I have the right not to do what you call God's will." The releasing statements were, however, only partially effective; she reported a Believability Score of 40%.

I then asked Rona to dialogue with God. God's message to her was: "I wouldn't punish you for breaking your engagement. I want what's best for you. I love you."

I told Rona, "Unfortunately, the Inner Critic gets woven into religious doctrines quite easily. If you conceive of God as punitive, you may, of course, fear retaliation if you begin to individuate and exercise your personal power. You may, on the other hand, see God as loving, as wanting you to be free from emotional punishment."

Armed with this new concept of God, Rona raised her Believability Score to 90%, and she was able to tell Bob she didn't want to marry him. They each went through some pain but, as Rona told me, "Better a little pain now than a lot of pain later."

■ **Fear of becoming a lazy bum.** This is one of the most common fears. The Inner Critic creates it by saying, "Without me, you wouldn't get anything done; you wouldn't even get up out of bed in the morning and go to work. You wouldn't get good grades in school. You'd never get promoted at work. You'd never improve yourself." Of course, the Inner Critic wants to survive, and one of its propaganda messages is "You need me to motivate yourself."

People find, however, that once they disarm their Inner Critic, they become motivated by the natural self. The natural self is a much more powerful motivator than the Inner Critic, partly because it provides more positive energy, partly because there is no need to resist it.

No one who has done Inner Critic challenging has so far become a lazy bum, though some people have begun taking life easier (which the Inner Critic *calls* "becoming a lazy bum").

■ **Fear of giving up all standards.** "If I give up my Inner Critic as a guide, I'll have to give up all my standards, and I like my standards; I don't want to give them up."

This is a common fear. We want to assure you that as you achieve freedom from your Inner Critic, you'll still have standards. But your standards will no longer be backed by your Inner Critic—that is, no longer enforced by the threat of emotional punishment. Instead, they'll be freely chosen and grounded in your natural self and therefore even more solid than Inner Critic standards, because you'll feel no need to rebel against them.

■ **Fear of growing up.** "If I give up my Inner Critic," said Bonnie, "I'll have to grow up, and I don't want to grow up; I want to stay the way I am." Prototype work revealed a message to Mom as follows: "If grown up is being like you, I don't want to grow up." This had been converted into an Inner Critic command that said growing up was being like Mom, so you shouldn't grow up. Bonnie was able to easily challenge this command by saying, "Just because I grow up doesn't mean I have to be like Mom."

■ **Fear of hurting other people's feelings.** If you have this fear, it has made you live a life of pretzelization as you twist and turn to make sure no one's feelings get hurt. So you spend time with people you don't like in order to avoid hurting their feelings. You tell lies so you won't make waves. In your attempts to maintain a low profile, you withhold much of your natural self from people.

Now, however, you are facing the possibility of disarming your Inner Critic, and along with this, the possibility of giving up your low profile. As you start living from your natural self, you'll be free to say what you don't like, and this may alarm your Inner Critic, which will do its best to silence your voice so you don't trigger other people's discomfort and anger.

If you do trigger someone's pain simply by being honest about what you want, you can get released by saying, "I'm not responsible for other people's negative feelings." (At the same time, you can behave in a caring way toward that person.)

It May Feel Uncomfortable at First

Remember the story of the armor in Chapter 6? As a child, you put

254 DISARMING YOUR INNER CRITIC

on a suit of armor to defend yourself—to ward off the two kinds of overwhelming pain you were feeling (one kind from the harshness of your Inner Critic; another from the rejection you were getting from the people around you).

Now that you're an adult, that armor is still in place, and it is weighing you down. Unfortunately, the armor feels familiar and, in a sense, comfortable. You know what to expect from it.

So when you begin to dismantle your armor piece by piece, you'll feel some discomfort. As this process continues, you may feel disoriented from time to time, or you may even feel some anxiety. That's what the armor was designed to protect you from—the anxiety of becoming psychologically liberated.

We want to assure you that such feelings of discomfort are perfectly natural. They seem to happen in about one out of ten people who do this work. If you feel them, it is simply your natural self uncramping and unfolding; it has been cramped for years and now feels a little stiff and awkward. We also want to assure you that such feelings will pass.

Remember: you are making a major shift in your philosophy of life. Your value system will be changing from one of constrictedness to one of inner liberation, non-reactive love, and genuine caring.

Here's what Mary said: "To me, Anthetic challenging was like a new pair of shoes. It was a little uncomfortable and unfamiliar at first, but the other day I suddenly started using it without thinking about it. I was berating myself for doing something stupid, and I was able to say, 'Wait a minute! Just because I did that thing, that doesn't mean I'm a bad person.' Then I was able to jump to the next step: "Just because my Inner Critic said that what I did was stupid doesn't mean that it *was* stupid. It was just a mistake, and I have the right to make mistakes.'

"Now, this isn't the way I usually think; I usually beat myself up about mistakes. So when I started learning the challenging skills, this way of thinking was very uncomfortable. But what helped was that there were payoffs right away. I felt free for the first time in my life that I can remember, and I got used to the discomfort. And now my old self feels like the uncomfortable one, and I'm very comfortable with this new way of thinking. But it was quite strange at first to think with these new concepts."

Your Growing Edges

Whenever you are up against a psychological boundary that limits you and that you think you can't go past, we want you to understand two things: One, the boundary comes from your Inner Critic, and two, it's simply a growing edge that you are confronting.[4]

As you progress in therapy and learn to make the Anthetic challenges described in this book you will be able to move past the edge, and what was formerly edge will now become familiar territory—whereupon a new growing edge will appear, and the horizon of your world will have expanded.

And the next step is to grow beyond this new limit created by your Inner Critic and then continue your growth, edge by edge. As you proceed in this way, you will continually reclaim new psychological territory, just as the Dutch reclaimed land by building dikes against the sea.

NOTES

1. To help the client replace reactive values with new values, we use methods from a discipline called Anthetic Philosophy (AP). Jim created AP in 1973 when he added it to his counseling work and gave lectures and workshops on the new approach in Berkeley, Calif.

AP's values are presented in Chapter 17; a book devoted to the subject will appear in a year or two.

2. When items are submerged because of condemnation by the Inner Critic, they are submerged into what Jungians call the Shadow . Note that Anthetic Therapy sees the Shadow as a domain, not an archetype or inner figure.

3. The Japanese have a saying: "The nail that sticks out will get hammered down."

4. Jim got the idea of the growing edge from Bob Botley, who led growing edge groups in San Mateo, Calif. in 1969 (Elliott 1969). Bob got this term from Richard C. Cabot, M.D., who described the healing of injured tissue as taking place only at the growing edge.

17

Toward A New Foundation For Morality

WHEN I (JIM) BEGAN TEACHING MY CLIENTS to do Anthetic challenging in the 1960s, I thought I was simply helping them gain inner freedom—that is, freedom from the Inner Critic. What they did with that freedom, I believed, was up to them.

But as I continued to help people do this work, I made five discoveries that showed me that my clients could achieve much more than inner freedom. If they pursued Anthetic challenging in a thoroughgoing way, it would lead them to a new and more solidly grounded morality.

The five discoveries have been mentioned in other parts of this book, but I want to bring them together here in the context of what I have come to call Anthetic morality.

Discovery #1
JAV and The Inner Critic

The first discovery I made was that judgmentalism, anger, and vengefulness (the "JAV triad") result from Inner Critic functioning.

Although these JAV feelings seem ego-syntonic to many people, they are destructive—especially when acted out. They are not caused by some mysterious evilness, "destrudo," aggressive instinct, or terminal meanness. They are the end-reactions of a chain of events that has its origin in the Inner Critic. This revolutionary discovery has not appeared anywhere else in the psychological literature.

What this discovery means is that judgmentalism, anger, and vengefulness are neither normal, valid, justified, appropriate nor legitimate, in the sense of being "not material to work on."[1] Each of them is always stuff to process; that is, each is a clue to Inner Critic functioning. So if you value inner freedom in a thoroughgoing way, you will be willing to work on these JAV feelings and not simply accept them as terminal elements.

To help people do this kind of advanced work, I developed a series of Anthetic processing skills that consist of step-by-step sequences for exhibiting the linkages between JAV feelings and the Inner Critic. There isn't enough space here to explain these sequences in detail; they will be presented in future journal articles and books. For now, however, let me comment briefly on the general strategies necessary to process each element of the JAV triad:

■ **Judgmentalism.** What you are judgmental about in others is the same thing you are judgmental about in yourself. Your judgmentalism is thus a clue (sometimes the only clue) to the operations of your Inner Critic. When you make releasing statements, you reduce your self-judgmentalism. As you do this, you also reduce your judgmentalism toward others.

■ **Anger.** Much of your anger comes about as a result of the disempowerment you experience at the hands of your Inner Critic.[2] Once you take back the power you have given away (by challenging your Inner Critic), the psychodynamic force that drives your anger will decrease.

■ **Vengefulness.** Any revenge you take on others serves as a compensatory buffer. However, if you challenge your Inner Critic successfully, you will no longer need this buffer, and you will no longer be driven to seek revenge.

Discovery #2
Anthetic
Love

My second discovery was that once my clients and group members learned the skills for processing the elements of the JAV triad, they were wonderfully able to feel loving toward other people. It was amazing to watch. The JAV feelings had been blocking the free flow of love.

We've discovered three other blocks to the expression of love. One block is the fear of getting hurt. Another was Inner Critic pejoratizations of love as "wimpy," weak, mushy, and childish. Supporting these pejoratizations are shoulds to be strong, tough, practical and mature. The third block consists of Inner Critic commands to be distant: "Don't express affection; Don't touch people; Don't get too close; Be self-sufficient."

Each of these mechanisms had been blocking the flow of love that comes from the natural self. Each block could be removed by Anthetic Therapy methods, so that love could flow freely.

The truly revolutionary thing we discovered about love was that when people were able to neutralize these blocks, the love that they expressed seemed quite different from what usually goes by the name love. It was sufficiently different to merit a special name: Anthetic love.

Anthetic Love And Reactive Love

Most people think they know how to love. The truth is, however, that much of the time they are engaging in reactive love: love that is given as a kind of commodity that requires a return; or love that is controlling and possessive; or love that demands that the other person surrender identity and autonomy.

We propose instead the concept of Anthetic love as a new way of thinking about healthy love. Such love consists simply of having warm (or very warm and passionate) feelings about someone. If you express them, you do so only for yourself—simply because it feels good—never because you require love in return. That's all it is: having (and perhaps expressing) loving feelings because it feels good to you, whether you get love back or not.

When our clients learned to do Anthetic processing, the channels were unblocked so this kind of love could flow freely. It felt wonderful to them to have this loving force pervade their lives. It was wonderful for us to see the love expressed, and we wish we had the space here to say more about it.

A book on Anthetic love is in the planning stages; meanwhile, here are some important principles to keep in mind in thinking about this new approach to love:

■ **Anthetic love need not be voiced; it may just be felt.** For example, voicing your love may be misinterpreted by the other person as a sexual invitation or an invitation for mutual commitment, when neither is what you want to express. So you may choose not to say anything at all about it.

■ **Anthetic love must be distinguished from caring behavior.** Whereas it's possible to *love* a great many people, it's usually not possible to engage in *caring behavior* toward them, simply because of time and energy limitations. So Anthetic love may or may not be expressed in caring behavior.

■ **Anthetic love must be distinguished from commitment.** You may voice Anthetic love (and even engage in Anthetic caring) with or without any commitment to continue doing so in the future.

Because it consists simply of feelings, Anthetic love can be expressed unconditionally. Whereas reactive love wants something in return, Anthetic love says, "I radiate my warmth like the sun—because it feels good and for no other reason. You don't have to do anything in return."

Discovery #3
Anthetic Caring

My third discovery was the concept of Anthetic caring: a kind of caring behavior that has its source in Anthetic love and, like such love, is also engaged in simply because it feels good.

Once people learned to process their JAV feelings and once Anthetic love was able to flow freely, that kind of love could serve as the moving force behind Anthetic caring. Thus, caring came from love, not from the Inner Critic; it was felt as a joy, not as a burdensome obligation.[3]

Anthetic Caring
vs.
Reactive Caring

Reactive caring is often called caretaking. It's what codependents do. Here are some of the things this kind of caring means:

■ It may mean taking responsibility for other people's feelings, thoughts, and behavior and trying to "fix" them or rescue them from having negative feelings.

■ It may also mean trying to control other people from an Inner Critic position. A common example is reactive caring for children. Al and Millie, for example, told their 19-year-old daughter Margaret that she was being disrespectful, irresponsible and immature when she went out on dates instead of doing things with the family. "We only want what's best for Margaret," they said. "We love her and care about her." They were unable to see that they were enmeshed with Margaret and felt debuffered each time she behaved autonomously.

Reactive caring such as this comes from the Inner Critic, who requires that children be controlled so they can serve as satisfactory buffers. Anthetic caring, on the other hand, comes from the natural self and is based not on control but on helping children separate from parents and become individuated and autonomous.

Some Comments About Anthetic Caring

Anthetic caring means caring behavior; in general, it means being considerate of others. It also means being willing to give them practical help. It may or may not involve self-sacrifice (e.g., for children, spouse, or others), balanced with taking care of oneself. The point is that if self-sacrifice is engaged in, it expects no reciprocity (unless there is a specific contract for reciprocity); it is done for its own sake. Moreover, it comes not from a martyr position but from love.

Though it's a form of behavior, Anthetic caring requires motivaation through Anthetic love. Anthetic caring is based on empathy and sensitivity to others; it is the essence of genuine considerateness, civililty, politeness, good manners, respect, and courtesy.

Being honest with others is one form of Anthetic caring. This includes telling others what you really feel and what you really like and dislike about them and their behavior. It also means setting boundaries: being able to say No when you wish.

Helping others achieve inner freedom is another form of Anthetic caring. This kind of caring includes being willing to help someone with a problem, concern, or issue instead of saying, "Why talk to me about your problems? I'm not your psychiatrist!"

Anthetic caring is not limited to face-to-face relationships; it includes caring about and having a responsible relationship to your community, your environment, and the whole planet.

Unfortunately, a great many people obey an Inner Critic message that tells them to look out for Number One. If they were to hold moral principles that involve caring, they would be made fun of—and they would fall prey to an additional Inner Critic message: Submerge yourself in the reactive mass of people and conform to what they expect of you. The result is that cynicism, hatred, prejudice, and misanthropy become legitimized, and few people aspire to the individuated greatness necessary to protest against them.

Living A Responsible Life

Living a responsible life means first of all living a principled life instead of a life that is impulse-directed. In addition, the key element in a responsible life is Anthetic caring backed by love. If these elements are in place, a responsible person will be conscientious, dependable, and trustworthy. For example:

■ If a responsible person accepts a project, it will be done on time (or ahead of time).

■ If you lend money to a responsible person, it will be paid back on time, or ahead of time.

■ If a responsible person has problems, she or he will be accountable and will not blame society, or parents, or the Inner Critic.

■ A responsible psychotherapist will engage in procedures that alleviate your emotional suffering, not increase it.

■ A responsible person will not be sarcastic, judgmental, or otherwise verbally abusive.

■ A responsible person will not be self-centered.

In short, living a responsible life means that people can count on you to be caring, to have their best interests at heart, and to be a person of good will.

Why do people pursue irresponsible ways of living? Partly because they have not received moral training, but mostly because their irresponsibility is driven by reactive forces created by the Inner Critic. For example, they live by shoulds to be cool, tough, abrasive, and self-centered. To be concerned about the welfare of others is to be "a softy," "a weakling," and "a sucker." Or so the Inner Critic says.

Discovery #4
Genuine Connectedness

The fourth thing I discovered was that after people learned the Anthetic challenging skills, it became possible for them to learn more advanced skills leading to genuine connectedness with others on a very deep level. They could become close without getting into emotional tangles. They could have what we call a high-voltage relationship: a relationship in which the partners experience intensity and intimacy, while still being free and retaining their own identities.[4] Kathy and I now teach these skills in our Anthetic couple therapy program.

Connectedness vs. Alienation

Alienation might appear to be simply a fact of life; it has become so endemic that it seems normal. We think of alienation as disconnectedness, as knowing only the surfaces of others—the facades—the acts they put on.

As usual, it's the Inner Critic that creates the protective self-structure that keeps us alienated and disconnected from each other. For example, the Inner Critic says things like:

- "Don't get close to others; you'll only be hurt."
- "If you get close, they'll find out what you're really like and reject you."
- "If you get close, you might say something to hurt their feelings, and then you'll feel guilty."

Of course, if your Inner Critic is telling you these things, you may not know it. All you may know is that you seem to be the kind of person who just happens to dislike high voltage: the intensity of being really honest and close.

QUESTION: All this sounds too idealistic to me. Are you sure these goals are possible for people?

ANSWER: True, the goals are difficult, but only to the extent that reactivity gets in the way. The more you work on your Inner Critic, the more realizable the goals become.

Cynicism, generated by the Inner Critic, may lead you to think that achieving this kind of love, caring, and connectedness is so idealistic that you can never accomplish it. Cynicism needs to be challenged like any other Inner Critic belief.

Discovery #5
Critical Thinking As A Prerequisite

One additional thing I learned was the importance of critical thinking skills. If my clients and group members were not able to critique ideas and theories, they found themselves stuck in ideological commitments that were dysfunctional. I also found that it's not enough simply to tell people to think for themselves; they must be taught specifically how to question and evaluate the ideas of various schools of therapy and growth.[5]

The Anthetic Triad

What we have alluded to elsewhere in this book— and what we want to state strongly here—is our belief that the JAV triad is responsible for most, if not all, of the wars, crime, delinquency, exploitation, patriarchy, oppression, prejudice, and other evils in the world.

If we are correct, it follows that a major part of the solution to the problem of evil is the replacement of the JAV triad with what may be called the Anthetic triad: Anthetic love, Anthetic caring, and genuine connectedness.

Discovery #6
How to Reverse The Decline In Morality

Our society's current decline in morality cannot be exhaustively explored here; we mention it only as a reminder of what is all too obvious. It might be thought that this decline results from a weakness of the superego; that is, the Inner Critic. If only people had stronger superegos, it is contended, the threat of guilt and shame would keep them in line, and declining morality would be arrested and ultimately reversed. This position is based on three mistaken assumptions.

The first assumption is that immoral people have no shoulds. Clinical experience has shown that they do. Here are some:

■ "I shouldn't adopt society's values such as working hard to get ahead. Only fools plan for the future, save their money, and delay immediate gratification. I should live spontaneously; if I want something, I should take it. I should be cool and laid back; if that man didn't want his car stolen, he shouldn't have left the keys in it. Only suckers work for a living; smart people lie, cheat, swindle, and steal."

■ "I shouldn't be interested in intellectual pursuits; it's too wimpy. I shouldn't stay in school and get an education; I should drop out like my friends."

■ "I should be macho. I should use physical force to settle arguments, defend my honor, get revenge, and make people respect me."

■ "I should take a cynical and fatalistic view of the world. Nothing good is going to happen to me anyway. I was born to be bad. It doesn't matter much what I do."

The second assumption is that shame and guilt will make people into good citizens. Unfortunately, shame and guilt drive people to get revenge. The shame of the German defeat in World War I, for example, drove Hitler to right the wrongs of the Versailles Treaty so he, along with the Germans with whom he identified, could be rebuffered by conquest and the exercise of power.

The third assumption is that other Inner Critic punishments, like defectiveness and inferiority are innocuous. Such punishments, however, are so painful that they are often projected onto scapegoats, as Hitler did with Jews and as white supremacists do with minorities.

Anthetics As Moral Training

What we're suggesting is that Anthetics is more than the philosophical foundation of a school of therapy: it has turned out to be a new kind of moral training. It does with great elegance and effectiveness what reactive moral training tries to do without much success. (Or when it does succeed, it does so at great cost in creativity and happiness.)

Once JAV feelings are processed, love is liberated; once love is liberated, caring can occur; once love-based caring occurs, people can live in loving harmony with each other.

We want to say again that this whole process is neither automatic nor easy; it simply means that the technology for achieving loving harmony is now available, whereas before it had been a mystery.

There is, of course, one proviso—that one proceed all the way to the end with the Anthetic challenging methods. To explain this, let's take a look at the penultimate and ultimate stages of this work.

People In The Penultimate Stage

In California back in the 1960s and '70s I (Jim) saw a number of people (some of them therapists) who appeared to have achieved inner freedom and who then said, in effect, "From now on I'm looking out for number one. I do my thing, and you do yours, and if you don't satisfy my needs, the hell with you, and I have no reason to try to satisfy your needs."[6]

It was hard for me to understand such people until I saw that although they appeared to be totally free, they were not. What had happened, it seemed to me, was that each had broken through a rigid persona, which had formerly been driven by shoulds. They had removed this "false self" to reveal what they thought was a "true self" underneath. They then believed that whatever happened to be in this "true" layer was authentic and valuable.

The truth was, they hadn't gone deep enough. There were more layers to work through.

The result of this partial work was that they had become only partially free. They were free, for example, to speak their mind, but what this meant was that they had peeled away their facade of "niceness" and now felt free to express the anger, judgmentalism and vengefulness that lay beneath. They thought this was the way to be: blunt, abrasive, self-centered, and inconsiderate. They called this "being authentic." (As you might imagine, their relationships were not very satisfying.)

Although they had become free to express their reactivity, they were not free to be tender, sensitive, loving and caring, nor were they free to live a responsible life.

These people had reached a penultimate stage—a stage that gained them a certain amount of inner freedom, but one that stopped short of an ultimate goal that I will describe a few paragraphs further.

Some of these penultimates had shifted from an uptight, should-directed life to an impulse-directed life. "Don't think about the

266 DISARMING YOUR INNER CRITIC

future," they said. "Live in the here and now: the moment."

As I mentioned above, some of these people became therapists and spiritual teachers, and they taught their clients and students to be impulse-directed. "Get out of your head," they said. "Trust your feelings." "Pursue oneness and spiritual ecstasy." They never mentioned love toward other people. Or caring. Or being responsible citizens.

They were self-centered.

The "Penultimates" In My Groups

I saw some of these penultimates in my early groups: people who had learned the basic challenging skills but who:

■ were angry and judgmental and didn't see this as stuff to work on but instead thought of it as justified and appropriate; and

■ were self-centered and unable to empathize with others.

Often such people had built walls that prevented genuine closeness. They were afraid of love, either to give it or receive it.

These penultimates were unwilling to process the elements of the JAV triad, and so their relationships were characterized by judgmentalism, anger, and vengefulness. This was not very pleasant for their partners.

QUESTION: Why do you label people "penultimates"? That sounds pretty judgmental to me. Why do you have to label people at all?

ANSWER: The term "penultimate" is the equivalent of "a person in the penultimate stage of growth, Anthetically speaking." We use the label to avoid the longer phrase every time we refer to such people. It may sound as though such a label is *inherently* judgmental, but it isn't. It would feel judgmental only because your Inner Critic says so—and because you believe what your Inner Critic tells you. In other words, there's nothing "wrong" in being in a penultimate stage (if you are)—but your Inner Critic may pounce and tell you that you would be bad, defective, and inferior were you to be in this stage.

If, after reading the above, you feel some anger or indignation, that's simply an element in the JAV triad—something to be processed. If you choose to do this processing right now, you can probably get released by saying, "I have the right to be what you call a penultimate. If I am, it doesn't mean I'm a bad person."

The concept of penultimism is designed to help you realize that if you are willing to use Anthetic challenging to process your JAV feelings, you can achieve even more inner freedom. We care about your inner freedom, and we want you to have as much of it as possible.

The concept of JAV processing is also designed to answer questions such as the one asked me (Jim) at a recent lecture: "I know someone who has achieved inner freedom, but he is the most obnoxious person I ever met. Are you sure inner freedom is a good thing?" My answer was, "He's probably a penultimate."

The "Ultimates"

The ultimates among our clients and group members are those who are willing to pursue inner freedom in a thoroughgoing way. Not satisfied with processing their obvious shoulds, they also choose to work on their judgmentalism, anger, and vengefulness.

They also value Anthetic love and Anthetic caring. Like the penultimates, they have been able to get free from the Inner Critic commands that are glaringly apparent. Unlike the penultimates, they are also able to get free from the JAV commands, too, that the penultimates were overlooking. They were able to do this because they saw the JAV elements not as terminal events but as clues to Inner Critic functioning.

The Need For Moral Renewal

A moral crisis is facing humanity. For many people self-centeredness feels so normal that they can't imagine any other way of living. Instead of taking responsibility for their actions, they try to shift the blame to others or to society. People engage in an endless search for power and possessions as buffers. Alcohol and drugs are used to medicate the Inner Critic temporarily, but they destroy the family structure and create irresponsibility and crime.

The emotional, sexual, and physical abuse of children creates new generations of people who are so crippled by their childhood experiences that as adults they are dedicated to the search for vengeance to balance the scales. This growing vengefulness gives rise to a growing crime rate; it has produced Hitlers in the past and will continue to produce new ones in the future. (We call such people barbarians. Not those pounding at the gates, as in ancient history, but those among us.)

Our planetary civilization requires a moral renewal. Democracy is only the first step in this renewal; by itself it is not sufficient to solve our problems.[7] In addition, a free enterprise system is also a first step. Both democracy and free enterprise are what we call process structures—open frameworks that are prerequisites to a good society but that may be filled out either by reactive or nonreactive elements.

If we do not allow a new and more positive moral dynamic to be expressed through these structures and in our everyday lives, we may destroy ourselves. The goal of society must be neither self-centered individualism nor mindless submergence in a collectivity. Each has been tried, and each has been a dismal failure.

We cannot solve our problems simply by passing new laws. Our moral crisis cries out for a deeper transformation of character, so that positive values can pervade our whole society and provide a strong source of guidance for our lives.

If there is one lesson that this book teaches, it is that the effects of the Inner Critic are more than a minor annoyance. Those effects include most of the ills of our society.

Our narcissistic culture must be transformed into a socially responsible and caring one; we must create new norms and values that liberate our creative energies and encourage the unfolding and blossoming of everyone. We must legitimize the pursuit of individual greatness instead of trying to level everyone down to an average mediocrity.

Anthetics is offered not just as the source of a school of psychotherapy but also as a philosophy of life that calls for moral renewal. It proposes that people live a principled life, not an impulse-directed life. It points the way to a new type of moral character that preserves individuality and at the same time leads to sensitive and caring relationships.

Most important, it presents not a series of preachments and exhortations but a transformative technology that can benefit people the instant they begin using it.

Our society seems to be at the end of a long cycle of development that has seen the unfolding of all the implications of a materialist symbolic.[8] We have exhausted the philosophical re-

TOWARD A NEW FOUNDATION FOR MORALITY 269

sources of that symbolic, and our realization of its bankruptcy is manifested in two trends: our fascination by exotic but mindless cults and our fruitless attempts to recover moral certainties appropriate to the past but unsuited to the future.

Human consciousness is at the point in its evolution where it can choose to take a quantum leap forward into a new way of being. If it can avoid both mindlessness and regression to the past, it can give birth to an extraordinary new kind of human culture. Anthetics is offered as the best pathway to that culture.[9]

NOTES

1. JAV feelings are, however, valid, legitimate, and appropriate in the sense of being acceptable ("It's okay to feel them"), and they are normal in the sense that everyone has them. *[From p. 257]*

2. We've been able to identify five types of anger. What we're talking about here is "failed-trade" anger. The other four types (to be presented in a later book) are: black hole anger, entitlement anger, trappedness anger, and self-image disconfirmation anger. *[From p. 257]*

3. Note that Anthetic caring means caring *behavior*. Once you distinguish Anthetic love from Anthetic caring, you can experience love without necessarily expressing it. You can also experience and express love without necessarily engaging in caring behavior. *[From p. 259]*

4. Anthetic concepts of connectedness are closely related to the relational self theory being developed at the Stone Center in Wellesley, Mass. See Surrey (1984) and Kaplan & Surrey (1984). *[From p. 262]*

5. In 1973 I (Jim) created the new discipline of Anthetic Philosophy and added it to my work with clients and groups. Anthetic Philosophy is the application to everyday life of concepts and methods drawn from the field of philosophy. *[From p. 263]*

6. Those familiar with the work of Fritz Perls will recognize this adaptation of his Gestalt Prayer. *[From p. 265]*

7. Although it's the best system around, democracy is simply a formal structure, empty of content. If this structure is to provide us with an optimally-functioning society, it must be informed by a positive morality. Democracy is like a blank purchase order; we must be careful how we fill it in. *[From p. 268]*

8. See Spengler (1939) and Sorokin (1941) for discussions of the historical cycle that is now ending. *[From p. 268]*

9. We are aware of the programmatic nature of this chapter. A book that will present these ideas in greater detail is in the planning stages. *[From p. 269]*

18

Some Final Words

WE ARE NOW NEARING THE END of the journey that we began in Chapter 1. In this book we have presented the Anthetic model that thousands of people have found to be powerfully effective in overcoming personal problems and achieving happiness and fulfillment.

It is our hope that this book has helped you acquire a better understanding of yourself through the new perspective offered here. Now that you have almost finished the book, we'd like to talk about some responses you may have to the material that has been presented. Here are some possibilities, along with our comments:

■ You may say "I don't have an Inner Critic." If this is the case, we have not succeeded in our task of explaining that you do have one (we all do) and that your Inner Critic is simply so hidden that you think you don't. We hope that some day you may realize that you do indeed have an Inner Critic, and that it's just part of being human.

■ You may say "I do have an Inner Critic, but it can't be that bad; I need it sometimes as a guide and motivator." If this is your response, then we have failed to persuade you of the emotional suffering that comes from even a partial acceptance of the Inner Critic as a guide to living. We can only hope that you may come to realize the fact that much of your mental anguish and psychological pain —and many of your seemingly unsolvable personal problems—are

SOME FINAL WORDS 271

connected with your belief that your Inner Critic can somehow be useful.

■ You may say "Now that I understand how my Inner Critic has been sabotaging my life, and I see all the disadvantages of being guided by it, I want to begin getting free from it as soon as possible." If this is your response, our work has been done well. We hope you will indeed begin, either with a mental health professional who has been trained in Anthetic Therapy or in an Anthetic training group.

We want to assure you that it's common for people to say, "I didn't see how powerful an influence the Inner Critic was until I had an actual experience of Anthetic Dialogue. The more of this work I do, the more I see how my Inner Critic has blocked me—in ways I never realized. It was only when I got free that I could look back and see how unfree I was—without knowing it."

More Questions People Ask

QUESTION: Why do you criticize other writers? Why not let your work stand on its own?

ANSWER: Many writers let their work "stand on its own" to such an extent that they rarely mention the work of their colleagues or predecessors. Instead, they write from a decontextualized position. The result is that they appear to be reinventing a number of psychotherapeutic wheels.

We chose not to do that. We want to show how our work is connected to the work of others. If our ideas are in agreement with others' work, we say that; if our ideas contradict those of others, we say that, too. It seems to us unfair to the reader not to make these connections.

QUESTION: Why do you lump so many characteristics together in the concept of the Inner Critic?

ANSWER: Some of the characteristics we have ascribed to the Inner Critic may indeed seem at first glance not to belong together. The Inner Critic criticizes, commands, inflicts punishment, interferes with performance, predicts catastrophe, pressures people into doing things, makes people depressed, keeps them isolated from others, and makes them take responsibility for others' negative feelings. Each of these seems different. And as we mentioned in

272 DISARMING YOUR INNER CRITIC

Chapter 2, a better name for the Inner Critic might be "Inner Saboteur." But our clients and group members found this term too unwieldy. They liked the term "Inner Critic," and it made sense to them to apply it to a single source of all the negative influences. To put this another way: when you spot any negative belief you have, it's useful to see it as resulting from one source: your Inner Critic.

QUESTION: Whatever you call it, how do you know it's only one inner figure?

ANSWER: It may not be. We call it by a single name for two reasons: First, the single name reflects a single general function: sabotage. Second, years of clinical practice show that calling it by a single name seems to be the best way to work with it through Anthetic challenging. We have no objection, however, to analyzing it into different inner figures—e.g., Critic, Punisher, Catastrophe-Predictor, Pusher, Depressor, Isolater, Responsibility-Prescriber. It seems to make little difference from an ontological standpoint whether these are seen as separate inner figures or aspects of one inner figure.

QUESTION: Why do you sometimes state things so dogmatically?

ANSWER: The term dogma refers to a statement that is presented as an article of faith, neither supported by empirical evidence nor falsifiable by any evidence that might possibly be presented. Far from being dogmatic, the ideas in this book are based on more than 30 years of clinical research into what works and what doesn't. Though presented with a certain firmness and confidence, each idea is strictly provisional—that is, subject to revision should it prove to be wrong.

QUESTION: Will Anthetic challenging eliminate my Inner Critic?

ANSWER: Anthetic challenging won't totally eliminate your Inner Critic. It's inevitable that your Inner Critic will pounce from time to time, making you feel scared, depressed, defective, ashamed, inferior, and guilty. Anthetic challenging simply gives you tools so you can work your way out of these negative feelings. And, ultimately, Anthetic Therapy will give you methods to open your heart so you can love others and receive love from them.

SOME FINAL WORDS 273

QUESTION: Will Anthetic challenging make me more human?
ANSWER: Anthetic challenging is not about becoming human; you are perfectly human right this minute—with all your hangups, problems, and negative feelings. That's the way humans are.

QUESTION: Then what will Anthetic challenging help me accomplish?
ANSWER: It will help you accept your humanness, thereby reducing inner conflict and turmoil. As it helps you get free from the oppressive and constricting forces of your Inner Critic, it will enable you to access and deploy the resources, talents, and vitality of your natural self.

QUESTION: Will Anthetic challenging make me happy?
ANSWER: Yes. The more you live from your natural self, undistorted by reactivity, the more you will be able to seek out and enjoy all the things in your life that will give you true happiness—whereas before you were blocked by your Inner Critic.

QUESTION: Will Anthetic challenging eliminate all my suffering?
ANSWER: No. For example, it won't eliminate any physical suffering. Nor will it eliminate some forms of empathic suffering; as, for example, when you empathize with someone's pain. And it will have only a moderate effect on feelings of abandonment that come from your Black Hole. Anthetic challenging will, however, reduce the pain and suffering that come from the emotional punishments that are inflicted by your Inner Critic.

QUESTION: Don't you think that life just has its ups and downs? That happiness comes and goes when it wants to?
ANSWER: Our years of experience doing counseling and therapy have taught us that happiness is not capricious. It occurs when reactive unhappiness is reduced or eliminated.

QUESTION: Don't you think you promise too much when you say we can all be happy all the time—or even a lot of the time?
ANSWER: We're certainly not saying that using the Anthetic challenging methods described here means you'll be happy all the time. The challenging methods are just one part of Anthetic

274 DISARMING YOUR INNER CRITIC

Therapy. They are simply the first step in working your way out of the unhappiness generated by your Inner Critic. However, we do say that the more you do this work, the happier you will be. If you can do it almost all the time, you'll be happy almost all the time.

However, additional steps are needed, too. You may need to do prototype work, unearthing and challenging the sources of dysfunctional beliefs in early childhood. You may need to work on your Black Hole—the part of you that feels pain when you don't get enough love. And you'll need to work on Inner Figure Orchestration—deployment skills for focusing the energies that are liberated when you challenge your Inner Critic.

QUESTION: It seems to me that your methods simply strengthen the ego. Don't you think the ego needs to be transcended, not strengthened?

ANSWER: It depends on what you mean by ego; the term has many meanings. If you equate "ego" with "reactive self" (a definition we highly recommend), then of course the ego should not be strengthened. It needs not only to be transcended but replaced.

On the other hand, suppose we equate "ego" with "natural self." Then the natural self does need to be strengthened—but you need to be capable of transcending it, too, in the sense of disengaging from it and reflecting on it.. In fact, the process of Anthetic liberation is a method leading to radical transcendence.

A third possibility is to equate "ego" with "transcendental self." Then the ego cannot, in principle, be transcended, since it is that which does the transcending.

QUESTION: I still can't quite believe that I have an Inner Critic, or that it's causing most of my problems, or that your methods will work. Is there anything helpful you can tell me?

ANSWER: Many people find the Anthetic challenging methods so useful that they can see right away how the Inner Critic has been oppressing them—and how to get free from it. Others find the methods so difficult that they can't even see how the Inner Critic functions in their lives, let alone get free from it. Unfortunately, there's a limit to how much help a book can give; actual experience with Anthetic Dialogue is needed.

It's not uncommon for people to say "I couldn't understand this whole approach until I actually did some of the challenging with my therapist guiding me."

QUESTION: Is there a place for religion and spirituality in Anthetics?

ANSWER: Yes. The only reason for omitting this topic is that there is not enough space in this book. There are powerful connections between Anthetics and spirituality, and this issue will be addressed in a future book.

QUESTION: Can I do this work on my own?

ANSWER: Many people have asked this question. Our answer is that while it's possible to make a *beginning* by yourself, the Inner Critic can be so subtle that you'll need the help of a trained professional to continue the work. So this book is designed as something of a road map—as an introduction to and supplement to Anthetic Therapy, not a substitute for it.

When people have tried to do extensive Inner Critic work on their own, they have later discovered that some elements of the Inner Critic's oppression have become unconsciously woven into the work they've done. Once you have thoroughly learned the Anthetic challenging skills, however, either in a group or in one-to-one counseling or therapy, you can continue to do Inner Critic work on your own—although you'll find that a support group will be enormously helpful.

From Old Self To New Self

It's common for people to speak of the contrast between the new self that is emerging as a result of Anthetic Therapy and the old self that existed before it. "My girlfriend got angry at me last night," said Craig. "If this had been my old self, I'd have just said the hell with it and written her off. But now that I know how to work on my Inner Critic, I made some releasing statements, and they shifted me into a different place, and we began talking rationally."

Comments From Clients And Group Members

■ "Before I learned about my Inner Critic," Margaret said, "I knew that something was wrong, but I didn't know what it was, and

I didn't know what to do about it. Now that I have some understanding of my Inner Critic and some ways of working with it, I know what the problem is and I know exactly what to do about it."

■ "I'm working on my Inner Critic now," said Maria, "and I'm a little bit OK now. About ten percent. Before, I was very seldom and only slightly all right. I've made some progress. I know I've got a lot more to do, but I know what it is I have to do now."

■ "When I came here," said Bob, "I was all set to kill myself. It was only a matter of when. Life was pretty bad. I even gave away my books and records. And then I learned to work on my Inner Critic. Now it's hard to remember that I wanted to commit suicide. I still feel lousy once in a while, but now I know that's just my Inner Critic. You know, it feels weird to think I'm making plans for the future. I didn't use to do that."

■ When Angie dialogued with her Inner Critic, the name she gave it was Satan. "It's like I made a deal with the devil," she said. "To live I have to have the approval of others, so I said, 'Satan, I'll sell you my soul and give up being a person if you'll just let me avoid everyone's anger and criticism. I'll be a zombie; I'll live just to please others.'

"And there's more. 'If I didn't listen to you, Satan, nobody would take care of me; I'd be shunned by everyone; I'd die an emotional death.'"

I (Jim) asked Angie to tell Satan what she thought of that bargain.

"I don't like that bargain at all," she said. "I can take care of myself; I don't need others' approval. I don't have to numb myself and be a zombie. It's my birthright to be a real person. I cancel that agreement. I'm going to live the way I want from now on, as much as I can."

■ After two months in an Anthetic training group, Megan told us, "I thought for a while this way of working would keep me from ever getting depressed, and when I got depressed, I thought, 'Oh, my God, it's not working!' But that's not what it's about. It's not so you'll *never* get depressed; it's so when you do get depressed, you'll have some way of getting yourself back to being happy."

■ "I no longer want to pretzelize myself," said Dan, "by reactively caring so much about what other people think. If they don't like who I really am, I don't want their approval anyway. I only want the love and approval of people who love and approve of the full me."

■ "I've been in the Anthetics program for about three months now, and I've gotten in touch with a lot of my shoulds, and it's really been blowing my mind," said Zoe. "I didn't know that a lot of the things I thought I wanted were just shoulds. And when I work on them and challenge my Inner Critic, I can feel my shoulders relax. My son says, 'Hey, Ma, there's something different about you. You're calmer.'"

■ "I think about my former life," said Ralph, "like it was B.A.—Before Anthetics. My life was on a treadmill. I wasn't very happy. Now I wake up each day looking forward to what adventures I'm going to have. Life is exciting."

■ "Before I came to this group," said Bert, "I thought it was normal not to be happy. Not to feel joyful. So when I started feeling good, it was a bit of an uncomfortable thing for me. My Inner Critic was getting on my case, telling me to watch out and be careful, not to be too happy, because I'll come crashing down. So I had one more thing to challenge. After I did that, I began to feel even happier. It was so new and strange, I didn't know how to handle it. But I learned."

■ Sam summed up what many people have reported as a result of Inner Critic work: "It's great! I feel like I've given birth to a new way of being that will have its own development from now on."

A Final Note

Our journey together is now over. As we mentioned in the beginning, this is a book to be used in conjunction with Anthetic Therapy sessions. Right now, all it can give you, perhaps, is a taste of what this new way of personal transformation is like.

The central message of this book is one of inner liberation; we hope you find Anthetics a useful way of thinking about your own progress toward such liberation.

If you would like information about Certified Anthetic Therapists in your area, or about our Training Program for Mental Health Professionals, please call or write:

ANTHETICS INSTITUTE
P.O. Box 81097
Lafayette, LA 70598-1097
(318) 234-8221 or (337) 234-8221

19

Epilogue: The Rat Story

ONCE UPON A TIME THERE WAS a very young rat who lived in a psychological laboratory. He didn't know it was a laboratory, of course; he thought it was "the world." In any case, he learned to run through any maze in the laboratory and wind up with the cheese very quickly. He was a clever rat.

When he was a little older, he was put at the entrance to a new kind of maze. This maze had lots of wrong turnings and also certain hazards: swampy places he had to struggle through, narrow openings he had to wriggle through, and obstacles he had to push his way through by poking at them with his little pink nose. He learned to do these things, too, and was still able to get to the cheese very quickly.

Finally, when he was a grown up rat, he was put in an even more complicated maze. Not only were there wrong turnings, swampy places, narrow openings, and obstructions to break through—there were also a very large number of branchings he could take, some of which were dead ends.

But since he was a very bright rat, he got through almost all the obstacles. Only one remained. He had discovered a passageway that seemed to lead to the very end of the maze. And then he came to a plate of clear glass through which he could see a large piece of delicious cheese. If only he could get through this last barrier!

He poked at it with his little pink nose, but it didn't give way. All that happened was that his nose started to hurt. When he thought about this, he said to himself, "I'm so close to the cheese, all I need is to make a few more pokes." So he did, but his nose just started hurting more.

At the suggestion of a friend, he went to a rat psychotherapist, who listened very sympathetically and suggested that the rat learn to become more adjusted to the pain and realize that trying to avoid pain was a bit unrealistic. "The pain you are feeling," said the psychotherapist, "is a necessary part of your struggle. It's an existential condition, and you must learn to adjust to it." But although this helped temporarily, the rat couldn't seem to adjust. Every time he returned to the glass panel, he kept trying to break through it, and his nose kept hurting, and he didn't like it.

The rat had read a lot of books on maze-running, breaking through glass plates, and overcoming nose pain. While most of the books provided detailed descriptions of these problems, they had little to say about how to overcome them. Many of the writers of the books said they just didn't have all the answers and even suggested that a search for answers was wrong. "There's no magic way out of this," the writers would say. Mostly, they suggested getting into a support group, going to lectures, and reading even more books. They also suggested "letting go of pain" or "banishing it" or "rising above it." The rat tried these strategies, but none of them worked.

Finally, the rat came across a book whose title was "Getting to the Cheese by Backing Out of the Maze." "No, no," the rat thought indignantly. He felt contempt for such a simplistic idea. "I've spent my whole life learning maze work, and I'm not about to give that up now. Besides, I've gone through all these hazards to get to the cheese compartment. The only thing that prevents me from final success is that silly glass plate. I can't back out; I've got too much invested. Backing out is just not me; I'm not a quitter. Besides, what would the other rats think if they saw me backing out of the maze? They'd think I was a fool."

And so the rat kept bumping his nose against the glass panel.

And he never did get to the cheese.

And he suffered from a lot of pain.

And he wondered why life was so hard.

Because the truth was that all he had to do was back out of the maze and go around to where the cheese was and eat all he wanted.

As you may have already gathered, the book you are holding in your hands could well be titled "How to Get The Cheese by Backing out of The Maze."

Appendix A:
Training Programs

Anthetics Institute offers a variety of workshops, seminars, and classes for both professionals and nonprofessionals. Presented throughout the United States, Canada, and England, these programs provide participants with practical tools they can use to increase insight, effectiveness, peace of mind, and deep joy and satisfaction in everyday living. Programs are scheduled as all-day sessions, weekends, or longer. The skills you'll learn can be used the rest of your life so your growth can continue after the training session is over.

For more information, write to Anthetics Institute, P.O. Box 81097, Lafayette, LA 70598, or call (318) 234-8221 or (337) 234-8221]. Or E-mail us at Anthetics@AOL.com.

■ Disarming Your Inner Critic

DYIC offers intensive training in the methods and ideas presented in this book, with opportunities for supervised work in disarming your Inner Critic.

■ Anthetics: A Psychotherapy-Based Way of Life

This program might well be called "What do you do after you've become liberated?" It presents methods for choosing a principled life based not on the sado-masochistic morality so commonly found in our society but on Anthetic morality: the morality of love, connectedness, and genuinely caring and responsible behavior.

Three types of philosophy of life will be discussed: Type I, based on revelation; Type II, based on the personal intuitions of its founder; and Type III, based on clinical practice. The workshop will explain how Anthetic Therapy can serve as the foundation for satisfaction.

In other words, because of its scope and depth, and because of the fact that it teaches skills, Anthetic Therapy transcends the symptom-by-symptom approach used by conventional therapies.

Special attention will be given to methods of critical thinking so you can evaluate the pronouncements of "the authorities," as well as the ideas of Anthetics itself. In addition, an expanded ontology will be presented in terms that are philosophically respectable as well as understandable by the average person.

Of special importance is Anthetic Spirituality, a unifying meta-spiritual framework within which any specific religion, religious practice, or religious belief may be evaluated. This pioneering approach offers practical ideas that are sensitive to your spiritual needs and at the same time are in harmony with the principles of empiricism. In other words, we offer deeply moving experiences based on the reality of a "supernatural" realm which is still quite natural.

As you might imagine, the loving God, not the "Inner Critic" god, is a feature of this new approach to spirituality. The emphasis, however, is not on whether God loves us but on how God is the source of love that flows through us to others. A surprising new (and thoroughly empirically grounded) definition of God will be offered, which leads to new understandings of traditional religious concepts.

■ Professional Training Program In Anthetic Therapy

Unlike other professional programs, this one does not simply offer a set of techniques that can be added to whatever the therapist is currently doing. Instead, it requires considerable work on oneself in order to eliminate the influences of the Inner Critic. Otherwise, these influences will be unconsciously woven into the work done, and the client may feel even worse after the session is over.

Prerequisites for admission to the program are at least state licensure as a Mental Health Counselor or equivalent (e.g., Marriage and Family Therapist; Licensed Professional Counselor). Please write for a detailed description if you are interested in this program.

Appendix B:
The High-Voltage Relationship®

VOLTAGE IS A CONCEPT WE DEVELOPED in our couple counseling work, and our couples have found it useful in understanding their relationships. At one time we thought that every couple wanted the most optimal relationship possible: the High-Voltage Relationship (HVR). We found, however, that some couples wanted a less intense Low-Voltage Relationship (LVR).

Let's take a look at the meaning of high voltage. First of all, it does not refer to dramatic emotionality, histrionics, impulsivity, agitation, uncontrolled expressiveness, or having stormy arguments. Nor does it always refer to passionate love. It doesn't even necessarily refer to ecstatic sexuality. Instead, high voltage is characterized by the following:

■ An everyday emotional intensity that is often experienced as thrilling.

■ Deep and freely-flowing love that is easily expressed in words. HV couples can easily say "I love you," and they say it often—usually several times a day.

HV partners like hearing the question, "Do you love me?", and they respond quickly in the affirmative. An LV partner, on the other hand, finds it difficult to express love. If asked "Do you love me," the LV partner may say, "I told you once, and I'm tired of your asking all the time. If I didn't love you, I wouldn't be here, would I? Stop being so insecure."

■ Genuine connectedness. HV partners respond directly. Responses of LV partners are often vague, evasive, and tangential. Often LVs do not respond to topics or even answer questions.

■ Lots of affectionate touching.

■ The desire for a conscious relationship; one in which each partner has a strong desire to analyze and reflect on what is said or done instead of saying "let's just immerse ourselves in life and not stand back and think too much about it."

- The desire for total immersion in life once the analysis and reflection are concluded.
- Wanting to be with your partner as much as possible. LV partners, on the other hand, often say "I need my space" or "I need to go into my cave." They have frequent nights out with the boys (or girls). They may have separate beds or bedrooms. Each person has her or his own separate interests. For example, the husband is interested in sports, hunting, fishing, and going out with the boys. The wife has her church groups, her woman friends, and the children.

HV partners like to do things together.
- HV sexuality is passionate, creative, and constantly exploring new possibilities. HV partners sometimes like to make appointments for sex, so they have something exciting to look forward to for several hours in advance. Most important, HV partners like to talk to each other about their sexual relationship, saying what they like and don't like.

LV partners like standard sex—or not much sex at all. When they do have sex, they like it to be always unplanned and "spontaneous." (NOTE: Sex is not a necessary part of the HV relationship. Friends can have HVRs, as can parents and children.)
- HV partners engage in lots of talk about here-and-now feelings about each other, usually positive but sometimes negative, too. HV partners can handle the "voltage" of feeling-talk. They can listen to negative feelings without becoming defensive or angry.
- HV partners like to talk a lot about their relationship. They like to talk about what they like and dislike about it and how they might improve it.
- LV people typically handle arguments by withdrawing. HV people handle them by processing negative feelings, then negotiating.

We also found that if couples are evenly matched in voltage, their problems were relatively easy to solve. For example, if marriages are LV-LV or HV-HV, they have a good chance of succeeding.

Serious problems may occur, however, when the relationship is LV-HV. The HV becomes the pursuer, demanding that the LV open up, listen more, connect more, be more loving, be more affectionate, and spend more time together. However, the more demanding the HV becomes, the more the LV withdraws. The LV is usually (but not always) the husband, and he typically says "I feel suffocated," "I need my space," and/or "You're too demanding." This is the typical Pursuer-Distancer pattern that is described as a mystery in the literature.

Most couple counselors, as well as the experts who write retionship books, will tell you that the husband simply needs more space (or needs to retire to his "cave"). The wife then thinks there's something wrong with her to need so much closeness, and she does her best to cultivate other interests.

Unfortunately, many couple counselors and authors of books on relationships happen to be Distancers. They're LVs. And the advice they give is usually contaminated by their LV reactivity.
They advise more distance. They say: "Realize that your partner needs his space. He must retreat to his cave. Realize that you're the one with the problem: you're too needy."

We're here to tell you there's nothing wrong with you if you want an HV relationship. You're feeling needy because your partner lacks the skills for handling all the voltage you long for.

What skills are needed? Inner Critic challenging is the most important one. A partner with a strong Inner Critic will find it impossible to handle high voltage.

Our workshops entitled "The High-Voltage Relationship," are designed to help LVs overcome their blocks to high voltage. (We also help HVs reduce their judgmentalism, which they mistakenly believe is necessary in order to get more intimacy and intensity in the relationship.)

Appendix C:
"Psychotherapy Today"

Consider these topics:
- **Hypnosis:** Does it really work? Are there any dangers?
- **Redecision Therapy**—An offshoot of Transactional Analysis, RT seems to be an important ingredient in any psychotherapy. Is it more effective than TA? How does it compare with Decision Therapy?
- **Solution-Focused Therapy.** It looks simple and effective, but does it leave out important elements?
- **Philosophical Counseling.** Most therapists lack a philosophical dimension to their work. PC offers this dimension, but is it too intellectual? And does it really help people?
- **Recovery, Inc.:** It's free to anyone, but are there disadvantages?

PSYCHOTHERAPY TODAY is a new four-page quarterly bulletin, the purpose of which is to bring you information on topics such as these. Aimed at both professionals and non-professionals, PT will be full of useful information about the many therapies that are currently available, including new ones being created almost every month. Each school of therapy will be evaluated from an Anthetic standpoint. (Plans call for increasing the number of pages and frequency of publication as soon as possible.)

Each issue will describe and analyze one school of therapy. In addition, an article section will deal with such topics as research on therapeutic effectiveness, nuggets of helpful information from the professional journals, and recent developments in our own Anthetic Therapy. (Would you be surprised to learn that some seemingly positive religious doctrines—for example, The Golden Rule—can lead to dysfunctional relationships?)

If you'd like more information about PSYCHOTHERAPY TODAY, please write us at P.O. Box 81097, Lafayette, LA 70598.

References

Adler, Alfred (1969). *The science of living.* New York: Doubleday.
Adler, Alfred (1973). *Superiority and social interest.* New York: Viking.
Ansbacher, Heinz, & Ansbacher, Rowena (1964). *The individual psychology of Alfred Adler.* New York: Harper.
Assagioli, Roberto (1965). *Psychosynthesis.* New York: Hobbs, Dorman.
Bach, George R. (1985). *The inner enemy.* New York: Berkley Books.
Bandler, Richard (1985). *Using your brain— for a change.* Moab, UT: Real People Press.
Bartlett, F. C. (1932). *Remembering: A study in experimental and social psychology.* Cambridge, UK: Cambridge University Press.
Baumgardner, Patricia (1975). *Legacy from Fritz.* Palo Alto, CA: Science & Behavior Books.
Bergler, Edmund (1957). *The psychology of gambling.* New York: Hill & Wang.
Bergler, Edmund (1962). *Tensions can be reduced to nuisances.* New York: Crowell-Collier.
Berne, Eric. (1961). *Transactional analysis in psychotherapy.* New York: Grove Press.
Berne, Eric. (1964). *Games people play.* New York: Grove Press.
Berne, Eric (1973). *What do you say after you say hello?* New York: Bantam Books.
Bradshaw, John (1988). *Healing the shame that binds you.* Deerfield Beach, FL: Health Communications, Inc.
Branden, Nathaniel (1987). *How to raise your self-esteem.* New York: Bantam Books.
Butler, Pamela E. (1981). *Talking to yourself.* New York: Harper & Row.
Campbell, Colin (1974, August). You're too kind: The consequences of compliments. *Psychology Today,* p. 43.
Campbell, Susan M. (1984). *Beyond the power struggle.* San Luis Obispo, CA: Impact Publishers.
Carson, R. D. (1983). *Taming your gremlin.* New York: Harper & Row.
Clance, Pauline R. (1985). *The impostor phenomenon: Overcoming the fear that*

haunts your success. Atlanta: Peachtree Publishers.

Coopersmith, Stanley (1967). *The antecedents of self-esteem.* San Francisco: W. H. Freeman & Co.

Cornell, Ann Weiser (1993). *The focusing guide's manual* (3rd ed.). Berkeley, CA: Focusing Resources.

Dusay, John M. (1977). *Egograms.* New York: Harper & Row.

Eidelberg, Ludwig (ed.) (1968). *Encyclopedia of psychoanalysis.* New York: The Free Press.

Elliott, James E. (1969). Growing edge groups. *The Group Leader's Workshop,* #2.

Elliott, James E. (1976). *Personal growth through interaction* (also titled: *The theory and practice of encounter group leadership*). Berkeley, CA: Explorations Institute.

Elliott, James E. (1991). Defusing conceptual fusions: The 'just because' technique. *Journal of Cognitive Psychotherapy, 5,* 227-229.

Elliott, James E. (1992a). Compensatory buffers, depression, and irrational beliefs. *Journal of Cognitive Psychotherapy, 6,* 175-184.

Elliott, James E. (1992b). Use of Anthetic dialogue in eliciting and allenging dysfunctional beliefs. *Journal of Cognitive Psychotherapy, 6,* 137-143.

Elliott, James E. (1994). Using releasing statements to challenge shoulds. *Journal of of Cognitive Psychotherapy, 7,* 291-296.

Elliott, James E. (1995). Three challenges to conventional thinking about "shoulds." *Journal of Mental Health Counseling, 8,* 89-95.

Elliott, Kathy J. (1995). The WILFY method: Unlearning lessons from the past. *Journal of Cognitive Psychotherapy, 9,* 259-266.

Ellis, Albert (1962). *Reason and emotion in psychotherapy.* Secaucus, NJ: Citadel Press.

Ellis, Albert (1979). The practice of rational-emotive therapy. In A. Ellis and J. M. Whiteley (Eds.), *Theoretical and empirical foundations of rational-emotive therapy* (pp. 61-100). Monterey, CA: Brooks/Cole.

Ellis, Albert (1990). *How to stubbornly refuse to make yourself miserable about anything—yes, anything!* New York: Carol Publishing Group.

Ellis, Albert; McInerney, John; DiGiuseppe, Raymond; & Yeager, Raymond (1988). *Rational-emotive therapy with alcoholics and substance abusers.* Elmsford, NY: Pergamon Press.

Ellis, Albert, and Yeager, Raymond J. (1989). *Why some therapies don't work.* New York: Prometheus Books.

Evans, C. O. (1970). *The subject of consciousness.* New York: Humanities Press.
Fantz, Rainette. (1975). Polarities: differentiation and integration. In F. Douglas Stephenson (Ed.), *Gestalt therapy primer.* Springfield, IL: Charles C Thomas.
Farmer, Steven (1989). *Adult children of abusive parents.* Los Angeles: Lowell House.
Fenichel, Otto (1945). *The psychoanalytic theory of neurosis.* New York: Norton.
Freud, Sigmund (1900/1955). *The interpretation of dreams.* New York: Basic Books.
Freud, Sigmund (1914/1949). On narcissism: An introduction. *The international psycho-analytic library*, vol. 4. London: The Hogarth Press.
Freud, Sigmund (1915/1957). The unconscious. *The international psycho-analytic library*, vol. 14. London: The Hogarth Press.
Freud, Sigmund (1923/1949). The ego and the id. *The international psycho-analytic library*, vol. 12. London: The Hogarth Press.
Freud, Sigmund (1928/1964). Dostoevsky and parricide. *The international psycho-analytic library*, Vol. 21. London: The Hogarth Press.
Friel, John C., & Friel, Linda D. (1988). Adult children. Deerfield Beach, FL: Health Communications, Inc.
Goulding, Mary M., & Goulding, Robert L. (1979). *Changing lives through redecision therapy.* New York: Brunner/Mazel.
Grof, Stanislav (1985). *Beyond the brain.* New York, NY: State University of New York Press.
Handly, Robert, & Handly, Jane (1990). *Why women worry...and how to stop.* New York: Prentice Hall.
Harvey, Joan (1985). *If I'm so successful, why do I feel like a fake?* New York: Random House.
Heidegger, Martin (1962). *Being and time.* San Francisco: Harper.
Heidegger, Martin (1966). *Discourse on thinking.* New York: Harper & Row.
Horney, Karen (1950). *Neurosis and human growth.* New York: Norton.
Hume, David (1978). *A treatise of human nature.* Oxford: Clarendon Press.
Husserl, Edmund (1960). *Cartesian meditations.* The Hague: Nijhoff.
Janov, Arthur, & Holden, E. Michael (1975). *Primal man: The new consciousness.* New York: Crowell.
Kant, Immanuel (1900). *Critique of pure reason.* New York: Co-operative Publication Society.
Kaplan, A. G., & Surrey, A. L. (1984). The relational self in women: Developmental theory and public policy. In L. E. Walker (Ed.), *Women and*

mental health policy (pp. 79-94). Beverly Hills, CA: Sage.

Kaufman, Gershen (1989). *The psychology of shame.* New York: Springer.

Keyes, Ken (1979). *A conscious person's guide to relationships.* St. Mary, KY: Living Love Publications.

Keyes, Ken (1987). *Gathering power through insight and love.* Coos Bay, OR: Living Love Publications.

Kurtz, Ernest. (1981). *Shame and guilt: characteristics of the dependency cycle.* Center City, MN: Hazelden Foundation.

Latner, Joel (1973). *The gestalt therapy book.* New York: The Julian Press.

Laughlin, Henry P. (1970). *The ego and its defenses.* New York: Appleton-Century-Crofts.

McGavin, Barbara (1994). The "victim," the "critic," and the inner relationship: Focusing with the part that wants to die. *The Focusing Connection, 11,* pp. 3-5.

McKay, Matthew; & Fanning, Patrick (1987). *Self-esteem.* Oakland, CA: New Harbinger.

Mahrer, Alvin (1989). *Experiencing: A humanistic theory of psychology and psychiatry.* Ottawa: University of Ottawa Press.

Maslow, Abraham (1962). *Toward a psychology of being.* Princeton, NJ: Van Nostrand.

Maslow, Abraham (1970). *New knowledge in human values.* Washington, DC: Regnery Gateway, Inc.

Maslow, Abraham (1971). *The farther reaches of human nature.* New York: Viking.

May, Rollo. (1939). *The art of counseling.* New York: Abingdon Press.

May, Rollo. (1958). Contributions of Existential Psychotherapy. in May, R., Angel, E. & Ellenberger, H. (Eds.) *Existence, a new dimension in psychiatry and psychology.* New York: Basic Books.

Mellody, Pia (1989). *Facing codependence.* San Francisco: Harper & Row.

Paul, Louis. (1970). The cruel inner critic. *Psychotherapy: Theory, Research and Practice. 7,* 178-180.

Peale, Norman Vincent (1992, April). Trust your censor. *Plus: The Magazine of Positive Thinking,* pp. 14-23.

Peck, M. Scott. (1983). *People of the lie.* New York: Simon & Schuster.

Pepper, Stephen C. (1961). *World Hypotheses.* Berkeley, CA: University of California Press.

Perls, Frederick S. (1969). *Gestalt therapy verbatim.* Lafayette, CA: Real People

Press.
Piaget, J. (1926). *The language and thought of the child.* New York: Basic Books.
Polster, Erving & Miriam. (1973). *Gestalt therapy integrated.* New York: Brunner/Mazel.
Ray, Sondra. (1976). *I deserve love.* Berkeley, Calif.: Celestial Arts.
Reich, Wilhelm (1972). *Character analysis* (3rd ed.). New York: Farrar, Straus & Giroux.
Resnick, Stella (1975). Gestalt therapy as a meditative practice. In John O. Stevens (Ed.) *Gestalt is.* (pp. 223-228). Moab, Utah: Real People Press.
Ridgway, Roy (1987). *The unborn child: How to recognize and overcome pre-natal trauma.* Brookfield, VT: Gower.
Rowan, John (1990). *Subpersonalities: The people inside us.* New York: Routledge.
Ryle, Gilbert (1949). *The concept of mind.* New York: Barnes & Noble.
Safran, Jeremy D., & Segal, Zindel V. (1990). *Interpersonal process in cognitive therapy.* New York: Basic Books.
Sandler, Joseph (1960). On the concept of the superego. *The psychoanalytic study of the child,* v. 15, 128-162.
Sandler, Joseph; Holder, Alex; & Meers, Dale (1963). The ego ideal and the ideal self. *The psychoanalytic study of the child,* v. 18, 139-158.
Sartre, Jean-Paul (1956a). *Being and nothingness.* New York: Philosophical Library.
Sartre, Jean-Paul (1956b). Existentialism is a humanism. In W. Kaufmann (Ed.), *Existentialism from Dostoevsky to Sartre* (pp. 345-369). Cleveland: Meridian.
Schafer, Roy (1960). The loving and beloved superego in Freud's structural theory. *The Psychoanalytic Study of the Child, 15.* pp. 163-188.
Shapiro, Stewart B. (1962). A theory of ego pathology and ego therapy. *The Journal of Psychology, 53,* 81-90.
Shapiro, Stewart B. (with James Elliott). 1976. *The selves inside you.* Berkeley, Calif.: Explorations Institute.
Sifneos, P. E. (1973). The prevalence of "alexithymic" characteristics in psychosomatic patients. *Psychotherapy & Psychosomatics, 22,* 255-262.
Simkin, James S. (1976). *Gestalt therapy mini-lectures.* Millbrae, Calif.: Celestial Arts.
Sorokin, Pitirim A. (1941). *The crisis of our age.* New York: Dutton.
Spengler, Oswald (1926/1939 & 1928/1939). *The decline of the West.* New York: Knopf.

Stone, Hal, & Winkelman, Sidra (1989). *Embracing our selves.* San Rafael, CA: New World Library.

Stone, Hal, & Stone, Sidra (1992, March/April). Talking to our selves: Interview with Hal and Sidra Stone. *AHP Perspective,* pp. 6f, 10f).

Stone, Hal, & Stone, Sidra (1993). *Embracing your inner critic.* San Francisco: HarperCollins.

Surrey, J. L. (1984). Self-in-relation: A theory of women's development. *Work in progress,* Stone Center Working Papers Series, No. 13. Wellesley, MA: Stone Center, Wellesley College.

Suzuki, Shunryu (1970). *Zen mind, beginner's mind.* New York: Weatherhill.

Taylor, G. J., Bagby, R. M., & Parker, J. D. A. (1991). The alexithymic construct. *Psychosomatics, 32,* 153-164.

Vaihinger, Hans (1935). *The philosophy of 'as if.'* London: Kegan Paul.

Verny, Thomas R. (1981). *The secret life of the unborn child.* New York: Summit.

Verny, Thomas R. (Ed.) (1987). *Pre- and perinatal psychology: An introduction.* New York: Human Sciences Press.

Walen, S. R., DiGiuseppe, R., & Wessler, R. L. (1980). *A practitioner's guide to rational-emotive therapy.* New York: Oxford University Press.

Watzlawick, Paul (1990). *Munchausen's pigtail.* New York: Norton.

Wegscheider-Cruse, Sharon (1985). *Choicemaking.* Deerfield Beach, FL: Health Communications, Inc.

Weiss, Joseph & Sampson, Harold (1986). *The psychoanalytic process.* New York: Guilford Press.

Whitfield, Charles L. (1987). *Healing the child within.* Pompano Beach, FL: Health Communications, Inc.

Wilber, Ken (1977). *The spectrum of consciousness.* Wheaton, IL: Theosophical Publishing House.

Wolinsky, Stephen (1991). *Trances people live.* Falls Village, CT: Bramble Co.

Woollams, S. & Brown, M. (1979). *TA: The total handbook of transactional analysis.* Englewood Cliffs, NJ: Prentice-Hall.

Wright, Beatrice A. (1983). *Physical disability—a psychosocial approach* (2nd. ed.). New York: Harper & Row.

Index

A

Acquittal statements 147
Adler, Alfred 93f
Affirmations 195
Alcoholism 100
Alexithymia 119
Anger 105, 256ff, 269
Anthetic
  Dialogue 4, 8f
  Master affirmation 143f
  Philosophy 255, 269
  Therapy 8
  Triad 263
Anthetics 9
Anxiety, overcoming 139f
Aphilia 167ff
Archetypes, Anthetic 40
Assertiveness problems 102f

B

Bad faith 120
Bergler, Edmund 26, 73
Black hole 34f
Blaming others for problems 115
Branden, Nathaniel 94
Buddhism 95
Buffer training 82, 94
Buffers 78ff, 130, 141f

C

Caring 259ff, 269
Catch-22 229
Challenging 131ff, 149ff, 175ff
Clues to Inner Critic functioning 121ff
Compensatory self 76, 93f
Compliments, accepting 98
Connectedness 104, 261ff
Conscience 17, 24, 73
Converting shoulds to preferences 181, 199
Counseling, reluctance to begin 114f
Creativity blocks 112f
Critical thinking 263
Criticism, difficulty listening to 100

D

Decision problems 111
Declaring your importance 153f
De-fusing 149f
Defectiveness, feelings of 50ff
Dehypnotizing the devalued self 175
Depression 94, 98f
Disengaging the present from the past 151f
Disputing 147
Double bind 130
Drugs 100

E

Ego in Eastern philosophy 95
Ego ideal 18, 48, 211
Ego-syntonic, ego-dystonic 121ff
Electric fence 46f

Ellis, Albert   49, 73f, 93, 197f
Emotional punishments   31, 50ff, 98
Emotional superiority   118f
Energy, low   109
Experience matching   119
Experiential disconfirmation   195
External unifiers   99f

F

Fear, magnified   69f
Fear, overcoming   139f
Fear of success   110, 166ff
Feedback & criticism, difficulties listening to   100
Feeling that you don't belong   106
Feeling unequal to others   106
Feelings, being out of touch with   113f
Fishing license   148
Forgetting process   86f
Forgiving yourself   191
Freud, Sigmund   24, 93
Frozen feelings   87

G

Gambling   72f
"Giving back" technique   193
Goals, difficulty reaching   109
"Good person" technique   138f
Growing edges   254
Growth, Anthetic   120, 148, 240
Guilt feelings   52ff
    Challenging   156ff

H

Heidegger, Martin   119
Horney, Karen   39, 49
Hume, David   159
Humility   73
Husserl, Edmund   159

I

Idealizing the other   101
Impostor phenomenon   110f
Individuation   148
Inferiority feelings   68f
Injustice collecting   73
Inner Critic
    Backlash   218
    Clues to   25f
    Definition of   16f, 24, 72
    Externalization of   20
    Fictional construct   25
    How it functions   16f, 41
    Judgmentalism of   47f
    Origins of   27ff
    Police   223f
    Projection of   20f
    Superego and   24f
    Thinking about   173f
Inner figures   15
Inner guide   58f
Insomnia   100

J

Janus words   74
JAV triad   256ff
Jealousy   108

Judgmentalism
   and the Inner Critic 73
   definition 79f, 104f
Judgmentalism vs. judgments 48f
Jung, C. G. 40, 148
"Just Because" challenge 150f

K

Kant, Immanuel 159

L

Learning, difficulties with 112
Learning model 29ff, 33f, 36ff
Life partner, wrong choice of 106
Love 108, 167, 257ff
Love addiction 101

M

Machinery 88ff
Mahrer, Alvin 241
Meditation 193
Mood swings 98
Morality, Anthetic 256ff, 263f, 267ff

N

Natural self 28f, 159
Natural self pleasures 81
Negative
   Comparisons 152f
   Feelings 147
   Predictions, challenging 157f

O

Other people's feelings, difficulties in handling 107
Overreactions 98
Overweight problems 100

P

Penultimates 266
Perfectionism 111, 153
Permissions 192, 199
Pleasure, lack of 98
Polarity types 29, 172
Power, lack of 106
Power, overvaluation of 104
Pressure from others 102
Pretzelization 101f
Pride 83f
Primary self 27f
Procrastination 110
Progress in challenging, evaluating 145f
Propaganda messages 201ff
Protective self 85f
Prototypes 32f, 40, 185
Pseudochallenging 229f
Psychosynthesis 212

R

Rational Emotive Behavior Therapy 49
Reactive self, polishing & improving 114
Reactivity 14, 31, 75ff, 91f
Reducing your concern about what other people might think 155

Releasing extensions 139
Releasing statements 139
Rescuing people 119
Resisting pressure from others 154f
Responsibility commands, challenging 156
Responsible life 261
Revenge 105, 119
Risks, fear of taking 110
Ryle, Gilbert 159

S

Sartre, Jean Paul 120
Schemas 28
Secondary self 28
Self-centeredness 103f
Self-sufficiency, addiction to 104
Sexual problems 107
Shame 52, 56ff
Shoulds 38, 41ff, 49
 advantages of living by 97
 consequences of living by 96ff
 vs. wants 42ff
 recipe 44ff
 self-created 40
Stage fright 110

Stress 101, 105f
Stuff 40

T

Taking orders, difficulties with 112
Terminalism 115f
Test anxiety 110
Thymophobia 119
Trance 91
Transactional analysis 39
Trauma resolution process in Anthetic Therapy 40
Triggering 70

V

Vocational problems 113

W

"What you call" technique 138
Willpower 91

Y

"YASNY" technique 138